WELSH REFLECTIONS:
Y DRYCH AND AMERICA 1851-2001

C000161754

Welsh Reflections: David Hughes (Arfonydd), *Y Drych*'s San Francisco correspondent, gazing into the waters of 'Llyn Y Drych' [Mirror Lake] at Yosemite National Park, California, with Mount Watkins in the background. From *Y Drych*, 18 September 1930. The photograph was accompanied by an account of Jones' vacation in the Sierra Mountains earlier that year.

WELSH REFLECTIONS:

Y DRYCH AND AMERICA
1851-2001

Aled Jones
&
Bill Jones

First Impression—August 2001

ISBN 1 84323 021 6

This book is published with the assistance of the University of Wales Academic Support Fund and the National Welsh American Foundation.

Printed in Wales at
Gomer Press, Llandysul, Ceredigion SA44 4QL

Contents

Preface

As the editor who has recently had the privilege of ushering *Y Drych* into the twenty-first century, I am humbled by this recounting of the vision and fortitude of those who have gone before. It is indeed an honour to be following in their train. All who read this book will be grateful to the authors for saving this piece of Welsh history in such an intriguing fashion.

My father used to tell two tales about his long train ride from New York City (after the long voyage to Ellis Island); he was with his mother and aunt on their way to meet his father in Denver. 'They were so happy when they finally got a proper cup of tea. I think it was in Ohio,' he recalled. 'And once they got to Denver they were so glad when *Y Drych* arrived and they could read the news in Welsh once again.' Little did any of them imagine that their offspring would one day edit the newspaper. Little did I imagine that when I read it as a child in the sunroom on the farm in southern Minnesota. After reading the following pages, I'd love to know if my predecessors *planned* to edit the paper, hoped to edit it, or just lived lives that one way or another prepared them for the task.

One image that arises from the following pages is that all of us – editors, writers, owners, publishers – have been and are stewards of this piece of American cultural identity, the Welsh piece. Stewardship always requires caretaking and the recognition that whatever one is a steward of has a life and importance of its own, not one given to it by the steward. Stewardship is a challenge and an opportunity. No steward can or should work alone. Not only have we all needed contributors and advertisers as well as reliable artisans and printers, but the whole project collapses without subscribers and patrons for advertisers. In every chapter of this book we see that owners and editors in each of the fifteen decades have needed readers who pay their bills on time, correspondents who submit copy of high quality, and businesses who advertise their goods. It's still true. And without all these vital ingredients, there cannot be a sequel to this book in another 150 years' time.

As you turn the following pages, you'll meet individuals with remarkable energy and vision. Such people are still needed in the Welsh

world on both sides of the Atlantic. You'll meet men and women who
were earnestly trying to help define what it meant to be Welsh in
America. That definition is still being honed. You are in for a good read.

Mary Morris Mergenthal
April 2001

Acknowledgements

At the end of every year throughout the nineteenth and early twentieth centuries, the editors of *Y Drych* habitually offered fulsome and extensive thanks to their readers and writers for supporting them during the previous twelve months. At the beginning of this book it is our pleasure to express briefly but no less sincerely our own deepest thanks to the many institutions and individuals on both sides of the Atlantic who have helped to make its publication possible.

Much of the research for this book was carried out during a one-year project on '*Y Drych* and American Welsh Identities', led by the authors and funded by the Board of Celtic Studies of the University of Wales. A University of Wales Academic Support Fund award enabled us to undertake research in the USA and contributed towards the production costs of this book. Publication was also made possible in part by a grant from the National Welsh American Foundation. We wish to acknowledge also the financial assistance of Dr Douglas Bassett and to thank Utica College of Syracuse University for so generously providing us with accommodation during our respective visits to the Utica area in April and June-July 2000.

An earlier version of some of the material included in this book appeared in an article '*Y Drych* and American Welsh Identities' in *The North American Journal of Welsh Studies*, Vol. 1 No. 1 (Winter, 2001). We thank the North American Association for the Study of Welsh Culture and History both for granting us permission to reproduce and for its interest in this project. We are grateful to the following archives and libraries and their staff for their willing help and good service, and where relevant, permission to reproduce illustrations: The American Antiquarian Society, The Balch Institute for Ethnic Studies, The British Newspaper Library, Cardiff County Library, Cardiff University Resource Centre, Harvard University, The Huntington Library, The National Library of Wales, The New York State Historical Association Library, Oneida County Historical Society, Remsen-Steuben Historical Society, Swansea Public Library, University of Wales Bangor Library, Utica College of Syracuse University Library, Utica Public Library, and The Western Reserve Historical Society. Unless otherwise indicated, the illustrations are reproduced from the files of *Y Drych* in Cardiff Central

Library. Our thanks also go to the *Western Mail* for kindly allowing us to reproduce a cartoon from a previous issue of that paper; to E. Emrys Jones and Billie R. McNamara for permission to reproduce photographs taken by them; to Kevin Thomas, who so skilfully copied most of the illustrations that appear in the following pages; to Gomer Press for its interest in this book, and to Francesca Rhydderch for seeing it through to publication so efficiently and professionally.

We have been privileged to have received the help, support and encouragement of many individuals. The ways in which the following have helped are myriad, ranging from giving us the benefit of their personal research, knowledge and experiences to kindly making material in their possession available to us or greatly facilitating our research and making us welcome: Yasmin Ali, Richard Aust, Andy Croll, Esther Evans Baran, Doug Bassett, Val Davidge, Martha Davies, John Ellis, David B. Evans, David W. 'Buddy' Evans, Laurie Jones Fox, Melinda Gray, Dave Harralson, William A. Hastie, Judith Surridge Heuser, Dorine Jones Jenkins, Larisa John, Beti Jones, Bob and Jeanne Jones, Bryn Jones, E. Emrys Jones, Walter O. Jones, Anne Knowles, Ron Lewis, Bethan Mair, Eugene Nasser, Darby O'Brien, John C. Owens, Laurence Roberts, Marion K. Roberts, Alun Trevor, Patricia Powell Viets, Huw Walters, Daniel Williams, and Leonard and Dorothy Wynne.

To conclude, three individuals deserve special mention. Sally Griffith Riesenberger cheerfully and selflessly gave up a great deal of her time to chase up references and photographs in the Utica area for us and send packages of invaluable material over to Wales. We owe an enormous debt to Huw Griffiths, our research assistant on the University of Wales Board of Celtic Studies project. His meticulous work and boundless enthusiasm for the topic provided us with a rich and enviable archive of material to draw on in the writing of this book. Finally, Mary Morris Mergenthal, present owner and editor of *Y Drych*, who first proposed the idea of writing a history of the paper and who since then has been a constant and unfailing source of advice, help and encouragement.

Diolch o waelod calon i bob un ohonoch.

Aled Jones, Bill Jones
Aberystwyth and Cardiff
April 2001

Introduction

This is a biography of a newspaper. The life-story of the Welsh-American journal *Y Drych* [The Mirror], from its birth in 1851 until 2001, is admittedly longer in the telling than is the lifespan of any single individual, yet its history shares certain identifiable human characteristics: a vulnerable childhood, an exuberant youth, a consolidating middle age, a late mid-life crisis followed by a change of direction, and a reinvigorated old age in which a younger competitor emerged to challenge its supremacy. Its remarkable tenacity over such an extended period of time alone demands an explanation. This study approaches the long and fascinating history of *Y Drych* principally from three directions. Firstly, it sees behind the surface of the paper a history of an extraordinary network of men and women devoted to the cause of its continuation and growth. The history of *Y Drych*, in that sense, is not so much the history of impressed ink on paper as a history of a group of people – among them editors, reporters, poets, short-story writers, letter-writers, advertisers, printers, travelling agents and readers – whose joint efforts made it possible to sustain a virtually unbroken tradition of Welsh journalism in North America for over a century and a half.

Secondly, it traces the title's changing relationship to the Welsh in both America and Wales, as reflected in its style, its news coverage and its choice of language. Most crucially in this respect, it examines in detail the language shift from Welsh to English that occurred in the middle years of the twentieth century, and considers its many meanings in relation to the changing composition of its readership. And thirdly, it regards *Y Drych* as a cultural project, a means of making the Welsh and their affairs in America (and beyond) more visible and more interconnected. News and cultural coverage in *Y Drych* provide us today with an incomparable source of information about the activities and movements of the Welsh in America, and its surviving copies should be appreciated, treasured even, for that reason alone. By the same token, it provided those contemporary Welsh Americans with a means of learning about developments in both America and Wales and of adapting their Welsh institutions to American circumstances. In so doing, those writers and readers were constantly re-fashioning their cultural identities.

It is debatable whether *Y Drych* ever acted as the mirror promised by its title by accurately reflecting that transforming sense of American Welshness, but there can be little doubt of its single-minded determination to seek to impose such an identity upon its readers. But if the values embedded in the newspaper's news coverage and style do not necessarily reflect an American-Welsh reality, they do, however, *reflect upon* the Welsh experience in America in diverse and highly revealing ways. In that more nuanced sense, *Y Drych* really was a mirror, its history being a long reflection on the condition of being Welsh in America. By offering through the medium of periodical print an array of 'Welsh reflections' on America, over such a long period, the story of this particular newspaper not only makes a significant contribution to the history of the Welsh, on both sides of the Atlantic. It also adds measurably to our knowledge and understanding of America's teeming multilingual ethnic press in the late nineteenth and early twentieth centuries.

Y Drych was not the first Welsh newspaper to be published in the United States, nor was it by any means the only one to be launched, either in the nineteenth or the twentieth centuries. Furthermore, editors and writers of Welsh descent have long been engaged in American journalism, including most prominently, perhaps, George L. Jones, the son of a Montgomeryshire weaver who established the *New York Times* in 1850, the same year as the first experimental issue of *Y Drych* was distributed in that city.[1] Clearly, the field of Welsh publishing in North America, in all its diverse forms, still awaits its historians. But *Y Drych* remains a special case. The grand sweep of its lifespan, its iconic status as an international Welsh newspaper, especially during its first hundred years, and its internal crises of political loyalty, religious belief and language, which appeared to presage those which were to disturb Wales itself, all serve to distinguish it from past or existing rivals, and makes its history an especially intriguing one.

Much of the research for this book was quarried from the pages of the paper itself, as well as from other printed material. Manuscript sources are rare, as are contemporary financial and administrative accounts. Newspapers, after all, are chiefly concerned with the 'now', about events and stories as they break. They are, as a consequence, hopelessly neglectful of their own internal histories. As far as they are concerned, history rests in their printed columns, their own record of their times.

The rest, including the edited proofs, the spiked stories, the letters to and from correspondents and distributors, and notes passed between editors and printers, were routinely swept into oblivion. Sources external to the paper that do survive often do so accidentally, and, except for illustrations of its editors, writers and publishers, relatively few were found in the case of *Y Drych*. The dependence of the authors on the content of the newspaper itself has to some degree shaped the story as it is told here, as the emphasis on format, iconography, language and the techniques of 'content analysis' demonstrate. This has its advantages. Not only does it provide a vivid picture of the paper's rich variety of content, but it also draws our attention to the ways in which Welsh America was being cumulatively defined by one of its key interlocutors in a relentless flow, week after week, month after month, year after year. No other single source allows us such unprecedented access to a people's history.

Consequently, the seven chapters that follow will reveal, in broadly chronological sequence, both the human energies that were invested in the production of *Y Drych* as an enterprise, and the changing contours and priorities of Welsh cultural life in North America, particularly in the United States. The paper was published almost exclusively in Welsh during its first hundred years, and one of the aims of this study is to render some of the richness and flavour of its contents accessible to those who may not have a reading knowledge of the language. Quotations included in the text have been translated by the authors and the original Welsh versions are reproduced in the notes at the end of the book. The first chapter considers the paper's first year of publication, while the second and third chapters describe respectively the uncertain years of Civil War and Reconstruction from 1852 to 1874, and the period of its greatest expansion and commercial success from 1874 to 1920. The fourth chapter stands back from the narrative to discuss its many contributions to the making of a Welsh cultural identity in the United States up to 1920, while the fifth returns to the story of its production through to the end of the Second World War. Chapter Six pays close attention to the symbolic consequences, as well as the demographic causes, of the shift in language from Welsh to English that occurred in the difficult years between 1930 and 1950, and, finally, the seventh chapter returns to the narrative of its most recent history leading up to its one hundred and fiftieth anniversary in January 2001.

Y DRYCH.

"A DDARLLENO, YSTYRIED; A YSTYRIO, COFIED; A GOFIO, GWNAED; A WNEL, PARHAED."

RHIF. I.   EFROG-NEWYDD, IONAWR 2, 1851.   CYF. I.

Barddoniaeth.

I GYMRU.

HYFRYDAWL ydyw tawel drych
Ar faesydd gwyrddion teg,
A gerddi ffrwythlawn Lloegr wych,
A'u haddurniadau chweg:
Hyfrytach fil im' golwg i,
O *Gymru*, ye'lh wylltineb di.

A thra hyfrydlon befyd yw,
Ar fynhoreawl hynt,
Gael peraroglau blodau gwiw
Yu nofiaw yn y gwynt;
Ond mil hyfrytach yw gan i
Un awel o'th fynyddgrug di.

Hyfrydawl ydyw gweled gwaith
Effaith Celfyddyd gain.—
A rhyfedd adeiladau braith
Eirianmaith aur a main;
Hyfrytach, *Gymru*, fil i mi
Dy greigiau llymion, noethion di.

A hyfryd gwel'd afonydd maith,
Mal moroedd bychain bron;
A'r llongau gwychion ar eu taith,
Gan ddawnsio ar y don;
Hyfrytach, *Gymru* fil i mi
Yw tyrddiad cryg dy ffrydiau di.

A hyfryd yw y ddinas lawn,
A phrysur wib ei llu,
A llon gymysgfa dyeg a dawn
A'u bywiol siriol ru ;
Hyfrytach, *Gymru*, fil i mi
Tawelwch dy bentrefi di.

Mi ddringaf draw i ben y bryn
I edrych tua'n gwlad,
Ond gwawd dyeithriaid gaf am hyn
Eu dirmyg a sarâd;
Ni wyddant hwy pa faint i mi
Sydd, *Gymru*, plith dy fryniau di.

CWYN Y FAM DROS EI PHLENTYN Y NOSON CYN EI DIENYDDIAD.

Na wyla, fy mhlentyn, ar fyr tyr y wawrddydd,
Ac y' fory taweleach yr hunai na thi;
Y beddrod a'm cuddia rhag gwarth a chywilydd,
Er mai goddef o gollfarn yr euog wnai i!

Nid hir y cei fraich tyner Fam i'th gofleidio,
Nid hir ar ei mynwes gorphwysi mewn hedd;
Ac yna pwy sydd a wna drosot dosturio,
Dy noddi a'th wylied pan b'wyf yn fy medd!

Fy mhlentyn anwylaf, trist iawn yw dy ddioffro,
I ganfod fy nhrallod a'm dagrau yn lli!
Galari wrth glywed fy nghadwyn mewn cyffro,
'A neb ond y traws cydalarant â thi!

Er hyn rhaid dy ddioffro, a phan yr och'neidi,
Atteliaf fy nagrau fu 'n llifo cyhydd;
Ah! gwenu yr wyt tra yn dawel breuddwydi,
Ow'l trum archoll i mi ydyw gweled dy bryd!

Ah! faban anwylaf, mor falch y'th godleidiwn,
Mewn mynwes aeth weithion dan arwydd a brad,
Pe gan rwymyn gwir rinwedd a serch y'th fendithiwn,
Tra croesawn di'n blentyn ar hoff enw'th dad!

Ond bellach rhy bwyr o dy blaid yw fy nghysutdd,
Heb gynsill, annddifad ar fyr bydd dy wedd;
Gan fyd pechadurus fe'th glwyfir â gwarthrudd,
Euogrwydd dy Fam a'th ddilyn hyd fedd!

PERORIAETH.—SEABORN. M. 16 (8. 8. 6.)   GAN J. M. THOMAS, EFROG-NEWYDD.

Yn Eden, coffaf hyny byth, &c.

Y Dôn uchod a gyfansoddwyd yn ngwaith yr awdwr yn dychwelyg'l wlad ei enedigaeth.

Â phan y doi'n hysbys o'm trawsedd a'm tynghed,
Oywilydd a dirmyg a wridant dy rudd;
Ac heb un a'th grwara ond Duw yr amddifad,
Am droesedd dy Fam y galeriwbob dydd!

Tra'n blentyn, y byd a ymdrecha dy dwyllo,
Un modd ag yr hudwyd dy fam i oer'frad,
Heb noddwr na chynghor, O pwy gaf i'th wylio!
O Dduw yr amddifad! bydd di iddo'n Dad.
GWENFFRWD.

CLYWEDOG.

O'n holl bleserau ar eu hynt,
Yr oeddwn ar fyr gyfraneg,
Am ddenu adgof—o bob man,
Di ail rai Glan Clywedog.

Yn nyddian mwyn plentyndod llon,
Pan oedd y fron yn fywiog.
Pa le y ceid ein chwareu fan!
Mewn dôl ar Lan Clywedog.

Pwy fedr ddweyd i mi mewn iaith,
Yr oruchafiaeth enwog,
O ddwyn y brithyll cynta' i dir,
O ddwfr elir Clywedog!

Pa le bum gyda hoyw fron,
A llangcian llon cyfoediog,
Yn cyd-ymdrochi'n fawr ein 'stwr!
Yn ngloyw ddwfr Clywedog.

Rhyw lawer gwaith y bum i gynt,
Yn rhodio hynt adlywiog,
Yn min yr bwyr, ar awel wan,
Môr fwyn ar Lan Clywedog.

Pa le 'r oedd anorddygol swyn,
Gan gôr y llwya gwyrddi-ddeiliog,
Pan ddaethient eu mwynneiddiaf gân
Yn nhâlgoed Glan Clywedog !

Pan y dygwyddaf imi loes,
Gan unrhyw groes adywiog,
Pa le yr awn i wella'r fron!
I lan y lon Clywedog.

Pan yunseilliduwn unrhyw bryd,
O drwst y byd amrywiog,
Pa le yr oedd fy newis fan!
Dan wyn ar Lan Clywedog.

Pan yw fy meddwl i yn brudd,
'N ol croesi 'r Weryid donog,
Pa beth yn fwy wna im' gofio'r fan |
Mae MAM ar Lan Clywedog.

Ond, Och! y'loes, y dwfn aeth,
Am brath fal saeth hedegog,
Pan gofiwyf na ddaw byth i'm rhan
Ail weled Glan Clywedog !

I'r lleoedd ce's bleserau mawr,
Nad wyf yn awr gyfraneg,
Erfyniaf fendith i bob man,
Ond penaf Glan Clywedog.
Efrog-Newydd.   B. LEWIS.

I ORIAWR.

DYMA flwch, edrychwch dro,—a'i lonaid
O olwynian cryno.
Trwy eu gilydd yn treiglo,
Un di fai, a dyna fo.

Maesurydd yr amseran,—mòr hyndd
Y rhenir o'n orian;
Ein dydd, a'i giwys nodwydd glan,
Nodi wna yu fynudan.

Oriawr, O! oriawr arian,—mòr ddifyr,
Oriawr, wyt yn mholmanu;
Oriawr glwys, llyw eira glas,
Oriawr ag anwiog arian.

First impressions: *Y Drych* in 1851

The first issue of *Y Drych* was printed in New York City in November 1850.[1] Dated 2 January 1851, it was an eight-paged tabloid-sized newspaper, printed, with the exception of a small number of advertisements and notices, entirely in the Welsh language. Two earlier attempts had been made to bring out a Welsh newspaper in the United States, but both had failed.[2] *Y Cymro America* [The Welsh American], the first Welsh newspaper of its kind on the continent, appeared in New York City in January 1832. The following year, in 1833, the coming of the penny press in that burgeoning city sparked the beginnings of American popular journalism,[3] but *Y Cymro* failed to appear after a cholera epidemic broke out in the city only twelve fortnightly issues later. The second attempt, *Haul Gomer* [The Sun of Gomer], was launched in January 1848 but failed in September of the same year. Prospects for the new venture of 1851, then, were not promising. Yet, the growth of Welsh-language religious periodicals in the 1830s and 1840s had at least indicated that a market existed for Welsh-American publications. The first to appear was the monthly *Y Cyfaill o'r Hen Wlad yn America* [The Friend from the Old Country in America] in New York City in January 1838, edited by the Revd William Rowlands of the New York Calvinistic Methodist Church.[4] Initially seeking to be of service to all the Welsh Nonconformist groups in America, the later appearance of journals specifically targeted at the Congregationalists and the Baptists effectively led *Y Cyfaill*, by the late 1840s, to become the principal mouthpiece of the Calvinistic Methodists. In January 1840, the Revd Robert Everett of Steuben, New York, launched *Y Cenhadwr Americanaidd* [The American Missionary], which shortly became the leading, though unofficial, organ of the Welsh Congregationalists. The Welsh Baptists followed suit in 1842 with the fortnightly *Y Beread* [The Berean], and in 1844 with the monthly *Y Seren Orllewinol* [The Western Star], printed in nearby Utica, New York, a major centre of Welsh settlement. However, none of these journals offered the kind of practical news and information required either by recent Welsh migrants seeking employment or opportunities in their new homeland, or those who had settled there and were seeking to be integrated, economically and politically, into the United States. Since large numbers were monolingual in Welsh, such information needed to be in their own language. But the paper was also aimed at those who had mastered English but who continued to regard themselves as Welsh through family ties or affiliation to Welsh religious organisations. It was that sense of identity, linking the Welsh in America with their language and their institutions, which *Y Drych* would foster for a further century and a half. Also, unlike its predecessors, *Y Drych* was from its inception a weekly newspaper, rather than a monthly journal.

The man responsible for launching *Y Drych*, and who owned and edited the paper in its early years, was John Morgan Jones (1818-1912).[5]

John Morgan Jones (1818-1912), late in life. He was the first owner, editor and publisher of *Y Drych*.

Reproduced by kind permission of Dorine S. Jones Jenkins, Frankfort, New York, his great-great-granddaughter.

Born in Glandulais Isaf, near Llanidloes, he had emigrated to America in 1832. Very little is known about his early years in the United States other than he first settled in Newburgh before moving to New York City by the mid-1830s. In the city at this time there was a network of Welsh churches and societies, including four chapels with Welsh language services, a Cambrian Association, a St David's Benevolent Society and a Welsh military company, the Cambrian Musketeers.[6] Starting as a porter, he worked himself up to be a broker in the bustling financial district on the southern tip of Manhattan, with an office at 51 Beaver Street. The renowned New York Welsh bookseller, bibliographer

Advertisements for Carnarvon Castle Hotel and Cambrian House, New York City, where John Morgan Jones (founder of *Y Drych*) and others gathered to discuss Welsh matters in the early 1850s. *From* Y Drych, *16 January 1851.*

and antiquarian Henry Blackwell suggested that Jones was one of a group of Welsh people

> who frequented the Cambrian House kept by Mrs Lewis and particularly the Carnarvon Castle, 14 Oak Street, kept by Mrs Jane Richards. This latter place was noted for its gatherings of Welshmen, who discussed Welsh matters . . . and here it was discussed that a Welsh newspaper should be published with the result that on Nov. 11, 1850 Jones issued from 51 Beaver Street, the first number of Y Drych.[7]

Given that in later years *Y Drych* would frequently refer to its subscribers and writers as 'teulu'r Drych' [*Y Drych*'s family] it is fitting that John M. Jones' wife Mary (née Griffiths) and children helped him to produce the early issues of the paper and his later publications. His

Mary Jones (née Griffiths), wife of John Morgan and one of the paper's first typesetters.
By kind permission of Dorine S. Jones Jenkins, Frankfort, New York.

son, Jonathan James, and one of his daughters, Sarah, became skilled printers.[8]

The first issue was printed by Edward O. Jenkins, 114 Nassau Street, and offered to subscribers for $1 a year.[9] Evidently, many took out subscriptions but failed to pay for them, as notices urging readers to pay their fees ran in *Y Drych* throughout its first year. An equally difficult task was to arrange the paper's distribution across the continent. Post offices became critical in this process, but a network of travelling and local agents was also constructed in centres of Welsh-American population across the country. Fortunately, the names and addresses of these vital links in the chain of Welsh cultural communication were printed in early issues of the paper.[10] These show how its circulation extended from its core areas of support in those critical early months. Of the thirty-one agents listed in 1851, seventeen lived in Welsh settlements in Pennsylvania, six in New York State, five in Ohio, two in New Jersey and one in Massachusetts. From the outset a travelling agent served the whole of North America; two others, intriguingly, were appointed to extend the paper's circulation in Wales (one of whom recruited Augusta Hall, Lady Llanover, as a subscriber), while yet another sought to cover the remainder of the United Kingdom.[11] From the very start, therefore, the producers of *Y Drych* had transcontinental and international ambitions for their fledgling weekly newspaper. Within a matter of months, the paper was also being sold in Louisiana, Michigan, Wisconsin, Vermont and Maryland.[12] Impressively, it also secured the reporting services of some well-known journalists in Wales, among them Evan Jones (Ieuan Gwynedd) for south Wales and Thomas Manuel, former editor of *Yr Amserau* [The Times], for north Wales.[13]

The paper's most powerful advocates in America were Welsh Nonconformist ministers, who broadcast news of its launch from pulpits across the continent. H. P. Griffiths of New York Mills took out a subscription, along with several others, following an announcement made in his chapel. Shortly thereafter, *Y Drych* was to be found 'in every Welsh family in the neighbourhood, apart from a few exceptions'.[14] Griffiths said that never before had he seen such willingness to receive a Welsh publication among his fellow nationals.[15] For John Morgan Jones, whom it appears had invested $2,000 of his own money in the venture, and who worked 'six days and two nights – sometimes part of a third and fourth night in the week' in order to get the paper out, the commercial success of the paper was of paramount importance.[16] To extend further the geographical range of the paper, Jones sent free issues to preachers who contributed news from far-flung Welsh communities. The prize of a copy of Warrington's *History of Wales*, worth $10, was offered to the person who collected the highest number of paid subscribers before 31 December 1851.[17] But the paper's capacity to survive depended as much on attracting advertisers as readers. In its first year, a fifth of the paper was devoted to advertisements, the vast majority of which were inserted by shipping companies or emigration agents.[18] Others were for items of food, books, clothes and oil lamps. This suggests both the immediate concerns of companies based in and around Wall Street, and the immigrant nature of the readership. Iconographically, the print style in 1851 was simple, and included few illustrations other than those stereotyped in advertisements.

Responses to the appearance of the new paper were generally positive on both sides of the Atlantic. In Wales, the weekly *Yr Amserau* congratulated Jones, observing that

It is about time that the Welsh in America possessed a weekly publication in the language of the country of their birth: . . . The Germans and French have papers in their various languages, and the Irish have several that are edited by their countrymen, and why cannot Gomer's race maintain one as well?[19]

For *Y Dysgedydd* [The Teacher], the publication of *Y Drych* marked the beginning of 'a new period in the history of our nation'[20] while others saw in it a means of bridging the divide between the Welsh in both countries. *Y Gymraes* [The Welshwoman] emphasised that

> The course of events in America cannot be considered unimportant in this country while so many thousands of our countrymen are there, and thousands likely to follow them before long. This makes some form of correspondence between the two countries a necessity, and the "Drych" promises to fulfil this need.[21]

The only ruffled feathers were those of Robert Everett in Steuben, editor of *Y Cenhadwr*. This may have been because in 1850 he had planned to launch a monthly periodical entitled *Y Detholydd* [The Selector] to print extracts from newspapers sent to him from Wales.[22] In marked contrast, the English-language New York papers regarded the first issue of *Y Drych* with benign bemusement. In general they welcomed it as a medium of communication that would help Welsh migrants settle in America.[23] Sardonically lamenting its ignorance of Welsh, the *Morning Star* (New York) informed its readers that it had been assured by 'a Cambrian friend . . . that the paper is an exceedingly entertaining sheet',[24] while the *Williamsburgh Daily Gazette* extended a conditional welcome while congratulating itself on having

> mastered one word, *very nearly*, namely 'Whigiad.' 'By ciphering', we have discovered that this word signifies either *Whig*, or *Whigs*, or *Whiggery*. If we were *sure* that the Mirror was a Whig journal, we should at once advise every Welshman to patronize it. The proprietor will therefore please to recollect, that if he is on *our side*, we wish him all sorts of good luck.[25]

The paper's own mission, however, was to provide a balanced coverage that transcended religious or party political divisions. Only by these means, its editor argued, might it hope to provide useful information to a relatively heterogeneous Welsh readership.[26] News coverage of all Welsh and Welsh-related affairs thus became a high editorial priority. In a letter to the editor printed in October 1851, John William Jones, who later became the paper's editor and owner, explained that a newspaper like *Y Drych* was important because 'many in this country cannot read English, and consequently they are deprived of practical information'.[27] But it was emphatically news with a purpose. The two major news stories from 1851, for example, centred on attempts to establish a separatist Welsh homeland in America, and on a campaign to install a Welsh memorial in the Washington Monument. From the outset *Y Drych* took the view that many more of their kinsfolk from Wales should join them in the New World. Religious and cultural oppression at home were contrasted to the privileges and freedoms afforded by America. *Y Drych* thus became a powerful voice in enticing others to emigrate.[28] Furthermore, it took the view that in order to preserve their identity the Welsh should settle in ethnically exclusive 'homelands'.[29] Many such schemes were advocated, the most prominent in 1851 being Nova Cambria in Brazil[30] and Vancouver Island.[31] Although these schemes, like many others, proved futile, the dream of establishing a Wales beyond Wales remained a key element of editorial policy for at least the following twenty years. However, the paper quickly came to prefer that homeland to be sited within its own geographic domain rather than outside the United States.

The second major running news story during its first year advocated the placing of a Welsh memorial stone in the Washington Monument, then in the process of being erected. Following the publication of a number of editorial articles advocating the idea, a Central Committee was formed in Utica to co-ordinate the work of raising the required $400.[32] Other committees were quickly formed in Radnor, Ohio; Chicago; New York City; Remsen, New York; and the Pennsylvania towns and cities of Philadelphia, Summit Hill, Catasauqua, Blossburg, Ebensburgh, Pottsville, Big Rock and Welsh Creek.[33] Exemplifying the kind of sentiments expressed at meetings were the words of the Welsh in Pottsville, Pennsylvania, who declared in a resolution in support of the scheme:

> That we, although foreigners through birth, are Americans and Republicans in sentiment; and have made Washington's country our adopted land; and appreciate the Freedom and Conveniences that we are allowed to enjoy.[34]

Others, though, objected. The Welsh in Bradford, Pennsylvania, for example, refused their support because 'it is not consistent with our principles to build a memorial to the first slave-holding president in our country'.[35] The storm that broke in the pages of *Y Drych* in the weeks following the publication of that letter only strengthened the editor's own, favourable line on the matter, and he urged the Bradford Welsh to reconsider their position.

These two issues suggest two things about *Y Drych*. Right from the start, it knew how to mobilise its readers as well as to inform them. It was also unafraid to create controversy, or to divide the Welsh on political or linguistic lines. But even more significantly, perhaps, its early campaigns had encapsulated the ambivalence that was to characterise its dominant, editorial attitude towards the Americanisation of the Welsh. They wanted to be recognised as Americans, but they also wanted to be different, to be Welsh in their American-ness, to be American with qualifications, and on their own terms.

While the paper's aims included informing and educating its readers on matters of American political structure and values, however, in its early years it succeeded only very partially in doing so. For example, in 1851 the question of slavery overshadowed the political landscape in the United States, yet apart from the Washington Monument controversy, only one article on the subject appeared in *Y Drych* during the whole year.[36] The only political issue that received widespread coverage in *Y Drych* in 1851 was temperance.[37] Neither, surprisingly, did it devote much space to matters of religion (typically less than 10 per cent of content during most of its first one hundred years), nor did it ally itself with any particular current within Welsh Nonconformity. This policy reflected an interesting and significant deviation from the practice of news journalism in Wales, where the major Welsh-language newspapers, most of which were launched after 1855, were closely associated with religious organisations. By so doing, *Y Drych* could legitimately appeal to as wide a readership as possible and could claim to rise above the theological and other sectarian arguments that had so disfigured the sense of Welsh identity in Wales. Even the denominational journals welcomed this distance from their internal quarrels, perceiving in it a medium that, while not secular, was at least non-sectarian and which served the material and cultural needs of the Welsh in America along a far broader front.[38] Balancing the often-conflicting interests of the four major Welsh denominations (the Calvinistic Methodists, the Congregationalists, the

Baptists and the Wesleyan Methodists), however, called for diplomatic skills of a high order. One correspondent ('Trentonite') in December 1851 asked the paper's editor why so many articles on the Wesleyan Methodists were included in the paper 'when there is never any favourable mention of the denomination in the monthly publications'.[39] Jones tactfully replied that all other Welsh denominations save the Wesleyans had their own periodicals to keep their members informed of events within their churches. Thus the paper had a responsibility 'to make up their want in so far as it conforms to the nature of our publication'.[40] To avoid further argument, the editor repeated his non-denominational policy and added that all the churches were welcome to supply him with news and notices of their activities.

Thus the mainstay of the paper's early content was neither political nor religious news, but the richness of Welsh cultural life in the United States, with occasional sidelong glances at cultural production back in Wales. It actively encouraged the numerous eisteddfodau and cymanfa-oedd canu (cultural and musical festivals) held by Welsh communities across the country, advertising their locations and competitions and printing their winning entries. Poetry was a central ingredient in the editorial mix. 'Colofn Y Beirdd' [The Poet's Column] provides a unique source of information on the Welsh-American psyche. The poets address almost every conceivable subject, including political attitudes, Christian values, their longing for home and family in Wales, cultural identity and the fate of the language in their new land. The inclusion of poems composed by Welsh Americans was an integral and popular feature of every issue of *Y Drych* for at least the next eighty years – it is possible that at least twenty thousand of them were printed during this period. They are thus a major Welsh literary resource whose potential is only beginning to be tapped, and the same is true of the various novels serialised in the paper during the nineteenth and early twentieth centuries.[41]

On 20 December 1851, in the fifty-first issue of *Y Drych*, an editorial article felt bound to thank the Lord and faithful friends for allowing the venture to be carried out thus far. And there was a boast: 'we have published the first Welsh Weekly Newspaper to have been published this side of the Atlantic for a full year.'[42] In terms of its distribution networks and targeting of a market, the paper had succeeded in laying foundations that might enable future expansion. Its basic format and style had also been established. Variations to these would come aplenty in subsequent years, but as far as content was concerned, the paper would not have been completely unrecognisable to later generations. Yet although by the end of 1851, *Y Drych* had indeed survived longer than any other Welsh-American newspaper up to that time, its future was still insecure, and ahead lay two very difficult decades. Indeed, those involved in *Y Drych* in the first year of its existence would probably have been astounded to learn that their paper had survived into the twentieth century let alone the twenty-first.

CHAPTER 2

Making a mark: *Y Drych* 1852-74

Few issues of *Y Drych* from the 1850s and 1860s have survived. Relatively complete runs exist only for 1851, 1856-7, 1863 and 1866 onwards, and it is particularly unfortunate that the missing years include four of the five years during which America was in the throes of the Civil War (1861-1865). Consequently, many aspects of the history of *Y Drych* for the first fifteen or so years of its existence are still largely unknown, and the glimpses of Welsh-American life it provides us with are tantalisingly brief. Even so, there is little cause to doubt that *Y Drych's* first years were very difficult ones, in which the new arrival struggled to make its mark. During the 1850s, while it was based in New York, it had, as one commentator put it, 'many ups and downs'.[1] There were frequent changes of ownership and editors, and more than likely it was not only failing to make money but also incurring heavy losses for its owners. These were also years of deadly rivalry between competing groups who strove for control of the paper. Nor would the 1860s be any less troublesome, as the paper's own precarious state was compounded by its embroilment in controversies arising from the American Civil War. Only in the late 1860s and early 1870s did signs of continuity and stability become apparent.

The first decade

The 1850s were a particularly turbulent period for *Y Drych*. A number of individuals became involved with the paper, some of whom would remain associated with it for many years to come. Most of them had the surname Jones. On 16 December 1854 John Morgan Jones, the paper's creator, relinquished ownership to a company formed by a group of Welshmen in New York City.[2] One source credits *Y Drych's* circulation at the time as 2,750.[3] The circumstances surrounding the transfer remain unclear as no issues from this period seem to have survived, and, as we shall see, subsequent reports are fraught with accusations between

William B. Jones (Ap P. A. Mon)
(1815-1887), one of the owners of *Y
Drych* and *Y Drych a'r Gwyliedydd*,
1854-58, and a writer for the paper for
the remainder of his life.

From The Cambrian, *January 1888.*

vendor and buyer. However, it appears the purpose of the sale was to avoid the paper's termination, and John M. Jones may well have requested that the new owners purchase the paper from him.[4]

The company who bought *Y Drych* comprised William B. Jones (Ap P. A. Mon), Daniel L. Jones, Revd Thomas R. Jones and Lewis Roberts. The chairman, William B. Jones, was a New York entrepreneur and owner of the Columbia Hall Dry Goods Store in Brooklyn.[5] A native of Holyhead, Anglesey, and son of the renowned writer Benjamin Jones (P. A. Mon), William B. Jones had emigrated to the USA in 1848 from Liverpool, where he had been an apprentice dry goods clerk. His interest in *Y Drych* and Welsh migration was continued with the establishment of Welsh settlements in New Cambria, Missouri, and Arvonia, Kansas, in the 1860s, and he was a regular contributor to the paper for the rest of his life.[6] Little is known of the early life of Daniel L. Jones, other than that he was born in south Wales in 1807, emigrated to the United States in 1832 and settled in Brooklyn. His business activities in America seem to be shrouded in mystery, being variously described as a plumber, manufacturer of lucifer matches and a real estate agent. He enjoyed a high profile in the Welsh community in New York City and was a founder member and president of the New York State St David's Society.[7] There does not appear to be any surviving biographical information on the other two members of the company, Revd Thomas R. Jones and Lewis T. Roberts.

The new owners appointed as *Y Drych*'s sole editor John William Jones, co-editor of the paper since December 1852 and editor of

Y Cylchgrawn Cenedlaethol [The National Journal] and *Yr Adolygydd Chwarterol* [The Quarterly Review].[8] In early 1855 they bought the rival newspaper *Y Gwyliedydd Americanaidd* [The American Sentinel], which had been launched in opposition to *Y Drych* the previous year and which appears to have had a circulation of 1,800 at the time of the purchase.[9] The combined paper was published by Richards and Jones, 138 Nassau Street, New York City.[10] In 1855 John William Jones was joined temporarily as editor by Morgan Albert Ellis, former editor of *Y Gwyliedydd*,[11] and in 1859, by T. B. Morris (Gwyneddfardd).[12] The amalgamated paper was temporarily re-titled *Y Drych a'r Gwyliedydd*, and this title was retained when Lewis T. Roberts became the sole owner in March 1857.[13] But when Roberts sold the paper to John William Jones in early 1858, the latter reverted to the simpler and more direct original title, *Y Drych*.[14] It was suggested that Jones had bought the paper because he had come to believe that it was easier for him to make a living from running it himself than it had been for a number of people, each with their own independent views, to do so and pay an editor's wages as well.[15] What appear to be the only

Morgan A. Ellis (1832-1901), editor of *Y Gwyliedydd* and then joint editor of *Y Drych a'r Gwyliedydd* until May 1856.
From The Cambrian, *August 1901.*

John William Jones (1827-1884). He began writing for *Y Drych* from the paper's inception in 1851, served as its sole or joint editor 1852-64 and 1871-1884, and also owned the paper between 1858 and 1865.
Photograph from the Archives of the Oneida County Historical Society at Utica, New York, reproduced by kind permission.

surviving copies from 1858 and 1859 suggest that after John William Jones took over the paper, its printer was Benjamin Parry, at Richards and Jones' former establishment on Nassau Street. However, on 1 May 1859, *Y Drych* reverted to Richards and Jones, and the paper's office moved to their premises in 201 Williams Street, New York City.[16]

Both Morgan Ellis and Gwyneddfardd were noted bards and men of letters, much sought after adjudicators and prolific eisteddfod prize winners. Born in 1832 near Machynlleth, Montgomeryshire, Ellis had come to the USA in 1853, and after his association with *Y Drych a'r Gwyliedydd* was to serve as minister in a number of Welsh Calvinistic Methodist churches in the United States as well work for other Welsh-American papers and periodicals.[17] Gwyneddfardd hailed from the Dolgellau area and was ordained as a minister with the Welsh Congregational denomination before he left Wales in the mid 1850s. He worked for *Y Drych* until 1869, principally as its poetry editor, although he may well have had other editorial duties in addition. In that year he became editor of the Scranton-published Welsh newspaper, *Baner America* (for which Ellis also worked for a time).[18]

But renowned though Ellis and Gwyneddfardd were, they were overshadowed by the man who was the key figure in the paper's history during these years, John William Jones.[19] Born in Llanaelhaearn near Caernarfon in 1827, he emigrated to Racine, Wisconsin, in 1845 before moving on to Sag, Illinois, and then to Utica, where he received further education at Clinton College. He was an able, trenchant, if imperious, journalist, with a reputation for getting involved in bitter quarrels; his editorial columns were described by a contemporary as being invariably 'strong, sweeping and one-sided; but truly powerful'.[20] One of the most gifted writers the paper has ever possessed, he expanded the range of its content through contributing articles on travel, science and astronomy. He also left an indelible mark on the paper's style and, as a strong supporter of the temperance movement and the Republican Party, on its political direction.

Evidently, the 1850s were difficult years for the *Y Drych* as a commercially viable venture. It was later alleged that during this decade the paper lost the owners a great deal of money.[21] Subscription rates were raised in January 1856 by 50 cents a year to $1.50 for US readers, $2 for Canadian subscribers and $2.50 for readers in Wales. In an announcement in January 1856, the owners patiently explained the financial difficulties faced by the paper, and justified the price increases

> The cost of publishing *Y Drych a'r Gwyliedydd* for the year 1855 will be over five thousand dollars ($5,000) without mentioning nearly two thousand dollars ($2,000) for the Subscription lists of the two newspaper, for which we had paid over fifteen hundred dollars ($1,500) during the year; . . . for which we received under three thousand dollars ($3,000). From this it will be seen that it is impossible to bring out a Newspaper like *Y Drych a'r Gwyliedydd* for a dollar a year without incurring large losses.[22]

By October 1855, the paper had also taken the step of printing lists of monies received 'so that everyone will know directly that their payments have been received safely'.[23] The initials and places of settlement of subscribers and the sums received from them were included. What was then a crisis measure, today provides the only detailed information on the extent of the paper's early distribution. Analysis of the lists for the year 1856 demonstrates that, as in 1851, nearly a quarter of the paper's subscribers resided in the state of Pennsylvania, while growing numbers were to be found in New York State and Wisconsin (around 18 per cent each). Furthermore, whereas copies of *Y Drych* were received in ten states in 1851, by 1856 that number had risen to twenty-one. Much of the paper's success in extending its circulation may be attributed to two travelling agents, 'M. A. E.' (possibly Morgan A. Ellis, who retired as joint editor in 1856) and John Jones (Eryr Merion), who between them generated $260 in new subscriptions.[24] In sharp contrast, and despite the efforts of its three agents there, the paper was sent to only two subscribers in Wales. Significantly, in view of later schisms, only seven subscribers were to be found in states in the American South, eleven in Virginia, two in Texas, and one each in Louisiana and Kentucky. Welsh settlers moving further west into such territories as Minnesota and Oregon, however, were receiving copies, while by 1856 California had become the state with the sixth largest number of subscribers to the paper. At the beginning of that year Revd William Roberts gave it the seal of approval, agreeing that it now looked and felt like a newspaper of substance. It had a

> . . . form and present bearing that is very pleasing to me. As you pick it up you are at once struck by the idea – Well, here is a 'new paper' that has a pretty good grasp to it. Its clothing and trimmings are respectable. It surely deserves a place on the Welsh gentleman's table, amongst English newspapers, like the *New York Recorder*, the *Tribune*, and the *Observer*. . . . Its mannerism and content are on the whole interesting, constructive and amusing.[25]

H. O. Rowlands (1845-1930), originally from Waukesha, Wisconsin. He served as a minister in Welsh churches in Whitesboro, New York; Oshkosh, Wisconsin; Elgin and Chicago, Illinois; Lincoln, Nebraska, and Davenport, Iowa. The 'Dean of Welsh-American Reporters', he was already writing for *Y Drych* by 1865 and wrote his last columns in the year of his death.

From Y Drych, *24 April 1930.*

By the end of the decade, John William Jones was sufficiently confident of his paper's chances of success as to design a more ornate masthead and to make the bold claim that *Y Drych* was 'The National Newspaper Serving the Welsh Nation in the United States'.[26]

Yet behind these expressions of confidence, *Y Drych* was embroiled in a fratricidal circulation war against a rival title until the end of the decade. Dissatisfied with the course taken by *Y Drych* under its new management, as well as being angered by his belief that the current owners had refused to provide adequate compensation – a claim *Y Drych* vehemently denied – John Morgan Jones, its original owner and editor, had on 1 May 1855 established *Y Cymro-Americaidd*.[27] In its first issue, he launched a ferocious attack on *Y Drych*, branding it a supporter of slavery.[28] The latter, and John William Jones especially, responded in kind: John M. Jones and his supporters were 'y celwyddwyr' [the liars].[29] Never would *Y Drych* recoil from doing its fair share of brawling in the in-fighting between rival camps that characterised the world of Welsh publishing in America around this time. H. O. Rowlands noted that 'between John W. and John M. there was an implacable and eternal enmity which would continuously break out in vitriolic and butcher-like writing',[30] and which continued long after *Y Cymro-Americaidd*, the weaker of the two newspapers, collapsed in May 1861.[31]

But John Morgan Jones' criticisms of the paper's politics had raised the important issue of how the paper should address the key political questions of the day. In 1851, as we have seen, it had largely ignored them, but political coverage in the paper increased during the 1850s. By February 1855 editorials on slavery and politics were appearing[32] whilst the 1856 presidential campaign, and the political loyalties of the Welsh, were discussed in intricate detail.[33] In November 1856 *Y Drych* asserted that never before had the Welsh in America shown so much interest in politics.[34] Particular emphasis was put on the Republican opposition to slavery.[35] The Welsh were urged to support that party's presidential candidate, John C. Frémont, and a biography of him, adapted from two English-language works, was translated into Welsh and serialised in the paper between August and October 1856.[36] This Republican and anti-extension of slavery policy was to dominate the paper's political direction as the United States descended into civil war in 1861. Indeed the late 1850s were crucial years in the formation of *Y Drych*'s political identity, for loyalty to Republicanism would remain as one of the strongest voices emanating from its columns for generations after General Robert E. Lee's surrender at Appomattox on 9 April 1865 brought the carnage of domestic warfare to a close.

Civil War and the transfer to Utica: 1860-74
Sometime in May or June 1860 John William Jones moved *Y Drych* from New York City to Utica in upstate New York, though precisely when and why he did so is uncertain. (The only issue from those months that appears to have survived, 12 May, was published in New

York City.) According to Digain Williams in 1921, the first Utica issue came out on 9 June 1860 and three weeks later John W. Jones revealed that friends of *Y Drych* had been regularly and earnestly urging it to go to Utica for the previous two years.[37] An advertisement for the paper in another Welsh periodical during this period welcomed the relocation as a rational step, as 'Utica is the most advantageous place to publish a weekly paper, because the city is in the middle of a country of Welsh people, and is more central to the Welsh in general.'[38] As we shall see more fully in the next chapter, setting up business in Utica was a propitious step for the paper's long-term future not only because of the city's strong Welsh community base. It also brought *Y Drych* into contact with its later owner and financial benefactor, the redoubtable Thomas J. Griffiths, who was awarded the new printing contract at his offices at 131 Genesee Street, Utica.

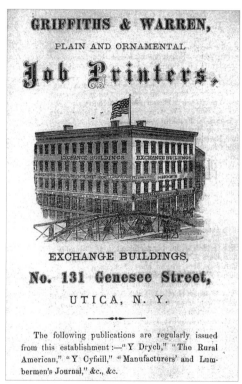

GRIFFITHS & WARREN,

PLAIN AND ORNAMENTAL

Job Printers,

EXCHANGE BUILDINGS,

No. 131 Genesee Street,

UTICA, N. Y.

The following publications are regularly issued from this establishment :—"Y Drych," "The Rural American," "Y Cyfaill," "Manufacturers' and Lumbermen's Journal," &c., &c.

Y Drych's first home in Utica: the Exchange Building, 131 Genesee Street. Around this time T. J. Griffiths had temporarily gone into partnership with one of his employees, Charles Warren.

From Utica City Directory 1868-69.

An article on the Welsh press in America by *Baner ac Amserau Cymru*'s United States reporter in 1862 provides a rare and intriguing glimpse into the condition of *Y Drych* during the early 1860s. The article approved of *Y Drych*'s efforts but asserted that editor and owner J. W. Jones had not so far succeeded in making much money from the paper and was owed hundreds of dollars; two thousand out of the approximately three thousand subscribers were

Calling the Civil War draft for the city of Utica, Mechanics Hall, Utica, 28 August 1863.
From 1922 until the 1950s *Y Drych* was published in this historic building.
*Photograph from the Archives of the Oneida County Historical Society at Utica, New York,
reproduced by kind permission.*

not paying fully or promptly. It seems *Y Drych* would undoubtedly have
folded had Jones not used the proceeds of his lecture tours on
astronomy to pay for printing the paper, and that Jones could have made
much more money following his craft as a furniture maker than through *Y
Drych*. As far as the writer of the article himself was concerned,
producing *Y Drych* was an unenviable task; if he was the owner 'he
would go to stand on his head, or shout boo hoo out on the streets,
rather than crucify himself for such unprofitable and thankless work'.[39]

It was in this ambiguous position of being journalistically respected
but financially precarious that *Y Drych* faced the challenge of the
American Civil War. When war was declared in 1861, it swiftly
demonstrated its passionate support of the Northern cause, interpreting
the conflict as a crusade to free the slaves from 'high treasonous
murderers and thieves'.[40] The Welsh-American press as a whole was
anxious to portray the Welsh as above reproach in their patriotic fervour

for the Union; in 1863 one correspondent called for *Y Drych* to print the names of all those who fought for the Union, and those who did not do their constitutional duty as citizens of the USA by refusing to fight.[41] From the start of the conflict the paper also advocated the formation of Welsh soldier regiments and companies to fight for their adopted country.[42] *Y Drych* was swept up by this nationalistic zeal and began to criticise the position of neutrality towards the conflict adopted by both Welsh and British leaders. Highly critical articles by John William Jones were printed in their entirety in the Welsh weekly newspaper *Yr Herald Cymraeg*,[43] where they were condemned for the savagery of their attack on Britain.[44] In response, *Y Drych* in 1863 printed a series of front-page letters on 'The Welsh Press and the American Crisis',[45] which typically included such sentiments as the following, by 'Undebwr' [Unionist]:

> I can hardly believe that my own kinsfolk, although totally ignorant of the true nature of the civil war and the enormous outcomes that depend on it, are willing to turn traitor to their blood-bought principles, by defending the slaveholding deserters in their attempts to destroy our country and to establish a slaveholders' empire on its ruins.[46]

As it appears that only issues for the year 1863 have survived, it is difficult to provide an overview of *Y Drych*'s content during the conflict. It is clear, though, that the paper established a pattern that would be repeated in its later coverage of the First and Second World Wars. Beyond commentary on the war and, as we have seen, the keeping of a close, and increasingly outraged, eye on opinion in Wales itself, *Y Drych* also sought to bring news of Welsh people, and Welsh soldiers in particular, to its readers. Impersonal general news of the various campaigns and battles was vivified by glimpses of individual experience, in the form of letters from Welsh soldiers in the various combat zones. For example, on 24 January 1863, the paper printed a letter from Gwilym Ap Ioan (who in 1855 was *Y Drych a'r Gwyliedydd*'s poetry editor),[47] writing on behalf of a group of Welsh in the Cattaraugus Regiment (154th New York Volunteers). Among other things, the letter described how they cooked their Christmas dinner. Two weeks earlier, John W. Rowlands of Slate Hill, Pennsylvania, writing from a camp near Fredericksburg in early December 1862,

Some Welsh soldiers from Iowa and Minnesota who volunteered for the Union army during the American Civil War. From Thomas E. Hughes, David Edwards, Hugh G. Roberts and Thomas Hughes, *Hanes Cymry Minnesota, Foreston a Lime Springs Iowa / History of the Welsh in Minnesota, Foreston and Lime Springs Iowa* (Mankato, 1895), pp. 116-120, English-language section. The book records details on some of these soldiers. James Edwards and James Roberts were among the first four men to enlist from Mankato; Lewis Lewis was wounded, captured, and died in Andersonville Prison Camp in 1864; Stephen Walters, David Walters and William Edwards of Courtland, Minnesota, and Joshua Wigley of Lake Crystal survived.

provided readers with an arresting description of soldiers bravely going into battle as heroes, and then when it was over

> in an instant the iron men take on the character of tender children, and they can be seen searching, anxiously, for a brother, or a friend among the dead and wounded that lie in their blood. [The men] pull one [body] off the back of another while their hearts beat in sadness, and while bright tears roll down their cheeks. Oh what gravity! Oh what anxiety! Oh what damage to life! Oh War![48]

A survivor of the battle of Antietam, Rowlands believed he had seen more in an hour than he wished to see in a lifetime again. Such accounts frequently found their way back to the homeland. Although *Y Drych* undoubtedly had its quarrels with the press in Wales during this time, the latter nevertheless relied on the former for Welsh-language accounts to include in their own columns. On 18 February 1865, for example, the Aberdare newspaper *Y Gwladgarwr* [The Patriot] reprinted from *Y Drych* a letter E. D. Williams, Company D, 117th Regiment, New York Volunteers, had written on New Year's Day 1865 to his parents in New York Mills, Utica. At the time of writing he was with the James River Army near Richmond.[49]

In 1864, in the midst of this national and international crisis, John William Jones relinquished his editorship to John Mather Jones, to whom he also sold the paper in August the following year.[50] Originally from Bangor, Caernarfonshire, Mather Jones had settled in Brooklyn in 1849 and, after a period as a mortgage and real estate trader, had just returned from travelling widely in Asia, Australia and Europe.[51] Like John William Jones, he was an ardent abolitionist and Republican. He also firmly believed that the Welsh needed to settle close together rather than being scattered over the continent, and no doubt this in part explained his developing a number of land settlement schemes during the course of his life. Again, no copies of *Y Drych* covering the time of the change of ownership and editorship have survived. However, it is highly probable that the principal motive behind the acquisition was less the result of the crisis precipitated by the Civil War than of a desire by both new and old owner to establish Welsh homelands in the United States. In 1863 John Mather Jones had bought tracts of land in Macon County, Missouri, for the purpose of settling his 'New Cambria' with fresh immigrants from Wales. Mather Jones may have become involved in *Y Drych* and later purchased it specifically to publicise the venture. In 1864 John William Jones returned to Wales to act as an emigration agent with the task of drawing attention to the New Cambria settlement scheme. We can only surmise whether the two worked in collaboration, but their later partnership in 1869 to buy between 70,000 and 100,000 acres of land in Osage County, Kansas, to establish the Welsh settlement of Arvonia lends plausibility to the existence of a co-ordinated and emigration-led business strategy in which the newspaper played a central propagandist role.[52]

Rival homeland settlement schemes may also have intensified *Y Drych*'s rancour towards any who appeared to be associated with the Confederacy or who criticised the Republican North. The most ferocious attacks were made on the formidable preacher-politician Samuel Roberts (familiarly known as S. R.), who had announced in *Y Drych* in February 1856 his plans to establish Brynffynnon, a Welsh homeland in Tennessee.[53] (He left Llanbrynmair, Montgomeryshire, for Brynffynnon the following year.) From the outset, his scheme brought him into conflict with *Y Drych*, which was pursuing its own settlement schemes elsewhere in the United States.[54] In July 1856 S. R. was already complaining of the paper's unfavourable attitude towards him.[55] In 1861, the strongly pacifist S. R. publicly

Advertisement for the Welsh Settlement in Arvonia, Kansas.

From *Y Drych*, 24 March 1870.

Samuel Roberts (1800-1885): an implacable critic of *Y Drych* during the last thirty years of his life.

opposed the Civil War,[56] and suffered as a result repeated assaults on his character and judgement in the pages of the by now militantly Republican *Y Drych*. The publication in 1865 – ironically by T. J. Griffiths – of S. R.'s apologia, *Pregethau a Darlithiau*[57] [Sermons and Lectures], led to a further deterioration in relations. The book sold well and S. R. later alleged that he had agreed to T. J. Griffiths retaining the proceeds in order to save the latter from bankruptcy, a claim Griffiths flatly denied.[58] But *Pregethau a Darlithiau* also appeared at a time when the nation was in deep mourning, both for its fallen war dead and for its recently assassinated president. S. R.'s bitter conclusion that Welsh-American support for the war was evidence of an entire community's abandonment of Christian values was particularly resented. In its equally intemperate reply, *Y Drych* referred to him as 'a worse traitor and a more zealous supporter of slavery than the Southerners themselves.'[59] Such devastating criticisms, and equally acrimonious rejoinders, appeared in the paper throughout 1865 and into 1866.[60]

In sharp contrast, in the immediate aftermath of war, *Y Drych* sought to produce a history of the war that would further legitimate its own patriotic record. This extraordinary volume, *Hanes Y Gwrthryfel Mawr yn y Talaethau Unedig* [A History of the Great Rebellion in the United States], ran to more than six hundred pages, and was intended to be the first of a series of volumes.[61] Written by a past and current editor of *Y Drych*, John William Jones and T. B. Morris (who appears to have made the greater contribution), it was largely financed by the paper's owner,

John Mather Jones, and its grandiose aim was to be a 'HISTORY that the Welsh people can depend upon, and the age to come can refer to as an authentic authority'.[62] Unfortunately for them, it was a publishing disaster which was to have serious financial consequences for the newspaper.[63]

In 1867, following his return to Wales the previous year, S. R. defended his position on the American Civil War in a closely argued polemic, *Hunan-Amddiffyniad S. R.* [The Self Defence of S. R.], in which he refuted the allegation of being pro-slavery made against him in *Y Drych*. In typically vivid fashion, he alluded to the 'quack doctors of *Y Drych* administering the strychnine of war to counteract the arsenic of slavery'.[64] He alleged that the paper's editors had consistently refused to allow him a right to reply in its pages and in so doing were 'breaking their word, tearing up their covenant, trampling underfoot all the honour of their agreements, and transgressing the rules of all free thinking, and the laws abided by the offices of every publication of any worth.'[65] 'Not even the most hot-headed slave holders that were ever in the South', he concluded, 'were more rabid in misrepresenting and persecuting any anti-slavery man, as were the unionists of Y Drych in persecuting S. R. for being an anti-war man.'[66]

The running feud between *Y Drych* and S. R. could still fizzle in the columns of the paper as late as 1881.[67] Nor was this the only quarrel it had with a leading Welsh figure and a momentous colonial scheme during the 1850s, 1860s and 1870s. From 1856 onwards the paper granted much column space to details of Michael D. Jones' plans for a Welsh 'Gwladfa' [Colony], eventually established in Patagonia in 1865, and to discussion of the positive and negative aspects of the scheme. Letters in favour and against appeared regularly.[68] (The paper continued to publish news reports and other items on the Welsh there, and the subsequent migration of some of the colonists to Canada in the early twentieth century was covered in depth.[69] Indeed news from Patagonia continues to appear in *Y Drych* in the present day.) *Y Drych* soon adopted a critical stance towards the Welsh colony in Patagonia and Jones himself. In 1856-1857 a serialised novel entitled 'Y Carcharor yn Mhatagonia' [The Prisoner in Patagonia], sought to discourage migration to the area, which was already being mooted as a possible site for a Welsh colony. As if to emphasise the dangers, the novel's episodes

John C. Roberts (1840-1911), editor 1869-1911.

From The Cambrian, *15 November 1911. Reproduced by kind permission of the National Library of Wales.*

were accompanied by illustrations of ferocious natives and scorpions.[70] By the early 1870s, enmities had seemingly become set in stone, and *Y Drych* regularly condemned Jones and the colony in the columns of the paper.[71] Not that Jones was reluctant to return the compliment. When he visited the USA in 1871 to drum up support and encourage more Welsh Americans to emigrate to Patagonia, he publicly and vehemently attacked John W. Jones and *Y Drych*. In return John W. Jones, never one to shy away from confrontation, sarcastically christened Michael D. Jones 'Ei Anrhydedd' [His Honour] and in 1872 wrote a series of articles entitled 'Y Wladfa Gymreig yn Ynfydrwydd' [The Welsh Colony is a Madness].[72]

But despite these continuing disputations, as passions cooled in the post-Civil War period of reconstruction after 1865, both the conduct of *Y Drych* and the composition and mood of the Welsh community it served underwent important if subtle changes. From 1869, the considerable energies of John Mather Jones were devoted increasingly to the Arvonia settlement, and while he remained the paper's proprietor until his death in December 1874, he relinquished the editorship of *Y Drych* in favour of Joseph W. Nichols (Neifion) and John C. Roberts.[73] The latter, appointed fresh from Wales, filled the post of editor with great distinction through arguably the newspaper's most successful years, until his death in November 1911. And despite the paper's continuing enthusiasm for Welsh land settlement schemes and the fortunes that could thereby be made by its owners, other evidence from the newspaper at this time suggests that during the late 1860s Welsh society in the United States began to take on a more settled countenance. Compared to the 1850s, the numbers and proportions of emigration advertisements were beginning to decline, while retail businesses with Welsh connections increasingly used the paper to sell their goods. At the same time, the geographical sources of these commodity advertisements become noticeably less diverse. In the early 1860s notices had appeared in the paper from locations as disparate as Montgomery House, San Francisco, and Ystordy Newydd [New Store], Birmingham, Pennsylvania.[74] However, in subsequent years they were mostly derived from Utica itself. This is not surprising, perhaps, given that Utica was the paper's home. By the late 1860s nearly all commercial advertisements in *Y Drych*, be they from grocery stores, clothes shops or undertakers, were from addresses on Genesee Street, Utica, making it one of the most well-known and famous streets in Welsh America.

But while advertisements were undeniably an important source of revenue for *Y Drych*, and a major factor in its commercial viability, the paper's managers remained acutely conscious of the need to extend its numeric and geographic circulation. To boost both, it offered inducements in the form of gifts to yearly subscribers who paid their dues in advance. The first of these was a carved image of the leading

New masthead introduced in April 1872.

Welsh Calvinist divine, the Revd John Elias, awarded to those who dutifully paid their subscriptions for 1861 before the 31 December 1860.[75] Such tactics appear to have had some success, for the number of subscribers had almost doubled to over 5,000 between 1856 and the late 1860s,[76] when the paper's circulation was said (in English) to be 'extending, more or less, into almost every State in the Union'.[77] In 1868, to mark the beginning of this renewed process of expansion, a new branch office for Pennsylvania was opened in Pottsville, where the Revd E. R. Lewis was appointed the paper's 'General Agent for the State'.[78] In the same year, the format was enlarged to broadsheet size, which allowed greater newsprint space for editorial and advertising content. This more profligate use of space was celebrated after April 1872 by a more ornate masthead which retained some of the older symbols and introduced a centrally located mirror on which the paper's name was superimposed.[79]

The years between 1851 and 1874 thus saw *Y Drych* making its initial mark, both on its target community in the United States and on its readers and critics in Wales. Free of irksome competition from *Y Cymro-Americaidd* and other rival titles, it consolidated its position as the single most important medium of communication for the Welsh in America. However, these early years were not without their difficulties. Political arguments, tactical errors and financial problems beset the venture, and the Civil War severely tested its ability to speak for the Welsh in the United States as a whole. But the foundations had been laid for its future growth, most importantly by securing the support of the man with whom it was to become most closely identified, Thomas J. Griffiths of Utica. As an editorial of January 1870 presciently noted, the newspaper's prospects were 'promising and encouraging'.[80] *Y Drych* was about to enter its 'Golden Age'.

CHAPTER 3

Y Drych in its 'Imperial Phase', 1874-1920

The flourishing of *Y Drych* in the half-century leading up to the First World War may be attributed to a combination of favourable circumstances. These included, as we have seen in the first two chapters, enthusiastic business leadership, solid journalism, strong local support and a continuing influx of Welsh-speaking readers. But it was also fortunate to ride the crest of another wave, namely the huge increase in American newspaper production and the nationwide expansion of their readerships that coincided with the growth of a 'new journalism' to match the 'new immigration' of the 1880s and 1890s.[1] This was an era characterised by such brash, confident and commercially successful newspapers as William Randolph Hearst's *New York Journal* and Joseph Pulitzer's *New York World* that, particularly in the 1890s, informed and entertained their readers with a heady mixture of anti-corruption campaigns, sensationalist reporting, cartoons and photographs. It was also a time when a foreign-language press blossomed to serve the millions of new migrants from Central and Eastern Europe. In 1900 *Y Drych* was only one of 1,163 non-English-language newspapers in the United States.[2] Thus, popular newspapers, printed in a rich variety of languages besides English, not only became an established part of the social fabric of the USA, but also were among the most accessible and potent means of integrating newly arrived immigrants into the customs and structures of American society.

Y Drych, too, performed a dual role as both a commercial commodity and a means of cultural integration. In 1850, when John Morgan Jones had proposed the new Welsh newspaper, fewer than 30,000 foreign-born Welsh people were living in the USA. In 1890, however, their numbers exceeded 100,000.[3] This period of high Welsh immigration coincided with, and provided the principal basis for, the remarkable expansion and commercial success of *Y Drych* as a weekly newspaper. Of course, not all migrants from Wales could read Welsh, and because of the lack of sources, we do not know precisely how many could or could not do so.

According to the 1891 Census in Wales, 54.4 per cent of the resident population spoke Welsh. It would not be unreasonable to assume that a broadly comparable proportion of new Welsh immigrants at the end of the nineteenth century, and an even higher proportion of those who arrived earlier in the century, had knowledge of the language. In his *Hanes Cymry America* in 1872, Revd Robert D. Thomas estimated that there were in the United States 115,716 Welsh people who understood their native language, whilst in 1913 Daniel Williams discovered that about 60 per cent of the Wales-born population of Columbus, Ohio, spoke Welsh.[4] *Y Drych* was read most widely in the larger Welsh settlements clustered in Pennsylvania, where more than a third of foreign-born Welsh people lived in 1900, and New York State, but many had moved west, to Illinois, Wisconsin, California, wherever their industrial skills, especially in coal, iron and tinplate mining and processing, led them.[5] Soon, copies of *Y Drych* were being read in states across the Union by consumers long accustomed to the availability of newspapers in the Welsh language, whether of a regional nature, such as Thomas Gee's *Baner ac Amserau Cymru*, or those representing religious or industrial interests, such as *Y Goleuad* and *Tarian y Gweithiwr*. *Y Drych* was to provide not only a substitute for such reading, but would maintain a symbiotic relationship with those papers and their editors for much of its first century.

John Mather Jones' death in December 1874, and the subsequent purchase of the title by its printer and publisher, Thomas J. Griffiths, ushered in a new and dramatically expansionist phase in the paper's history. Griffiths, whose parents had emigrated from Bala, was born on 31 May 1835 at Deerfield, near Utica, and educated at Lombard's School in Utica, before moving on to the city's Academy.[6] In 1856 he began work as a compositor on the *Utica Morning Herald* and in 1860 purchased a share in D. C. Davies' printing company. In the same year, as we have already seen, he won the contract to print *Y Drych* even though he was unable to speak or read Welsh.[7] In 1862 he became sole owner of the firm. Although he later became very successful, his early years in business appear to have been more precarious. In 1877 he wrote to Samuel Roberts (in English): 'as for being short of money, why I have been often so, and always expect to be short at times, am not short at present time but may be many a time before the year is out'.[8]

Griffiths went on to publish more than a hundred Welsh language imprints, and became known as 'The Dean of Welsh Publishing in America'. He was also responsible for publishing the long running denominational periodical *Y Cyfaill* and, from 1887 onwards, the English-language Welsh-American monthly magazine *The Cambrian*, which he eventually purchased around 1900.[9] Following his death on 6 February 1924, control of *Y Drych* and the rest of his publishing company passed to his sons, Charles W. Griffiths and Thomas J. Griffiths, Jnr. Their father's name remained on the paper's masthead until it was sold to its editor, Arthur M. Roberts, in April 1951.

The success of *Y Drych* from 1874 can be attributed largely to

Thomas J. Griffiths (1835-1924), owner of *Y Drych,* 1874-1924.

Photograph from the Archives of the Oneida County Historical Society at Utica, New York, reproduced by kind permission.

Thomas J. Griffiths' financial acumen and support. As we shall see, he employed some of the best Welsh literary talents and printers around, equipping the latter with up-to-date machinery and in turn demanding the highest standards from them.[10] Writing in the 1920s, Henry Blackwell, the renowned Welsh-American antiquarian and bibliophile, was in no doubt about Griffiths' significance: 'The paper might not have survived but for his business sagacity and devotion. He acquired it when it was a struggling sheet and developed it into one of the best known journals in the Welsh world. . . . For what he has done to promote Welsh literature in America he was truly the best Welshman in America.'[11]

The city of Utica to which *Y Drych* was transferred in 1860 had first been settled by Welsh families in 1795, and by 1801 they had built its first Welsh Baptist Church.[12] It was also a cosmopolitan community, where a population of no more than 250 spoke a dozen languages. In 1812, 700 Welsh-born people were living there, and by 1850, the Welsh in the nearby settlements of Remsen and Steuben comprised three-quarters of the population. Welsh settlement reached its height in Oneida County as a whole in 1855, when its Welsh-born population exceeded 4,000. The great majority of them hailed from the counties in the north of the homeland; indeed in 1864 one observer believed it was not possible to differentiate Utica from some of the towns of north Wales.[13] Most of the Welsh boys and men were employed in construction as masons and carpenters, while both men and women worked in the local textile mills. By the late nineteenth century, however, a high proportion of the Utica Welsh might be considered to have reached middle-class status in commerce and the professions, in a town where they comprised the second largest ethnic group.[14] Partly as a consequence of this solid basis of 'old immigrants', Utica was a nationally known centre of Welsh publishing. The first Welsh hymnal, *Pigion o Hymnau,* had been printed there in 1808, although most book publishing occurred after 1840. By the early twentieth century, some two hundred Welsh books had been published in the town.[15] In the midst of this thriving industry, T. J. Griffiths, who printed material in both Welsh and English, had emerged by 1862 as the leading printer and publisher of Welsh books in the USA.[16]

The half-century that followed 1874 was also a period of astonishing stability, in terms both of the paper's ownership and editorial control, thereby providing an essential foundation for the successful programme of expansion on which *Y Drych* now embarked. The Griffiths family was to own the title for seventy-seven years, while John C. Roberts' hand remained on the editorial tiller from March 1869 until his death in 1911.[17] 'John C. y "Drych"' or simply 'J.C.', as he was generally known, became almost an institution in his own right. Born in Llysfaen, Caernarfonshire, in 1840, he had started work at *Y Drych* within a year of emigrating to America in 1866 following a brief career as a teacher in Wales.[18] Together with his brother, Richard E. Roberts, *Y Drych*'s book-keeper for over twenty years until his death at the age of only forty-eight in 1898, 'J.C.' also ran a Welsh book business in Utica.[19] In addition he was one of the pillars of the city's Welsh community in the city, giving years of service to the Utica Cymreigyddion Society and Moriah Welsh Church. Like his employer, T. J. Griffiths, John C. Roberts must be regarded as one of the most important individuals in *Y*

Drych's history. A memorial tribute to him in 1911 maintained that the success of the paper was 'to a high degree due to his diligence, faithfulness, good taste, and tireless commitment.'[20]

During his term of office John C. Roberts was joined in the shared editorial chair by a succession of talented individuals. All of them were, or became, respected writers, prominent figures in the Utica Welsh community and faithful servants of its social, cultural and religious organisations. Most were also ardent Republicans. According to Henry Blackwell, T. J. Griffiths 'selected the best Welshmen obtainable to conduct the paper – all he wanted of them was for them to do their best and give the news. He was against puffing'.[21] Until his death in October 1884, John William Jones co-edited the paper with Roberts. His successor was Griffith Henry Humphrey, a preacher, solicitor and Republican activist.[22] Humphrey had emigrated with his parents to Ixonia in Wisconsin less than a year after his birth in 1844 in Llanarmon near Caernarfon. Having been raised in a part of Wisconsin with a large German population, he had become fluent in that language as well as Welsh and English. Humphrey resigned as co-editor at the end of May 1892 in order to

Richard E. Roberts (1850-1898). The man who looked after *Y Drych's* subscription lists, and J. C. Roberts's brother.
From The Cambrian, *July 1898.*

Gwilym H. Humphrey (1844-1906), editor of *Y Drych*, 1884-1892.
From The Cambrian, *November 1906.*

Benjamin F. Lewis (1832-1897), editor of
Y Drych, 1892-1897.
*Photograph from the Archives of the Oneida County
Historical Society at Utica, New York, reproduced by
kind permission.*

devote more time to his legal practice, although he continued to write regularly for the paper.[23] John C. Roberts' next partner as co-editor was Benjamin F. Lewis, the paper's original typesetter and erstwhile editor of the rival *Y Cymro Americaidd*. Born in 1832, Lewis was a native of Llanidloes who had emigrated to New York in 1848. He joined *Y Drych* from the *Utica Herald-Dispatch*, where he had been working for twenty-seven years.[24]

A month before Lewis' death in June 1897, there arrived at *Y Drych* another well-known Welsh literary figure who, like John Roberts, was also to guide the paper editorially for a long, uninterrupted period. Dafydd Rhys Williams (familiarly known by his literary pseudonym, 'Index'), remained in post until his retirement and return to Wales in 1923.[25] Index was a prolific poet and prose writer who penned a number of classic Welsh-language works. The son of a cattle drover, he was born in Cefn Coed y Cymer near Merthyr Tydfil in 1851, and in early life worked underground in a coal mine whilst he taught himself to read and write in English, French and Latin. He emigrated to the United States in 1883, settling first in Brooklyn, Ohio, before moving to Utica when he joined *Y Drych*. Between March 1912 and 1918, R. Morris Williams worked alongside Index as managing editor.[26] Previously Williams had been a reporter for the *Scranton Republican*, having moved to Scranton, Pennsylvania, from his native Tanygrisiau, Meirionnydd, in 1908 when he was about twenty-four years old. He left *Y Drych* to establish his own printing company in Utica. After Williams' departure, R. T.

Dafydd Rhys Williams (Index) (1851-
1931), editor of *Y Drych*, 1897-1923.

From Y Drych, *4 January 1923.*

R. Morris Williams (1884-1950), editor
of *Y Drych*, 1912-1918.

From Y Drych, *27 December 1923.*

Williams served as second editor for about a year, but for the last four
years of his tenure Index had the editorial chair to himself.[27]

Throughout this time of editorial stability and continuity, *Y Drych*
was edited and printed in two locations in Utica, the first being the
Exchange Building (later the Foster Building) on the southeast corner of
Genesee Street and the Erie Canal. In April 1884, *Y Drych*'s travelling
agent William D. Davies described what he saw when he visited the
paper's office that month:

> Everything there appeared organised and lively – T. J. Griffiths cheerfully
> and industriously overseeing all; J. W. Jones and J. C. Roberts organising
> and selecting suitable things to appear in the DRYCH, for the benefit of
> the Welsh nation throughout the States: and Richard E. Roberts looking
> after one of the most important departments in the office, the accounts.
> And of course several other Welsh with literary talents were there
> facilitating the office's work.[28]

The Exchange Building, 131 Genesee Street, where *Y Drych* was published
1860-1900, October 1894.

Photograph from the Archives of Utica Public Library, Utica, New York, reproduced by kind permission.

Later, in April 1900, T. J. Griffiths' business, and *Y Drych* with it,
moved to the business block on the corner of Liberty and Hotel Streets
(No. 11 Liberty Street).[29] A visitor to the paper's office there in August
1914 suggested that those writers who always complained that their
contributions appeared late in *Y Drych* should 'see tens of letters
continually bubbling in, and every correspondent asking for space in the
next [issue]. . . . R. M. [Williams] was nearly out of sight behind reports
and could not see the desk.'[30]

It was from this stable base, rooted commercially as well as editorially
in the strong, well-established and relatively prosperous Welsh community
of Utica, that in the years after 1874 *Y Drych* began to tread the path
towards its domination of Welsh journalism in North America. The
clearest evidence of its ambitions to be the single most important Welsh
newspaper in the United States may be found in its expansionist policy

towards its real and potential rivals during the final quarter of the nineteenth century. As we have seen, in 1855 *Y Drych* had acquired and assimilated the Utica-based weekly, *Y Gwyliedydd*. Three further mergers were to be negotiated between 1877 and 1894, each of which extended the paper's geographical reach, expanded its readership and diversified its sources of news and other editorial content. They also further demonstrated the importance of Utica, and of T. J. Griffiths' publishing enterprise, over other centres of Welsh settlement in the United States.

The first paper to be purchased by Griffiths was the Scranton-based *Baner America* in 1877, which then had a circulation of around 2,000.[31]

Established in Scranton in 1868, it had long been at the centre of a large Welsh community, one that industrial migration from Wales to the anthracite coalfields in and around the city continued to replenish.[32] To meet the demands of this vibrant community, Griffiths retained the *Baner America* office in Scranton (at 310 Lackawanna Street) for a further seven years. In 1884 Griffiths claimed that the circulation of *Y Drych* exceeded that of all the other Welsh weeklies and monthlies in the United States combined.[33] In May 1890, he turned his attention to Pittsburgh, where he bought *Y Wasg*,[34] founded in May 1871, while in February 1894 he acquired *Y Columbia*, established in Chicago in 1888.[35] Like *Baner America* before them, these two papers

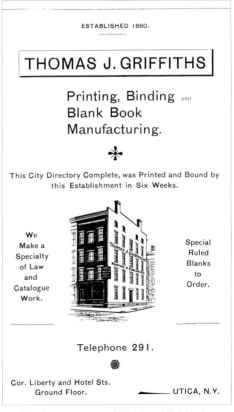

The headquarters of Welsh publishing in America between 1900 and 1922.

From Utica City Directory, 1902.

were said to be making heavy losses at the time of their acquisition. There had been several instances of friction between *Y Drych* and each of its former rivals, although because few issues of *Baner America*, *Y Columbia* and *Y Wasg* have apparently survived it is difficult to determine how these papers addressed *Y Drych* in their columns.[36] It was alleged, for example, that *Y Drych* had been less enthusiastic about the World's Fair Eisteddfod in Chicago in 1893, the year before its take-over of *Y Columbia*, because the latter had been the main mouthpiece of that event's organising committee.[37] However, one can only speculate to what extent these factors contributed to Griffiths' decisions. After *Y Wasg* had been purchased in May 1890, *Y Drych* triumphantly played down the challenge the former had presented: 'it has been recognised for many years that Y DRYCH had few competitors in the breadth of its circulation, the extent of its news and the character of its literature.'[38]

In the case of *Y Wasg* and *Y Columbia*, *Y Drych* justified the purchases on the grounds that both these papers were printed in a combination of Welsh and English. *Y Columbia* had, according to Griffiths, failed to capture a readership that preferred their weekly newspaper to be 'Welsh in language and sentiment'.[39] Whether that was strictly true remains a moot point, but Griffiths evidently regarded the Chicago newspaper as a significant competitor in a small market, declaring that the Welsh were not 'sufficiently numerous in this country to maintain two weekly newspapers'.[40] It seems *Y Drych*'s bullish policy ruffled a few feathers, as some of *Y Columbia*'s supporters established a new newspaper, *Yr Adlais* [The Echo], and the front page of its first issue was apparently full of hostility towards *Y Drych*.[41] The acquisition of *Y Columbia*'s subscription list further extended the readership and advertisement base of *Y Drych* into the mid-West and the Welsh settlements in Illinois, Wisconsin and Iowa. It claimed at this point to have a circulation of 12,000 a week.[42]

Each step in this process of expansion brought with it a more confident self-image, as expressed in the iconography of masthead design. An increase in the size of the paper in January 1879 was marked by the appearance of a new, enlarged and more baroque masthead. With the White House taking centre stage in an ornate tableau that balanced the Red Dragon and depictions of the ancient world on the left with the

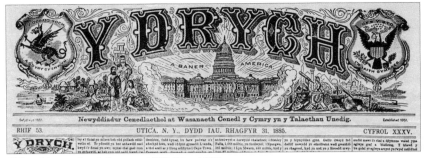

Y *Drych*'s masthead, January 1879-May 1890.

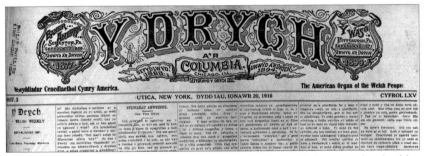

Y *Drych*'s 'imperial phase': new masthead introduced after 1894, incorporating the titles of the newspapers purchased by T. J. Griffiths.

American bald eagle and images of modernity on the right, Y *Drych* heralded itself as *Newyddiadur Cenedlaethol Cymry America* [National Newspaper of the Welsh in America].[43] The paper projected itself as an instrument of learning and progress, and explicitly associated the Welsh language with American patriotism. Following the acquisitions of 1877, 1890 and 1894, Y *Drych*'s masthead bore witness to its imperial expansion following the incorporation of the titles and dates of its conquests. More significantly, the emblems of Y *Wasg* and Y *Columbia* replaced the more explicitly Republican imagery.[44] Apart from mastheads and advertisements, Y *Drych* throughout this period contained little illustrated material. Until the end of the century most were engravings taken from other newspapers, including those of the exhibition buildings at the Chicago World's Fair of 1893.[45] It appears Y *Drych* printed its first photograph, of Baptist minister J. Gomer Lewis, on 18 May 1893.[46]

The format of the paper also acquired greater consistency during this period of growth. To the editorial, market price and poetry columns were added other regular sections. One of the most striking of these involved missing persons enquiries, which were a feature of the paper from the 1850s through to the 1930s.[47] Welsh Americans attempting to track down relatives with whom they had lost touch placed notices such as the following, from August 1891:

> DAVID R. JONES, son of the late Meredith Jones, Arthog, Meirioneth. He emigrated to this country 18 years ago. He was last heard from in Dakota. I would be grateful for any word from him or anybody that knows him. His brother – JOHN M. JONES, Box 389 Granville, N.Y.[48]

There is no way of knowing how many of these notices were successful although the paper did manage to reunite some dispersed families.[49]

Reunited by *Y Drych* in 1908. John Griffiths, Utica (seated left), and Thomas H. Griffiths, Iowa (seated right), with Mrs T. H. Griffiths (standing left) and Mrs William M. Williams, John Griffiths' daughter. See reports in *Y Drych*, 3 September, 1 October 1908.

Photograph from The Cambrian, *October 1908.*

In 1908 Thomas H. Griffiths, of Iowa, aged 82, met his cousin John Griffiths of Utica, aged 85, for the first time. The report of the meeting in *Y Drych* was seen by another cousin, Jane Reynolds, who had not seen Thomas for seventy years.[50] The paper may also have been more proactive as a dating agency than merely printing occasional 'Wife wanted' notices and letters which drew attention to a shortage of Welsh women in particular localities (the gendered dimension to this will be discussed in the next chapter).[51] In 1921 Digain Williams of California opined that *Y Drych* not only searched silently for lost Welsh people, but had also done so 'even more silently for husbands and wives for many Welsh who were available, but behaving as if they were lost'.[52] Other regular sections in *Y Drych* included music, which introduced the work of Welsh-American composers as well as those from Wales, culled principally from the north Wales magazine *Y Cerddor* [The Musician]; comic limericks, cartoons and short stories; a review of the press, religious news and agricultural information. Increasing space was devoted to eisteddfodic prose, including such prize-winning essays as 'The Search for the Madogiaid' that won the Poultney, Vermont, Eisteddfod in 1904 and which appeared in instalments over a five-week period.[53]

Another popular prose form was travel writing. Often this consisted of nostalgic return journeys to childhood homes in Wales but other writings in the genre took readers across the continent and even around the globe. Confirming its aim to be among the best of newspapers in whatever language, a notice in *Y Drych* in 1884 explained that overseas travel accounts were an important section in English newspapers so 'certainly the DRYCH's readers should be honoured with the same intellectual and interesting delicacies'.[54] One of the striking features of *Y Drych*'s pages during the late nineteenth and early twentieth centuries is the significant number of accounts of visits to new settlements in the United States, especially in the west, that they contain. People who would never have the opportunity – or the inclination – to visit distant places nevertheless wished to read about them. These items, many of which contain fine passages of vivid and evocative writing, invariably also included some reference to the Welsh in the areas visited – how many of them were there, the condition of their religious institutions, the names of famous and successful businesses and professionals and so forth. It is partly because of accounts like these that *Y Drych* is such a

William O. Thomas, author of *Dwywaith o Amgylch Y Byd* (1882), which first appeared in instalments in *Y Drych* in the late 1870s.

William D. Davies, travelling agent for *Y Drych* in the 1880s and 1890s. His accounts of his travels were published in instalments in the paper and also as *Llwybrau Bywyd* (1889) and *America a Gweledigaethau Bywyd* (1895).

valuable source for historians of the Welsh in North America. A typical example of travel writing in *Y Drych* during this period may be found in the recollections of Miss Maggie Jones of Bridgewater, New York, following the journey she and her sister undertook in late 1883 and early 1884 to see friends and relatives in Wisconsin and Minnesota before moving on to visit Dakota Territory.[55] As well as individual pieces, serialised travel writing was also common. Editor and owner John William Jones was an early and accomplished contributor in this vein,[56] whilst some series were later published by T. J. Griffiths as books in their own right. Notable here are the global wanderings of William O. Thomas in the late 1870s, which later appeared as *Dwywaith O Amgylch Y Byd* [Twice Around the World],[57] and William D. Davies' tours of Wales and of Welsh communities in America, which formed the basis of *Llwybrau Bywyd* [The Paths of Life] and *America a Gweledigaethau Bywyd* [America and the Visions of Life].[58]

In terms of content, *Y Drych* was far more wide-ranging than its contemporary Welsh-language newspapers in Wales. In 1883 the Cincinnati-published English-language Welsh-American periodical *The Cambrian* described it as being 'full of good reading – from the news of the week to the editorial squibs and comments,

'A Wedding in Philadelphia Welsh Church', which appeared in *Y Drych*, 3 November 1910. The bride and groom are Margaret Owen of Caernarfon (seated left) and J. Humphreys Griffiths (standing second left), one of the paper's Philadelphia correspondents. The couple had apparently been sweethearts in Wales.

from the generalizations and dissertations of the philosopher to the musings of the poet. Its columns have been fraught with a little of everything, civil, political, moral, religious, historical, archaeological, natal, hymneal and *disputational*.'[59] A good indication of *Y Drych*'s regular format and the variety of reading material it offered during its heyday can be gained from a brief survey of the five issues and forty pages of the paper that appeared in September 1898. The first two pages of each issue were usually reserved for items of important national or international news, feature articles discussing various topics, and tributes. On page one on 1 September, for example, there was an appreciation of one of Wales' biggest idols of the second half of the nineteenth century, the British Liberal Prime Minister, William Ewart Gladstone, who had died the previous May. Alongside it an article discussed the relationship between the Welsh Celt and the Pulpit, whilst another paid memorial tribute to the recently deceased Revd Richard Hughes of Pawnee City, Nebraska.[60] Much of page three was generally devoted to allowing Welsh North Americans to have their own say – the letters column, 'Syniadau y Bobl' [The People's Ideas]. Personal reports of Welsh people's successes, tragedies, promotions, visits and all manner of experiences were occasionally included in individual features in their own right, but were more usually incorporated in the reports

Rhys Lewis Dance Company, Rome, New York.   *From* Y Drych, *23 June 1910.*

West Pawlet, Vermont, Children's Choir, with their leader, Isaac Henry Hughes, and accompanist, Mrs Blanche Morris Roberts, 1911. The choir won many eisteddfod prizes in Utica and the New York-Vermont slate region around this time.

From Y Drych, *6 June 1911.*

from the various Welsh settlements or in the 'Nodion Personol' [Personal Notes] section alongside the editorial comments normally on page four. The columns of September 1898 typically blended news of sadness and joy: for example, the death of Thomas Jones, aged 19, of Scranton who had fallen down the 500 foot deep shaft of Storrs No. 2 Mine in the city, and the 'surprise' party given to Mrs Kendrick Hughes of Cincinnati, consisting of feasting on the lawn outside her house, interspersed with vocal solos, recitations and toasts.[61] Just as diverse were the subjects of the paper's editorials, where the paper opined on an amazing range of matters. As might be expected, political, religious and social topics of the day in both America and Wales came in for a good deal of scrutiny, as did issues and questions relating to the Welsh language and the condition of the Welsh ethnic group in the USA. But so, too, was there an editorial that welcomed the purchase by the Wesleyan University, Syracuse of the library of the late pioneer German historian Leopold von Ranke.[62] There was even one which condemned people who wore squeaky shoes in church and other gatherings,[63] whilst another pondered on what type of man could wear a moustache with propriety.[64]

At least three of the inside pages of each issue in September 1898 were almost entirely devoted to news from the various Welsh communities in the United States, among them settlements as diverse and different as Gomer, Ohio; Blue Earth County, Minnesota; Philadelphia; Granville, New York; Scranton; Utica; Emporia, Kansas; Chicago and Great Falls, Montana. No shortage of Welsh cultural gatherings that month – eisteddfodau in Newcastle, Pennsylvania, and Clear Creek County, Colorado, while the programme of competitions for the forthcoming Fortieth Utica Eisteddfod, to be held on New Year's Eve 1898 and 2 January 1899, was also printed.[65] The Old Settlers of Mahoning Valley, Ohio, held what generally seems to have been a highly successful picnic in Squaw Creek Park near Girard. Some of those who attended were unhappy, however, because the event took place amidst the Park's regular attractions. These included gaming tables, a beer tent and the fortune-teller, Madame Lewis.[66] The Births, Marriages and Deaths columns appeared regularly on page seven in each issue whilst on the back page every week could be found news and obituaries from Wales, divided into sections for north and south Wales. Items in the 'Newyddion yr Hen Wlad' [News of the Old Country] columns were gleaned from an impressive range of newspapers in Wales. By 1898 *Y Drych* was no longer listing them individually, but in 1884 they included *Baner ac Amserau Cymru, Yr Herald Cymraeg, Y Goleuad, Y Llan, Y Tyst a'r Dydd, Seren Cymru, Cambrian News, Y Dydd, Carnarvon and Denbigh Herald, Y Genedl Gymreig, Y Gwliedydd, Llais y Wlad, Tarian y Gweithiwr, Y Celt, Gwalia, Yr Wythnos, Liverpool Mercury, Cardiff Times* and the *Weekly Mail*.[67]

Y Drych kept a sharp watching brief on the news of the day in the USA, especially in order to report any Welsh angle or mobilize aid for distressed Welsh Americans. Lengthy accounts of catastrophes such as the 1889 Johnstown Flood or the San Francisco earthquake of 1906 were accompanied by bulletins on Welsh victims, casualties and survivors, and pleas for financial assistance to alleviate the suffering.[68] In similar fashion, *Y Drych* also observed events in Wales closely and helped to raise funds for a variety of Welsh causes, for example, during the 1900-3 Penrhyn Lockout in the slate industry in north Wales. In

'N EWYRTH SAM.—"A ydwyf I ddeall eich bod chwi yn dod o Bethesda, Arfon?
YR ENETH FACH.—"Oddiyno y deuthym, Syr. Clywais fy mhobl yn dweyd yr ewyllysient i ryw Roosevelt eu gwar-
edu a daethym drosodd i ofyn a allech chwi ei hebgor am ychydig amser."

Wales begs Uncle Sam to come over and settle the Penrhyn Dispute in the slate industry
in north Wales. This cartoon appeared in *Y Drych*, 1 January 1903, when the dispute had
already lasted for over two years.

1902 William W. Jones, president of the North Wales Quarrymen's
Union (and brother of John William Jones, previous editor and owner of
Y Drych) visited the USA and established a relief fund for distressed
slate-quarrying families. The paper played its part by giving extensive
coverage to the various meetings and by printing the names of
contributors and the size of their donations.[69]

But *Y Drych* not only reported events in Wales, it also commented on
Wales' changing society. Nowhere can all these aspects of *Y Drych*'s
relationship with Wales be seen with such stark clarity than in its
coverage of the First World War.[70] Scorning America's neutrality,[71] its
pages embraced the strongly pro-war lobby in Wales in the face of
Austrian and German imperial aggression.[72] A new column, 'Rhyfel yn
Ewrop' [War in Europe], which included items selected from
newspapers in Wales, was introduced in *Y Drych* on 13 August 1914
and continued throughout the war.[73] The majority of these articles saw
the conflict as a crusade for the rights of small nations against a
despotic European order personified by the German Kaiser, Wilhelm II.
In articles and poems the Kaiser appeared as everything from the devil

incarnate[74] to a comic character, 'Wili Wirion' [Silly Willy] or 'Wili Wyllt' [Wild Wili].[75] To reinforce its message, recruitment speeches by David Lloyd George[76] and the sermons of John Williams, Brynsiencyn,[77] were printed in *Y Drych*, often verbatim. Echoing John Williams' plea to the Welsh to 'praise the Lord and kill the Germans', the pages of *Y Drych* throughout the war years resounded with the warning that 'it would be to Wales' perpetual shame if it left England, Scotland and Ireland to defend Britain and its civilization.'[78] The paper never seemed to miss an opportunity to condemn those 'pasiffistiaid' [pacifists] in Wales who opposed the war; in June 1916, for example, an editorial article criticised conscientious objectors in Glamorgan for not killing Germans.[79] It also urged Welsh Americans to organise collections to aid the families of Welsh fighting men. On 1 October 1914 *Y Drych*'s editors at the time, Dafydd R. Williams (Index) and R. Morris Williams, together with the Utica Cymreigyddion Society, launched the Appeal Fund, urging all Welsh Societies, Welsh churches and Welsh clubs throughout the United States and Canada to contribute.[80] In return the paper promised that it would print the names of all those who donated more than a dollar. In the opinion of one letter-writer, fundraising would be made more effective

> if every Welsh church in the States and Canada conducted a special collection every Sabbath. . . . No Welshman of the right sort can allow such an opportunity as this to pass by. Let us tax ourselves for a certain sum every week that the thousands of our fellow countrymen will be on the battlefield.[81]

By early December 1914 the sum of £325 had been collected and posted directly to David Lloyd George, then Chancellor of the Exchequer, to distribute in whichever way he thought best. His letter of thanks printed in *Y Drych* in January 1915 declared that the donation had given him and his countryfolk more pleasure than anything else since the start of hostilities.[82]

In general during the war years *Y Drych* carried a great deal of news of latest developments in the various theatres of the war – even to the extent of offering its readers special atlases and maps showing the various fronts[83] – and about Welsh soldiers. Some of these, like the

Helping the Welsh in America to understand the geography of war. An advertisement in *Y Drych*, 16 May 1918.

A Welsh American at the front: Joseph Williams, Utica, in American army uniform. This photograph and his letter from 'somewhere in France' were published in *Y Drych*, 11 July 1918.

Nurse Edith M. E. Davies, Philadelphia, and originally from Gwaun-Cae-Gurwen, Glamorgan, who went to tend the wounded in France in May 1918.

From Y Drych, *6 June 1918.*

Some Welsh soldiers who celebrated St David's Day in Bombay in 1918 and Dr Harriet Davies, the famous missionary in India, seated, in Welsh costume. The photograph and an article by Davies, a subscriber to *Y Drych*, appeared in the paper 27 June 1918.

Caernarfonshire-born Sapper Harry Evans, of San Diego, whose photograph was featured in 20 July 1916, were emigrants who returned home to enlist in the British army when war broke out. Once America itself entered the war in April 1917, a development which *Y Drych* sarcastically described as 'better late than never',[84] the paper's attention shifted, perhaps inevitably, to Welsh-American involvement in the war. Features on, obituaries of, and sometimes letters from Welsh-American soldiers and female nurses at warfronts were printed in every issue. But reports from the living were far outnumbered by those of fatalities and casualties; some of the saddest pages in *Y Drych*'s entire existence are those which appeared during this war, with column after column of obituaries reflecting the horrific human carnage that occurred.

Despite the loss of life, to *Y Drych* the First World War was an opportunity for the Welsh to show their worth. Throughout the war it rejoiced in the part Welsh people were playing in the war effort, regarding it as an affirmation of the value of Welshness. But there was one supreme hero: David Lloyd George. His rise to become Prime Minister of Britain in December 1916, and eventually leader of the victorious Allies, was interpreted as epitomising the coming of age of the Welsh nation. *Y Drych* furiously fanned Welsh-American idolatry of him as the new King Arthur, 'the Little Big Man from our little nation' and 'David the Potent'.[85] The paper compared Lloyd George's becoming Prime Minister of Britain in 1916 to the

The conquering Welsh hero. Advertisement for replica of William Richards' Sculpture of David Lloyd George.

From Y Drych, *27 October 1921.*

rising of a new dawn and numerous correspondents marvelled at how one who had been so hated by Britain's aristocratic class was now saving them in the war. One writer believed *Y Drych*'s editorial comments on Lloyd George during early 1917 were 'like shining stars in the firmament, shooting light in every direction'.[86] A month later a brief editorial in the paper regretted that such a romantic and admired figure as Buffalo Bill was not of Welsh descent, but insisted that 'we have more than Bil in Daff [Dafydd/David]'.[87] It was Lloyd George's leadership that ultimately won victory for what the paper described as 'the Good Countries',[88] and after the end of the conflict, the eulogising of him among the Welsh in America reached frenzied proportions. Banquets to celebrate his birthday were organised all over the USA.[89] A touring lecture on the Welsh statesman by Revd R. R. Davies of Wilkesbarre was recommended to *Y Drych* readers because it would 'do your bodies and souls good'.[90]

As the years of the First World War and other seemingly innumerable commentaries on political, social, cultural and religious developments in Wales show, *Y Drych* maintained a close relationship with the homeland. From at least the 1860s, Welsh journalism on both sides of the Atlantic echoed each other's voices. By then *Y Drych* had established a simple but effective exchange scheme with Welsh newspaper offices where copies of the one would be sent to the other free of charge each week. Thus Welsh editors read *Y Drych* weekly, from the days of Gwilym Hiraethog and Thomas Gee to Beriah Gwynfe Evans and E. Morgan Humphreys.[91] They also copied news stories and inserted them into their own newspapers, without having to translate them.[92] *Y Drych* reciprocated in kind, as the two journalisms used each other's papers like news agencies.[93] *Y Drych* enjoyed a particular bond with *Baner ac Amserau Cymru*, both being regarded as peers, well above the others in terms of their status and quality.[94] The contents of the one found its way, regularly, for about sixty or seventy years, into the columns of the other.[95] A potent and early illustration of the potential of this symbiosis occurred in 1870 when Welsh Americans began to collect money for *Baner ac Amserau Cymru*'s eviction fund (in aid of tenants evicted for voting against their Tory landowner candidates in the 1868 general election) after seeing that paper's reports in *Y Drych*.[96] In that sense *Y Drych* and Welsh newspapers in Wales formed part of the one transatlantic newspaper economy. Yet in another way, *Y Drych* increasingly came to belong to a very different world, with its own pressures and its own agendas. Its news content progressively became more American-oriented. Whereas in 1856, 34 per cent of its news coverage, calculated in terms of column inches, originated in Wales, by 1950 the proportion had fallen to 2 per cent. Conversely, the ratio of news coverage of Welsh activity in the USA increased from 15 per cent in 1851 to 98 per cent in 1950.

By the time T. J. Griffiths' stewardship of the paper was nearing its end, *Y Drych* had established itself as the pre-eminent newspaper in Welsh America. It attracted readers from well beyond the cluster settlements of the Pennsylvania coalfields and upstate New York, and there is ample evidence that those readers felt great fondness for the paper. Their familiarity with its format and range of content may have affected the ways in which it was read. Writing in 1919, one correspondent, from Shell Lake, Wisconsin, likened its eight pages to a familiar home, and described how he preferred to enter it 'by the back door' of the obituary section, then to the 'kitchen' with its news from Wales, the 'front room', where religious and community leaders discoursed freely, the 'dining room', where the 'level table was always full of various delicacies' culled from local, national and international news reports.[97] The aura of permanence exuded by the paper's content and format, which had changed little since the 1880s, may have been misleading, however. Evidence suggests that *Y Drych* was in difficulty in the year immediately following the end of the First World War, when its sister title, the English-language weekly *The Cambrian* was discontinued by Griffiths.[98]

Y Drych, which remained a Welsh-language newspaper throughout this period, may thus be said to have ridden the wave of Welsh demographic expansion, and should be regarded primarily, in these years at least, as the organ of that shifting immigrant population. To take full advantage of these more propitious circumstances, the proprietors of *Y Drych* needed, firstly, to consolidate its commercial position within the North American Welsh newspaper market and, secondly, to establish an enduring sense of brand loyalty among its readers. In seeking to achieve these aims, its editors and publishers were compelled to position the paper in relation to the broader cultural processes of constructing and maintaining a Welsh national identity among a widely scattered and displaced ethnic community. The next chapter will explore the ways in which it pursued these two, not always compatible, objectives.

CHAPTER 4

American Wales: *Y Drych* and Welsh cultural identity, 1874-1920

The history of *Y Drych* recounted thus far contains a puzzling paradox. While on the one hand its entrepreneurial publishers sought to reach as many readers, and to attract as many advertisers, as possible, they also ensured that the paper's journalism could only ever be accessible to a segment of the Welsh in America. In other words, they deliberately, as an act of editorial policy, *excluded* a potential market for their product. This was largely, though not exclusively, achieved by its ninety-year insistence on the primacy of the Welsh language. An explanation of why this was so must pay due attention to the *purposes* of *Y Drych* as they were understood by successive editors and publishers during this period. Evidently, their mission extended far beyond the selling of news, and the paradoxical nature of their enterprise can only adequately be understood when it is recalled that *Y Drych* was intended also to act as an instrument that might help shape, and perhaps even to determine, the identity of the American Welsh. In short, it was more than a newspaper. It was also a highly ambitious cultural project that sought to define what it meant to be Welsh in America. By pursuing the question of identity, it may be possible to offer answers to the vexing question of whose newspaper *Y Drych* really was, and whose interests in the ever changing Welsh community it served. In 1911, *Y Drych*, especially under its dynamic editor John C. Roberts, was described as having 'exerted a tremendous influence on Welsh life . . . [and] had much to do with the shaping of Welsh thought on the questions of the day.'[1] The following chapter will explore some of the more salient and problematic issues embodied in this valedictory assessment of Roberts' editorial achievements, and in particular the tensions inherent in the paper's treatment of such elemental features of Welsh identity as language, religion, cultural institutions and the family.

For a newspaper, a medium of communication composed almost entirely of the printed word, language was the most elemental issue of all. From as early as the 1830s, other titles had acknowledged that a large proportion of Welsh migrants, let alone first- and second-generation settlers, did not read Welsh and had, as a result, printed news stories, editorial columns, letters, notices and advertisements in both English and Welsh. *Cymro America/American Cambrian* in 1832 had printed one of its four pages in English, as had *Cymro Americaidd/ Cambro American* in the 1850s. Later newspapers, such as *Baner America* and *Y Wasg*, regularly included English-language articles. The latter's amalgamation into *Y Drych*, in 1877 and 1890 respectively, shifted the language balance in the Welsh-American press back in favour of Welsh at a time when other titles, such as T. J. Griffiths' own *The Cambrian*, or the Scranton- and later Pittsburgh-based *The Druid*, were printed entirely in English. In light of the changing composition of the immigrant group, many more of which were coming from the industrial south than the rural west of Wales, and the declining significance of Welsh among later generations of settlers,[2] the Welsh-only policy practised by *Y Drych* throughout this period of expansion is, to say the least, unexpected. Yet, seen from the perspective of its Utica-based editors, the policy was entirely rational on two related grounds. Firstly, for them, the Welsh language, and the communities of belief and cultural practices in which it was uniquely embodied, was the only significant extant link between individuals of Welsh descent and their, by now displaced, national past. The language alone defined their Welshness. Without it, they were simply Americans of British descent. Even the *Y Drych* of the title, John Morgan Jones had explained to his readers in 1851, referred specifically to the Welsh language, which in its vocabulary, syntax, inflection and idiom 'reflected' the most fundamental characteristics, as he saw them, of the Welsh character.[3] Forty years later, that policy was still being strongly endorsed. In an editorial that appeared in *Y Drych* on 10 August 1893, the centrality of the language to Welsh-American identity was again unambiguously defended:

> In accordance with an unwritten but inflexible law, a man cannot be a Welshman without knowledge of Welsh. His veins can be full of the reddest, purest blood in the world; but if his tongue cannot speak the old language he is nothing but an excommunicant in our midst. . . . Outwardly the language proves you are Welsh, and it is too late in the day to change that law. . . . When a Welshman loses his Welsh, he is no longer in the eyes of his nation a Welshman. The thing is now an instinct and it

cannot be uprooted. . . . The Welsh will surely lose themselves in and melt into the American nation when the language is lost. The only hope of maintaining alive the Welsh character and distinctiveness is through adherence to the language. Be it wise or foolish, Welsh life in America is concealed in the language.[4]

The reference to loss of identity and the fear of assimilation into the 'American nation', is particularly revealing. America might have been a better place for the Welsh than British Wales, but the editorial discourse of this paper, as far as we can see, was anything but assimilationist. The insistence that the language was the most important distinguishing mark of a specifically Welsh kind of American nationality was also consistent with the homeland settlement schemes of the paper's early editors. Ironically, *Y Drych* was also a means of compensating for the failure of such ventures. If the Welsh could not be kept together as Dissenting, Welsh-speaking and eisteddfodic communities in grand isolation from the rest of America, the weekly newspaper could act as the nub of a nationwide network of Welsh people whose community was defined above all by their ability to read *Y Drych* and be mobilised by its campaigns.[5] There were a great many of these over the years, including some that were explicitly aimed at preserving the vitality of Welsh in North America. One such involved a movement, led by editorials and letters in *Y Drych*, to establish a Chair of Welsh (a 'Cambrian Professorship') at Marietta College, Cincinnati, to educate young Welsh Americans in their language, culture, history and literature. Despite their most strenuous efforts, over three months in 1898, the $50,000 required to endow the Chair was not raised.[6] *Y Drych* actually saw itself, too, as a medium through which to maintain standards as far as the Welsh language was concerned. On several occasions it insisted on the importance of correct Welsh whilst as early as 1860 John W. Jones, editor and owner of the paper at the time, published his instruction manual to writing in Welsh, *Yr Athrawydd Parod* [The Ready Teacher].[7] Chapters on grammar and containing advice to correspondents and letter-writers were also included in one of *Y Drych*'s occasional free gifts to new subscribers, *Y Trysor Teuluaidd* [The Family's Treasure].[8] However, some of its correspondents were less sanguine than the paper's editors about the long-term feasibility of preserving Welsh as a living language in America.[9] The Revd Erasmus W. Jones, for example, in an article on 'The Future of Welsh in America', predicted its eventual decline, but insisted that it would be 'preached in, spoken and read . . . for some lifetimes to come'.[10] Others, however, challenged the desirability of emphasising the language as the defining feature of Welsh identity. In 1909 Revd W. R. Evans deplored all attempts to sustain Welsh and every other minority language as 'a calamity beyond imagination. . . . The peace and civil and religious success of this country demands that one language should swallow all the others, and it will come to this despite every lament and effort to the contrary. The attempt to immortalise the Welsh language in this country is as futile as an attempt to drive back the ocean tide with a besom.' He advised that the best thing for those who wished Welsh to continue was to emigrate back to Wales.[11] America was, in this view, an English-speaking republic, and the Welsh would need to redefine their cultural identity in relation to that fundamental fact. The paper's Welsh-only policy, therefore, was the subject of lively debate throughout this phase in its history, a debate that extended beyond the printed page to touch a raw nerve among individuals of Welsh descent across the country.

Another reason why the use of Welsh may have been for its editors both rational and justifiable was that the mainstay of the paper's readership remained the first-generation immigrant. *Y Drych* was principally a newspaper for immigrants. Advertisements for emigration agents, shipping lines and the land purchase schemes of railroad and other companies alone testify to this. But *Y Drych*'s role as an immigrant newspaper went deeper. Its content, and its regularity, helped to establish and sustain supportive networks for migrants by providing them with advice on essential subjects such as travel, finance, and American civil and property law. Nor did these only appear in the paper itself. The publication *Y Trysor Teuluaidd* referred to earlier brought within one cover 'thousands of things worth knowing', including guidance on medicine, farming methods and agricultural technology, cookery, the American constitution, and its legal and political systems.[12] In this work as in its columns, *Y Drych* sought to answer the fundamental questions – such as how to become a citizen, or even how to post a letter bound for Wales – immigrants might have in their quest to survive in, and become comfortable with, their new environment. Further, *Y Drych* was an employment agency. It carried job advertisements for positions from maids to miners, some of which directly asked for Welsh workers.[13] These advertisements either took the form of weekly 'Situations Vacant'-type notices, or more extended calls for workers included in letters and other items. For example, on 9 January 1868 the paper carried a letter from a Dafydd Morgan of Rock Cabin, Pennsylvania, which stated that miners were needed in that area, whilst thirteen years later a group of Welsh who had opened a coal mine in Cadiz, Ohio, stated their preference for Welsh miners to come and work for them.[14] From its early years onwards the paper also printed feature articles on working conditions in mines and mills and updates on the fortunes of the economy in

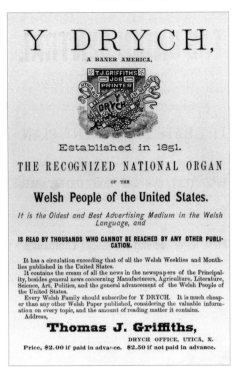

An advertisement for *Y Drych* which appeared in the English-language Welsh-American magazine *The Cambrian* in February 1884.

various localities: in the early 1870s, for example, there was an 'Adran Amaethyddiaeth' [Agriculture Section] and one entitled 'Sefyllfa y Gweithfeydd' [The Condition of the Works].[15] By such means *Y Drych* was creating a virtual directory of employment opportunities and prospects for the Welsh in the USA, and it performed a similar function in the world of real estate, be it for farms, houses or hotels.[16] In August 1884 James Williams emphasised that the house in Coalton, Jackson County, Ohio, he was selling was very near to a Welsh chapel, a revealing illustration perhaps of the target audience the paper was cultivating.[17] In each of the respects outlined here, *Y Drych* was no different to the hundreds of other immigrant newspapers in scores of languages other than English that strove to soften the impact of a new life and a new home on America's 'greenhorns' (recent arrivals).[18]

Of course, the paper's editors were themselves immigrants in this period, and they thought of their readers very much in their own images. If *Y Drych* set out to assist successive waves of these immigrants to orient themselves to their new homeland, it did so in the expectation that enough of them would continue to subscribe to the paper for the rest of their days. Every new Welsh immigrant processed through Ellis Island was, potentially, a new lifetime subscriber. And since enough of them continued to be Welsh-speaking up until the First World War, it made a degree of commercial, as well as ideological, sense to remain exclusively Welsh in language. In so doing, the best that might be said is that its presence may have slowed down the rate at which the language declined in America. One of *Y Drych*'s most regular correspondents of the late nineteenth and early twentieth centuries, Revd Daniel Williams of Storm Lake, Iowa, began to write for the paper in the 1880s as a means of retaining the language. He believed he would have lost it otherwise as he was living far away from any other Welsh families.[19] The following letter, written by Mrs Ellen Jones of Table Rock, Nebraska, in January 1912 poignantly illustrates a similar case:

A 'silent' reader of *Y Drych* for 60 years: Ellen Jones of Table Rock, Nebraska.

From Y Drych, *1 February 1912.*

The "Drych" is the only Welsh friend I have since my husband John A. Jones died 14 years ago. He was a subscriber to the "Drych" years before he left Carbondale Pa. to come to Nebraska in 1858. I came here in 1860 and we endured much hardship in new country. . . . We bought half a section of land and I live on one part of this and my son on the other. I suppose when I am gone the "Drych" will be stopped as none of my children can read or write Welsh. I believe I am among the "Drych"'s oldest subscribers, if not the oldest, and it is a great comfort to me.[20]

While her children did not read the copies of *Y Drych* that were

'Burning the mortgage' in the Welsh Calvinistic Methodist Church, Cleveland, Ohio, Monday evening, 13 December 1915, following full repayment. The vessel (centre) is being held by Mrs Thomas Llewelyn, oldest member of the congregation and the only surviving Charter Member. *Photograph and report in* Y Drych, *20 January 1916.*

delivered to their home each week, and in that sense it failed to help preserve the language into the second generation, Ellen Jones herself continued to read it religiously. Though very much part of her private domain – she read it 'silently' for sixty years[21] – it nonetheless kept her in regular touch with the written form of her native tongue, and with the activities of its other speakers. Even in her Nebraska fastness, *Y Drych* enabled her for more than half a century to remain part of a virtual Welsh community.[22]

That community was also built around an equally divisive phenomenon, religious faith. While virtually all Welsh-speaking migrants adhered to Dissenting Christian traditions, their denominational loyalties were often sharply at odds with each other, in terms of their Calvinist or Arminian doctrines, their forms of worship and organisation, and even the regions of Wales from which they originated. These denominations, referred to in *Y Drych* as the 'llwythau Cymreig' [tribes of Wales],[23] had in Wales for much of the nineteenth century strained loyalties and fragmented Welsh-language journalism into competing sectarian camps. The urgent

Old Saron Church, Sharon, Le Sueur County, Minnesota, the first Welsh church in the state, established 24 June 1856. From Thomas E. Hughes, David Edwards, Hugh G. Roberts and Thomas Hughes, *Hanes Cymry Minnesota, Foreston a Lime Springs Iowa / History of the Welsh in Minnesota, Foreston and Lime Springs Iowa* (Mankato, 1895), p. 53, Welsh-language section.

challenge in America was to acknowledge such divisions while subsuming them into an overarching cultural identity based on the transcendental qualities of the Welsh language. Such was the delicate diplomatic task that *Y Drych* was intended to perform. It sought to do so by emphasising the centrality of the Bible itself in the life of Welsh America, rather than particular readings of it. Thus, an editorial column in September 1899 explained that one of the functions of *Y Drych* was to act as a 'companion' to the Holy Book:

> In the obituary columns in the "Drych" it is often commented . . . that the deceased was very fond of both the Bible and the "Drych"; without doubt, this is no small compliment to the newspaper. Being a companion to the Bible is a mark of great respect. We do not mean by this that the "Drych" is equal to the Bible, but rather it resembles a disciple who follows the leadership of the Old Book and is fond of the teaching and morality of the Scriptures. Another excellent thing about the "Drych" is that it is Christian without being denominational, like the Bible itself. . . .

[Y Drych] is too magnanimous to be owned by party or denomination. The Baptist, Wesleyan, Independent and Calvinistic Methodist all have affection for it as they have for their Bible.[24]

While *Y Drych* did make a serious attempt to establish a different relationship between the press and the religious denominations to that which prevailed in Wales, it nevertheless continued to take a keen interest in religious developments in the old country, and in some respects moved to the same historical rhythms. An intriguing example may be seen in its response to the great religious revival of 1904-05, which was itself fanned by enthusiastic reports in such newspapers as the Cardiff *Western Mail*.[25] Articles on the Welsh revival began to appear in *Y Drych* on 8 December 1904, when it was noted in an unusually hyperbolic editorial that the charismatic young preacher, Evan Roberts, was beginning to be described as the John Wesley of his generation and 'another prophet risen from the bosom of society, like John the Baptist, his ability a secret, and his influence inexplicable'.[26]

From that point onwards, *Y Drych* urged its readers not only to take heed of the dramatic upsurge of religious observance in Wales, but actively to participate in it in their own communities.[27] Articles describing revival not only as a means 'to excite emotions but also to improve the heart'[28] appeared regularly into January 1905, when the first reports of Welsh revivalist meetings in America, such as those in Edwardsdale, Pennsylvania, began to be printed.[29] By the end of the month, further reports were printed of revivals in thirteen Welsh settlements.[30] The connection between revivalism and the intervention of *Y Drych* was noted by a correspondent writing in February 1905:

We feel grateful for so much news of the revival. The wonderful facts the "Drych" presents before us have warmed many hearts already, freezing out cold materialism . . . . The prayer week has already become prayer weeks in many places.[31]

Y Drych, then, while clearly setting a distinctive religious agenda in relation to the denominational loyalties of the Welsh, and acting as a conduit of news from the old country, also was a means of keeping American fingers on the pulse of Nonconformist Wales. In the case of the revival, its coverage and editorial support not only enabled its readers to be informed of its collective frenzy, but also to involve themselves in it. Significantly, interest in the revival in *Y Drych* declined sharply in the autumn of 1905, and, like the revival itself in Wales, had disappeared from its pages by 1906. The spasms of the revival on both sides of the Atlantic bore testimony not only to a crisis in religious life in Wales, but also to the power of journalism to help extend the revivalist experience into new areas, both geographical and cultural.

That *Y Drych* continued to take its religious role seriously in the North American context is evidenced by the introduction in March 1916 of the weekly 'Pwlpud Y Drych' [*Y Drych*'s Pulpit] column in which leading Welsh ministers of religion presented a guest sermon.[32] According to Digain Williams in 1921, the column was introduced because the paper wanted not only 'to transport news to the lonely extremes of massive continents' but also to 'transport a lot of the Gospel. The "Drych" is a preacher and minister to many an old Welsh man and Welsh woman who are so far from facilities that they would not have a sermon at all were it not for y "Drych".'[33] As a demonstration that *Y Drych*'s constructions of Welshness were rarely uncontested, he did acknowledge that some readers disapproved of its printing of sermons. Perhaps adverse voices were discontented at the paper's refusal to print any criticism of the comments in the columns.[34] But it is clear that to some, *Y Drych* and the Bible were inseparable after all. Evan Williams of Long Island, New York, told the paper in a letter in April 1935 that he took it for two reasons: to keep it alive, and the 'Pwlpud Y Drych' column. 'I cannot think about Welsh people without thinking about God', he confessed; '. . . we hope that we will not see the day when there is not some small corner for Jesus Christ in the Drych'.[35]

The paper performed a similar function in relation to other defining characteristics of Welsh life, namely the cultural institutions of the eisteddfod and the gymanfa ganu. The importance of these events in maintaining a distinctive sense of identity among the Welsh in America cannot be over-emphasised. Nor can their vitality and creative exuberance. During January 1893, for example, reports of, or programmes for, at least twelve eisteddfodau in states as far afield as Pennsylvania, New York, Illinois, Ohio and Iowa were printed in *Y Drych*.[36] Nevertheless, here, too, the all-Welsh policy pursued by *Y Drych* was subjected to critical scrutiny, and, seven years after the great Chicago World's Fair Eisteddfod of 1893, *Y Drych* abandoned its long-held principle. In a carefully worded editorial printed in January 1899, it explained the reasons for its *volte-face*:

> If we keep the Eisteddfod to ourselves, it will die, but by turning it into a gospel for the nations it will become beneficial from sea to sea and from the river to the ends of the earth. The way to perpetuate it (for ages at least) is to join it with the Stars and Stripes and place it under the special patronage of 'Uncle Sam'. . . . It is better for it to live in American cheerfulness than die in obscurity because of Welsh obstinacy.[37]

In opting for greater inclusivity through the use of English in eisteddfodau, *Y Drych* had effectively acknowledged the difficulty of associating Welsh identity exclusively with the Welsh language. Yet it was to be a further thirty years before the logic of its position *vis-à-vis* the eisteddfod would work itself out in relation to the use of the

The Cambria (Blue Earth County, Minnesota) Philharmonic Band, which made its debut in Cambria in July 1890. From Thomas E. Hughes, David Edwards, Hugh G. Roberts and Thomas Hughes, *Hanes Cymry Minnesota, Foreston a Lime Springs Iowa / History of the Welsh in Minnesota, Foreston and Lime Springs Iowa* (Mankato, 1895), p. 112, English-language section.

language in the newspaper itself. Among the many reasons for this was that *Y Drych* at the turn of the twentieth century continued to serve a substantial and highly active Welsh-language constituency. In the summer of 1909, for example, notices advertising Welsh events flowed into the paper's Utica office from all over the country, from the Hallowe'en Eisteddfod to be held in Poultney Opera House, Vermont, in October, or the forthcoming tour of the south Wales-based Cambria Glee Society's performance of Joseph Parry's opera 'Blodwen' in the Fall, to the Alaska-Yukon-Pacific Eisteddfod held at the Exposition Auditorium, Seattle, Washington, in August.[38] Welsh-language chapels, too, publicised their festivals, class and prayer meetings: in the paper on 3 August 1893, for example, there were advertisements for Cymanfa-oedd Canu and other religious events in Red Oak and Penuel, Iowa, and Wayne County, Nebraska.[39]

A Welsh 'rags to riches' story. George T. Matthews (1847-1932) was born in poverty in Crickhowell and died a very wealthy New York Tea Merchant. From *Y Drych*, 13 September 1923. He paid for a memorial window to Henry Ward Beecher to be installed in Plymouth Church, Brooklyn; part of the inscription was an extract from a Welsh-language hymn by the famous Welsh hymn-writer, William Williams, Pantycelyn.

Commercial advertising also imparted a Welsh flavour to the paper. By the early twentieth century, by far the largest number of businesses that advertised their wares in *Y Drych*, be they grocery stores, bookstores, clothes shops or undertakers, were located in Utica's Genesee Street, giving the distinct impression that Utica, '*Dinas Y Drych*' [The City of *Y Drych*], was America's Welsh business heartland. Of all the advertisements that appeared in *Y Drych*, however, none was so ubiquitous or as evocative as tea. Appeals to their readers to drink *Te'r Hen Wlad* [Old Country Tea] [40] *Te y Ddraig Goch* [Red Dragon Tea], *Te y Werin* [The People's Tea][41] and, most implausibly of all,

Londoners drinking George T. Matthews' 'King of Teas', c. 1902.

From an advertisement feature in Y Drych, *6 February 1902.*

Eryri Tea [Snowdonia Tea],[42] filled the advertising pages of *Y Drych* throughout this period. A non-alcoholic beverage for an idealised tee-total and devout people, whose quality and provenance was assured by its Welsh associations, tea was a staple of both the Welsh table and the account books of *Y Drych*. It also made fortunes for such Welsh immigrants as George T. Matthews, who rode the crest of the Welsh tea market and placed advertisements for his *Te y Brenin* [King of Teas] continuously in *Y Drych* from 1873 until his death in February 1932.[43] Matthews insisted that two things made the Welsh excellent: 'Yfed Te'r

Brenin a darllen y "Drych"' – drinking the King's tea and reading *Y Drych*.[44]

By linking the Welsh language with Christian commitment, temperance and historically Welsh cultural practices, *Y Drych* was directing itself primarily at a devout, Republican and patriotic readership. These it attempted to persuade to become subscribers by offering inducements in the form of gifts that included, in 1884-85, a photograph of the paper's recently deceased former editor, John W. Jones,[45] and, in 1890, a coloured image of 'Christ Before Pilate.'[46]

Y DRYCH AM 1885!

Y Newyddiadur Hynaf yn yr Iaith Gymraeg

ANRHEG YSBLENYDD

I Bob Un a Dalo Yn Mlaen am y Drych Hyd Ddiwedd' 1885 ! !

—SEF—

DARLUN LLIWIEDIG CYFLAWN-FAINT OR

DIWEDDAR JOHN W. JONES,

Yr Hwn wedi ei Fframio, a fydd yn Addurn i Unrhyw Ystafell.

Gwnaed y darlun bychan a uuddlangosodd yn y Drych ar ol marwolaeth Mr. Jones mewn brys ac ar rybudd byr; ac er ei fod yn rhagorol fel wood-cut, nid oedd yn gwneud cyflawnder a'r gwrthrych. Bydd y Darlun sydd yn awr yn cael ei barotoi gan un o'r ar feddydwyr goren yn y wlad, yn anrheg gwerth i bawb ymdrechu am dani. Mesura p modfedd wrth 24, a bydd yn addurn i unrhyw barlwr. Cydwynir ef

I Bob Hen Danysgrifiwr, ac hefyd i Danysgrifwyr Newyddion Dalant am y DRYCH hyd Ddiwedd y Flwyddyn Nesaf.

Cymered cefnogwyr y Drych fantais o hyn i helaethu ei gylchrediad, a hyny yn ddioed. Cyfeirier—

THOMAS J. GRIFFITHS, Drych Office, Utica, N. Y.

Commemorating a great man and boosting circulation: special offer following former editor and owner John William Jones' death in October 1884. Translated extract from the text: 'A Splendid Gift To everyone who pays in advance for Y Drych until the end of 1885; A full size coloured picture of The Late John W. Jones; Framed, and an adornment for any room. . . . The picture now in preparation by one of the best artists in the country will be a gift worth acquiring by everyone. It measures 18 inches by 24 inches, and will be an adornment for any parlour. . . . Y Drych's supporters should take advantage of this in order to expand the paper's circulation, and do so at once.'

From Y Drych, *27 November 1884.*

Hail the Presidents. A *Drych* Special Offer reproduction of the painting 'The Presidents of the United States' (up to Theodore Roosevelt). In the background are depicted famous symbols and scenes from American history: Liberty Bell (Philadelphia), the Boston Tea Party, the battles of Bunker Hill and Gettysburg, and they are brought up to date with the capture of San Juan Hill by American forces in the war against Spain, August 1898.   *From* Y Drych, *26 February, 1903.*

By the beginning of the twentieth century, such inducements had become far more substantial. On offer in 1903 was a reproduction of the famous oil painting 'The Presidents of the United States', which the paper believed would be 'an inspiration for a better life'.[47] In a circulation drive in 1904 Griffiths offered (in English) 'a handsome Morris chair, beautifully polished, quartered golden oak or imitation mahogany' to readers who recruited six new subscribers.[48] In the following year, a number of forty-three piece tea sets were to be won by readers who could attract four new readers each to take out annual subscriptions to *Y Drych*.[49]

But the greatest inducement of all was the quality of its journalism, and its ability to remain of relevance to readers across the country. In that respect, its most important function was to inform. News was its most fundamental commodity, occupying a consistent 50 per cent of the paper's column space between the mid-1880s and the mid-1920s. Yet,

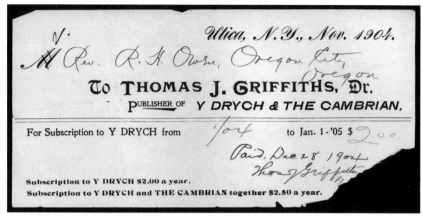

Securing Y Drych *for another year: subscription receipt, 1905.*

news came in different forms and the balance between different kinds of news changed substantially and in some highly significant and suggestive ways during this period. From the end of the 1880s, general American news practically disappeared from the pages of *Y Drych*, a decline that may be attributed to the growth of English-language dailies that contained far more up to date national news. The proportion of news items from Wales remained constant at around 20 per cent of total space. However, the proportion of specifically Welsh-American news grew from a little over half the paper's total news content in 1875 to nearly three quarters in 1910.

Increasingly, therefore, *Y Drych* was reorienting itself around the activities of the Welsh in America as a particular interest group, rather than the affairs of the republic as a whole. It was becoming a chronicler of, as well as a newspaper for, the Welsh, or at least a chronicler of those whose morality was broadly consistent with its own, and of whose lifestyles it approved. Its news values, that is to say the kinds of news items to which priority was given, overwhelmingly privileged the traditional and the conservative in both religion and culture. But the insistence on the intrinsic Nonconformist respectability of the Welsh, which was the hallmark of its news reports at this time, served a deeper purpose. As its extraordinary masthead designs of the 1880s had so clearly demonstrated, *Y Drych* was in the business of constructing the Welsh and their values as being archetypically American. And there was one further element to that American ideology: upward mobility and making money. *Y Drych*'s pages were a celebration of those Welsh Americans whose successful lives demonstrated the opportunities American capitalism had to offer. As the owner of a massive commercial empire based on tea, George T. Matthews is both an obvious and a very good example here. A feature on him in *Y Drych* in 1891 stressed how he had built up his enterprise from virtually nothing through his own commitment, perseverance and honesty.[50] At the very same time, *Y Drych* was also a vehicle for making material advancement possible on a large scale. This is what lay behind the consistent pleas that Welsh people shop with their ethnic group, the continual boosting of Welsh businesses, and even recommendations that the Welsh buy shares in companies established by members of their ethnic group.[51] In 1894 one of the paper's Chicago correspondents, Bismarck Davies, urged Welsh people to answer in Welsh to the advertisement his employers, the Woolf Clothing Company, placed in *Y Drych*, because it would gain greater respect for the language and create more jobs for Welsh speakers.[52] Typically, news of Welsh settlements that appeared in the paper regularly noted their Welsh businesses and professionals and urged their countryfolk to support them, especially those who had earned success through hard work and good service. As an article on businesses in Hyde Park and Scranton, Pennsylvania, in 1881 remarked of the Welsh-speaking emigration agent David W. Powell: 'Why trust in strangers when there is a young Welshman of good character, fully known to everyone here ready to serve you?'[53] Publicising traders and professionals who could understand Welsh was an important factor, of course, but so was the desire to raise the general prosperity and the economic profile of the Welsh ethnic group as a whole. By doing so the Welsh were showing how essentially American they were.

We might conceive of *Y Drych*, then, as a screen, a kind of cultural Ellis Island, through which successive waves of Welsh-speaking emigrants passed in their journey to become Americans. It was a screen that filtered out those who did not conform to its own strict codes of Welshness. While it allowed many, often conflicting, arguments to be aired, mainly through its letters columns, its most dominant voices were those that legitimated and promoted the idea of transforming the Welsh into a particular kind of American. In 1893 an editorial article entitled

'Ein Gwlad Ni' [Our Country] succinctly and forthrightly issued the following advice: 'The Welsh who come to make America their home should take the first opportunity to become citizens, so they can take an active part in government, through voting and influencing their society and politics. In doing so, they need not lose any of their love for the Old Country, its language and customs.'[54]

The particular kind of American-ness *Y Drych* had in mind was not open to all. In 1888 it expressed dismay about 'Peryglon Ymfudiaeth' [the Perils of Immigration], by which it meant migrants of Asian, African and East European origin. Further, it issued a challenge to the nation's statesmen 'to devise ways and means to avoid that which is threatening us – to prepare a plan which will be effective in keeping America American'.[55] In July 1895, Ieuan Ddu of Provo City, Utah, stressed that though the Welsh were perfectly entitled to be a part of the 'genedl fawr Americanaidd' [great American nation], 'it would be futile and foolish to argue that all the tribes and nations of our Republic should melt into each other. Would it be appropriate for Gomer's race to mix with the black Negro and the red Indian, or the bloody Dago?'[56] And in the heightened emotions of the First World War period *Y Drych* railed not only against Germans in the USA, but also against certain others who were making the country 'pitifully mixed . . . a Babel of nations and a wilderness of religions, and ideas and paganisms'. Typically drawing on a Biblical metaphor, it warned that America's open door policy towards all immigrants would, like Absalom's hair, ultimately prove to be its downfall. It insisted that as soon as Absalom's hair was cut, the better.[57] In stark contrast, the paper continued to expound the virtues of Protestant north Europeans (including Germans up to 1914) among whom the Welsh were a notably worthy national group. Furthermore, such civilized and civilizing cultures improved their many good qualities in the relative freedom of the United States. In 1892, an editorial article enumerated at length the ways in which the Welsh in America were superior to those who had stayed behind in Wales. They were less servile, more egalitarian, more tolerant and broad-minded, had expanded horizons, were more practical and adventurous in spirit, more ambitious and showed greater willingness to strive for money and fame, and more practical and better mannered.[58]

Part of the process of learning how to be American was the unlearning of the language of Britishness. By distinguishing in essays, letters and editorial columns between Americans and the English, that most powerful collective voice of the paper was encouraging a not-so-subtle process of de-Anglicisation. Acculturation was not a simple linear process, it entailed much more than the abandonment of subject status and the acquisition of citizenship, important as that constitutional change undoubtedly was. As early as 1870, a letter from 'one of the sons of the West' had demanded that *Y Drych* demonstrate its loyalties by printing the Stars and Stripes on its masthead.[59] It also involved the transformation of identity. On 16 March 1893, the Revd W. Tudwel Williams, Slatington, observed in *Y Drych* that it was better to be Welsh in the USA than in Wales, since here the Welsh were no longer under threat from 'John Bull'.[60] Three years later, during a bad-tempered debate in the paper on whether immigrants were 'better Welsh' than those born in America, R. C. Roberts, Utica, pronounced that he was 'proud to be a native of Merioneth, but prouder still to be a citizen of the United States'.[61] This was amplified later in 1896 by G. W. Prees, M.D., from Cambria, Wisconsin, who gave two reasons for leaving Wales. One was to improve his material circumstances, the other to escape the 'sickness that has taken hold of our moral constitution' and that had been caused by centuries of what he termed 'gorthrwm y Sais' [English oppression].[62] Only having fled his country could he fully comprehend the mess he had left behind. 'Having reached the clear air of independent America,' he triumphantly announced, 'we could see very clearly signs of the paralysing disease'.[63]

For the producers of *Y Drych*, the keystone of the moral identity of the Welsh in America was the integrity of the family, the single most important institution for the reproduction of the Welsh as a people and as a body of values. Within the family, the Welsh woman, as wife and mother, was the keeper of the faith. As one lonely farmer put it while advertising in *Y Drych* for a spouse:

> WIFE WANTED! – I wish to commence correspondence with a young woman or a young widow; no objection if she has one young child. Must be of good character and religious. The intention is to make two into one in order to take up a farm in the West, and to make home comfortable. No deceit or frivolity.[64]

Margaret E. Roberts (1833-?), indefatigable supporter of women's rights and temperance, and versatile and erudite writer who produced hundreds of thousands of words for *Y Drych*'s pages, 1870s-1911.

Photograph which appeared in The Cambrian, *December 1902, and* Y Drych, *24 October 1907.*

The puritan ethos of the Dissenting nineteenth-century male, perhaps, is not surprising, whether he was a farmer or a newspaper editor. But *Y Drych* took further the logic of its argument and began, towards the end of the nineteenth century, to advocate the 'civilizing influence' of women on American public as well as private life. A column on 'Y Rhyw Fenywaidd' [The Female Gender] appeared from July 1893 for a time,[65] and an editorial in 1899 maintained 'that it was an undeniable fact that women represented the best side of civilization; and certainly their presence in every city and national council would be likely to have a graceful effect upon their decisions.'[66] Women writers, such as Mrs M. Oliver Jones, described the socially positive effects of the advancements made by women in the fields of education, work, politics and religion during the second half of the century.[67] Chief among this small band of pioneering women was Mrs Margaret E. Roberts, née Evans, who rose to attain a position of literary and intellectual eminence and was widely regarded as being one of the most gifted Welsh writers of either sex in the America and Wales of her time.[68] Born in Carmarthenshire in 1833, she and her husband ran a store in Hirwaun, Glamorgan, and a farm in Iowa over the years, whilst she herself ran a bookstore in Scranton and was a much sought after lecturer. A Women's Christian Temperance Union activist, from the late 1870s until 1911 she authored scores of articles for *Y Drych* (and subscribed to it from 1862 onwards),[69] as well as other publications, on a dazzling range of subjects: religion, geology, astronomy, current affairs, and travel writing.[70] Another cause close to her heart was feminism, and she declared in January 1894 that 'the field of defending the rights of the female sex among the Welsh in this country has been left almost exclusively to me. I choose to magnify this privilege, even though many women lift their nostrils in incomprehension at me for doing so – I forgive them easily, as I would children who make necessary errors because of their childish nature.'[71] Roberts' campaigning for, and defence of, the rights of women inevitably earned her derision and criticism from men in the pages of *Y Drych* but there was also occasional male support.[72] However, her formidable debating skills, as evident in print as they were on the platform, usually ensured she got the better of her opponents.[73] To Miss Ellie Francis of Carroll, Nebraska, Roberts' writings were especially appealing as they 'included some support for her sex, against many who are trying to keep us in the gutter since Adam's time'.[74]

But though discussion of 'Pwnc Y Merched' [The Woman Question], as the paper's writers occasionally described it,[75] became more extensive in the early years of the twentieth century, Roberts and her kindred spirits were ultimately minority voices in *Y Drych*. The feminisation of the paper, which would become such a marked feature of its editorial composition from the 1940s, as we shall see in a later chapter, was restrained by the ideology that saw the domestic role as the most rewarding one for women. That mindset was uncompromisingly asserted in an 1899 editorial article which warned of a 'deterioration and awful danger to society, that is the apparent tendency in today's women to neglect and despise the office that belongs to them especially, that of keeping house'.[76] Further, participation in the public sphere could only be countenanced where women's work was of the most impeccably respectable nature. The employment of women in the south Wales tinplate industry, for example, was cited as further evidence of the moral and social chaos to which Wales had descended.[77]

All of these issues return us to the question of whose purposes were served by *Y Drych*. Without doubt, it served the interests of freshly arrived immigrants by providing them with a support network and advice about travel, finance, American civil and property law, agricultural and industrial conditions and employment opportunities. An aspirational text, it projected strongly positive images of 'successful' emigrants to entice and encourage others to join them. But, as the evidence discussed above suggests, it was more than an emigrant's guide to their new world. It also sought to define and sustain a distinctive cultural identity for the Welsh-speaking Welsh in America. Its pages projected an ethnically defined geography, an America of Welsh individuals, chapels, cultural societies and celebrations, of Welsh Days, the eisteddfod and the gymanfa ganu, interleaved with other news and features from the rest of the United States and beyond. What effect it had on the minds of its readers is, of course, open to question. As Rudolph Vecoli argues in relation to the Italian immigrant press in the United States, readers' minds were not 'simply a *tabula rasa* upon which print culture impressed its definitions of social reality. Rather, *they* filtered media messages through the sieve of their own experience. Finally, *they* decided what was reality – and its meaning'.[78] The danger facing *Y Drych* as it emerged from the First World War was that its definitions of Welsh reality in the United States no longer accorded with the lived experience of an increasingly English-speaking American-Welsh population. In the decades that followed, its moral and cultural construction of Welsh identity was to face its greatest challenge.

CHAPTER 5

Facing Hard Times: *Y Drych* 1920-1945

If success and expansion were the dominant themes in *Y Drych*'s history during the late nineteenth and early twentieth centuries, then the overriding concern for the paper during the remainder of the twentieth century would be survival. After 1920 the paper faced a number of serious challenges and on several occasions it seemed doomed to cease publication. It now found itself in a far tougher environment in which to publish a Welsh-language weekly newspaper. The economic depression of the 1930s and, later, the Second World War would play their part in adversely affecting *Y Drych*'s health. But to a great extent the ongoing crisis in which the paper found itself from the 1920s onwards was caused by fundamental transformations in the character of its main constituency and the Welsh ethnic presence in the United States in general. The number of Welsh speakers in the United States declined sharply because Welsh-speaking first-generation immigrants died and, as we shall see more fully in the next chapter, the second and subsequent generations were unable to read and write Welsh. American English emerged as the predominant language of Welsh-American life. Crucially, too, fresh immigration from Wales was drying up.

Sally Miller has noted that the fortunes of the ethnic press in America are shaped by an ebb and flow closely related to immigration patterns.[1] The Welsh-American case is no exception. It was recorded that 13,012 immigrants from Wales arrived in the United States during the 1920s, an almost identical number to the previous decade and significantly below the 17,464 that did so between 1901 and 1910. Almost certainly due to the adverse economic climate, the immigration of Welsh people into the United States dwindled almost to nothing during the early 1930s. A mere 735 arrived between 1931 and 1940, and 550 of those did so in 1931 alone. Similarly, Welsh emigrants to Canada fell away.[2] Severe depression in Wales and an equally savage one in North America thus brought an extended and extensive wave of Welsh settlement across the Atlantic to an abrupt and bitter end. With the fading of immigration, the number of foreign-born Welsh people in the United States inevitably declined. That figure fell from 82,488 in 1910 to 67,066 in 1920 and 60,205 in 1930, and then collapsed in the 1930s, to 35,360.[3] More and more during the twentieth century the Welsh presence was becoming a predominantly second, third or even fourth generation one. Already by 1920 immigrants from Wales were only one-third as numerous as the second generation Welsh; with the decline of immigration to fewer than 300 a year by 1970, they were only one-fifth.[4] Little wonder, therefore, that during the inter-war years a popular type of photograph that appeared in *Y Drych* was 'Pedair Genhedlaeth' [Four Generations].[5]

These profound social, cultural and demographic changes meant that after 1920 the writing was on the wall for *Y Drych*. As a result the paper was forced to reinvent itself drastically within the relatively short time frame of a quarter of a century. By the time the Second World War ended in 1945, *Y Drych* was a very different paper.

1920-29: Ends and Beginnings

As the United States strove to return to what new President Warren Harding called 'normalcy' in the immediate post-First World War period, in some respects *Y Drych*'s future appeared promising. With Index's steady hand still on the editorial helm the paper celebrated its seventieth birthday (albeit in March rather than in early January 1921) with a commemorative issue containing photographs of past and present owners and editors, and special features. In a long, celebratory history of the paper, Digain Williams of California asserted that *Y Drych* had been, and was still, one of the five best papers in the Welsh language even though it was more difficult to publish a newspaper in that language in America than in Wales. There was special praise in the issue for the owner, Thomas J. Griffiths, and he and the editor were apparently determined to make *Y Drych* better than it had ever been.[6] For T. J. Griffiths and Sons generally business was booming at this time and their expansion occasioned the first change of premises for *Y Drych*'s office in twenty-two years. In September 1922, along with the others sectors of T. J. Griffiths' company, it moved across Liberty Street into the Mechanics Hall (at 100 Liberty Street) 'in order to meet the growing demands of the business'.[7] The new home was an important historic building in Utica. Built in 1836, for many years it was the only

'Four Generations', from *Y Drych,* 25 July 1935. Seated centre is Elizabeth Morgan of Racine, Wisconsin, who reached her 80th birthday on 9 July 1935. Originally from Aberystwyth, she was one of the oldest Welsh people in Racine, and moved there in 1883. The other 'generations' in the photograph are, to her left, her daughter, Mrs Annie Morgan Clark of LaGrange, Illinois; to her right, Morgan, Mrs Clark's son, also of LaGrange; and his two children, Richard Morgan and, nestling in the proud old lady's lap, Barbara Dexter.

auditorium in the city, and it housed the local draft office during the American Civil War. From its windows to the waiting crowds below were called the names of those required to serve in the army, including Welshmen who had taken up American citizenship or had been born in America.[8]

Nevertheless, during the early 1920s there were more than enough indications that hard times were not just a-coming but in some respects had already arrived. Although in the absence of the company's records it is difficult to find direct supporting evidence, by this time the paper was probably, if not exactly running at a loss, then at least not making a profit. A tribute to the owners in 1951 declared that at one time the paper had been T. J. Griffiths' main publication 'but owing to its decline in later years, sentimentality largely accounted for its continuance'.[9] In the space of two months in 1922 Index twice pleaded that he was not receiving sufficient material and remarked that the deaths of veteran reporters was distressing his office.[10] *Y Drych* was suffering from a crisis in both demand and supply: on the one hand its market and consequently its income from subscriptions and advertisements were shrinking, whilst on the other it was receiving less Welsh-language material, the lifeblood of its columns. As we shall see in the next chapter, this would be one major reason for the later switch to English. Fundamentally, not only was *Y Drych* itself ageing, but so too was its army of writers and its readership. During the 1920s, and even more so during the 1930s, columns were regularly punctuated with reports of the passing away of long-standing, devoted correspondents and subscribers. In 1929 alone death robbed *Y Drych* of such perennial, gifted writers as Dr Jonathan Edwards of Portland, Oregon; Dr Richard Hughes of Holland Patent, New York (who wrote the first 'Pwlpud Y Drych'); and Jabez Williams of Wilkesbarre.[11] Losses were made more acute by the failure of a sufficient number of replacements to emerge. The same was true in the case of subscribers generally. In 1929-1930 the deaths of David L. Davies of Lebo, Kansas, and Job Morris, Colfax, Washington, deprived *Y Drych* of two who had each taken it for half a century.[12] The passing away of Mrs Margaret Parry of Chicago in 1930 was declared to be a double financial loss for the *Y Drych*. It removed one who had religiously paid up at the start of every year and now there was no one left in the house to subscribe to the paper.[13] In 1934 *Y Drych* revealed the names of thirty individuals or married couples who had subscribed to the paper for over forty years, including one who had done so for seventy years (W. Hughes, Fair Haven, Vermont), three for sixty-three years, and four for fifty-two years. The 'Ffyddloniaid' [The Faithful], as they were very appositely described, are at the same time striking testimony to the intense loyalty the paper could command and to the ageing of its readership.[14]

As well as these long-term problems which boded ill for *Y Drych*'s survival as a Welsh-language paper, during 1923 and 1924 it also suffered three hammer blows in the form of the removal of two key individuals and a disastrous fire at the new premises. On 10 May 1923 it was announced that Index's long reign had finally come to an end.[15] He had been an editor of *Y Drych* since 1897 and had edited it single-handedly since 1919 (as well being editor of its sister English-language magazine *The Cambrian*, which ceased publication in 1919). A large testimonial collection was made by the paper to aid his return to Wales, where he remained until his death in 1931.[16] Then, nine months after Index's departure, the man universally regarded as the most important factor in the survival and flourishing of the paper, Thomas J. Griffiths, suddenly passed away in Florida, at the age of 88. Ironically, he died whilst spending his first real

Thomas J. Griffiths Jnr. He and his brother, Charles W., owned *Y Drych* from their father's death in 1924 to 1951, when they sold the paper to Arthur M. Roberts.

From Y Drych, *27 June 1929.*

Charles W. Griffith, joint owner of *Y Drych* with his brother, Thomas, 1924-1951.

From Y Drych, *27 June 1929.*

vacation in sixty-four years.[17] His business concerns, and with them *Y Drych*, passed to his two sons, Thomas J. Jnr and Charles W. Griffiths, who would retain control of the paper for nearly thirty more years.[18]

Finally, to compound these losses, on the night of 12 December 1924 a disastrous fire occurred at the Mechanics Hall which caused $150,000 worth of damage to T. J. Griffiths' own business and others located there. It developed into one of the worst blazes seen in Utica for many a year and brave fire fighters spent three hours pouring over a million gallons of water on it before it came under control. Fortunately no one was injured in the actual inferno although *Y Drych*'s book-keeper, John E. Williams, broke his arm while attempting to rush to the building to rescue the paper's records. *Y Drych*'s production was affected, needing to publish two shorter issues before the normal format was restored at the beginning of 1925.[19] This tragic fire was not just a disaster for *Y Drych* at the time. As the paper itself acknowledged, the blaze also destroyed the stock of back issues of *Y Drych*;[20] in so doing it also robbed subsequent generations of valuable early issues of the paper

Front page of *Y Drych*, 8 December 1924, with two strikingly contrasted messages. Above, the paper wishes its readers a Merry Christmas and a Happy New Year. Below, reporting the events of perhaps the worst night in the paper's history. The headline states 'A Destructive and Frightening Fire Sweeps Through *Y Drych*'s Office'.

from the 1850s and 1860s that might otherwise have survived to this day. A good deal of *Y Drych*'s history literally went up in smoke that frosty December evening.

As well as marking the end of an era, the early 1920s also marked the beginning of yet another chapter in *Y Drych*'s history as a new team took over; it would remain in charge for the rest of the decade. Index's successor as editor in 1923, in a part-time capacity, was Hugh Hughes (1870-1945), a most respected New York State newspaperman who had worked for the *Utica Daily Press* since 1900.[21] Though born in Anglesey, Hughes had come with his parents to Remsen, New York, when he was two years old. Apparently,

Hugh Hughes (1870-1945), editor 1923-1933 and April to June 1945.
From Y Drych, *6 January 1921.*

he had been heavily influenced in early life by his father-in-law, Revd Edward Davies, editor of the Welsh-American Congregational paper, *Y Cyfaill*, for which Hughes wrote numerous articles and assisted with editing. Throughout his life Hughes also took an active role in Welsh societies in Utica, becoming president of the Cymreigyddion Society and director of the St David's Society. He also served as president of the National Gymanfa Ganu Association for two years and compiled a memorial volume to the former *Drych* editor, G. H. Humphrey.[22] With delicious hyperbole, in 1945 the *Utica Observer-Dispatch* suggested that being editor of *Y Drych* had put Hughes 'just a shade below Lloyd George. When he went abroad a few years ago, people in places like Llanhilleth and Abergavenny used to point to him and whisper: "Look, the editor of The Drych"'.[23]

By September 1923, Sarah (Sallie) Catherine Evans (later Surridge), a recent arrival from her native Rhosllanerchrugog, Denbighshire, had become full-time assistant editor of *Y Drych*.[24] Evans had been a schoolteacher in Wales but because she did not possess the necessary

The first woman to edit *Y Drych:* Sarah Catherine Evans, later Surridge (1901-1990), assistant editor 1923-1931 and editor 1931-33.

From Y Drych, *4 June 1931.*

qualifications to continue this career in the United States, she was training to be a librarian when T. J. Griffiths asked her to join the paper.[25] Working on *Y Drych* would take her all over the United States and to Wales, win her innumerable friends and tributes, and earn her the accolade of being the paper's first female editor. Thanks to a unique photograph of *Y Drych*'s staff published in the paper in October 1925, we have a glimpse of others involved in production during these years.[26] (Only very occasionally do *Y Drych*'s workers below editorial rank surface in the written record.) As well as Hughes, Sallie Evans, and the two Griffiths brothers who owned the paper, the camera caught foreman William E. Davies; three compositors, Thomas C. Jones, Allen H. Davies and Ellis F. Williams, the latter apparently being the main Welsh-language compositor; two pressmen, Jake Werthman and Arthur Jones; apprentice John Williams; two mailers, Catherine Roberts and Florence Williams; and another long-standing stalwart of the paper, John E. Williams, who had been injured during the fire at *Y Drych*'s offices some months earlier. Originally from Ffestiniog, Williams (Ioan Gwynedd) was book-keeper between 1912 and his premature death in 1933 aged only fifty-four. He was also an occasional writer for the paper and ran his own Welsh-language book business in Utica.[27]

The new editorial team soon made a rapid and permanent impact on the paper's style and presentation as it strove to make the content more digestible and easier to read. A greater use of photographs, bigger, bolder headlines, more by-lines and the introduction of cartoons – for example, Baker's 'Little Julius Sneeser' (in English)[28] – can be detected from the beginning of the 1920s onwards, but during the second half of 1923 these changes became even more prominent and noticeable. The first two pages were now devoted as much to news as to lengthy discursive articles, whilst generally articles were shorter and editorials fewer in number. There were more boxed features and photographs (until the mid-1930s at least), especially of groups and scenes from Welsh-American social and cultural activities, and not just individual portraits. Messages were often printed above the masthead such as 'A Merry Christmas and a Happy New Year to all the Readers of *Y Drych*'[29] or 'The 85 year history of the Welsh Church in Youngstown Ohio on page 2'.[30] This new look was well received in some quarters, judging by praise occasionally printed in the newspaper during the 1920s,[31] although there are indications that not everyone was in agreement.[32] *Y Drych* was finally responding, rather belatedly perhaps, to changes in taste and fashion. In his survey of the various phases in the paper's history published in 1929, Revd H. O. Rowlands believed that within the last few years *Y Drych* had entered a new period, one of changing trends. This was because 'in the present age the majority do not care for

The people behind the scenes. *Y Drych's* staff, October 1925. A photograph taken when Dr D. M. Phillips of Tylorstown, Rhondda (seated, centre) visited the paper's office.

From Y Drych, *22 October, 1925.*

long editorials, nor debates on religious and philosophical topics, and even less for personal quarrels . . . Now they look for short articles and news – (news, note) of the world and Welsh life in the States'. He thought Hugh Hughes was the ideal editor to introduce these innovations as previous editors would not have accorded with current tastes.[33]

As far as *Y Drych*'s content is concerned, with hindsight we might well regard the 1920s as the last fling of a Welsh-language social, religious and cultural life in North America. Its pages are replete with vigorous photographic and verbal images of religious meetings, eisteddfodau, concerts, Welsh Days and St David's Day celebrations (organised with unusual dynamism during the mid-1920s) held in an impressive range of Welsh communities in the United States and Canada. If anything, the paper took pride in the fact that it was becoming even more of an international Welsh paper and not just a Welsh North American one,[34] justifiably as the regular reports from correspondents in Wales itself, London and other English cities, Patagonia, India and Australia well demonstrate. In 1929 that long-standing source of advertising revenue for *Y Drych*, tea manufacturer G. T. Matthews, testified (in English) to the paper's

Welsh Ladies Quartette, Seattle, who had apparently already sung together for many years before this photograph appeared in *Y Drych*, 7 April 1932. From left to right, Ruth Burke (first soprano), Annie J. Jones (second soprano), Doris Jones McClusky (first contralto) and Annie Hughes Lea (second contralto), who wrote Seattle news for the paper in the 1950s.

Cymry Winnipeg yn Gwisgo'r Geninen

Officers of Winnipeg St David's Society committee who organised a successful banquet in the Marlborough Hotel in the city, in March 1927.   *From* Y Drych, *10 March 1927.*

St. David's Male Voice Choir, Ottawa, from *Y Drych*, 21 December 1933. According to the accompanying report this 'famous' choir was due to compete at the Utica Eisteddfod, New Year, 1934.

geographic range: 'Few indeed are the places on the map of the world where Y Cymry, few or many, cannot find y Drych and inquiries come from the interior of the Argentine Republic, the Klondike as well as Australia for our goods in response to the ad in y Drych.'[35]

Inevitably, extensive coverage was given to the new initiatives and some of the great events in the history of the Welsh in America during the 1920s. There was, for example, the excitement caused by the long-awaited visit of the all-conquering hero, David Lloyd George, to the United States and Canada in 1923, even if his inability actually to visit certain Welsh-American communities originally included on the itinerary caused disgruntlement and disappointment.[36] A less well-publicised visit, but in its own way just as symbolic in reinforcing links

Officials of the Chairing the Bard Ceremony, Wilkesbarre Eisteddfod, 1928. Front row, left to right, Bessie Thomas Flickenger (trumpeter), T. H. Williams, William T. Williams (Chief Bard), Olwen Williams (trumpeter); second row, Margaret Jones and Mollie Davies (flag bearers) and Mrs David John Jones (Liberty).

From Y Drych, *15 November 1928.*

Here at last! Nearly fifteen years after a visit was first mooted, David Lloyd George, seen here in Chicago, finally toured North America in October and November 1923.

From Y Drych, *25 October 1923.*

The caption for this photograph which appeared in *Y Drych*, 9 January 1930 reads [in translation] 'Mr and Mrs Lewis Evans, at work as missionaries in Assam, India'. It accompanied an article containing a letter from them written at the Welsh Mission, Shaistaganj, 18 November 1929. The couple had lived in Chicago for a time and their missionary work was sponsored by the American Presbyterian denomination.

'The Peace Missionaries' as *Y Drych* called them. From left to right, Mary Ellis, Annie Hughes Griffiths, Eluned Prys and Mrs H. G. Thomas, who presented 385,000 signatures of women in Wales in support of world peace to the the women of America in 1924.

From Y Drych, *20 March 1924.*

between the people of Wales and those of America, was that of the Welsh Women's Peace Mission in February – March 1924.[37] Looking in the opposite direction, there was pride about Welsh-American victories at the National Eisteddfod of Wales, notably that of Scranton's Anthracite Male Chorus, conducted by Luther Bassett, in Treorci in 1928.[38] An editorial acknowledged the joy and enthusiasm with which that news was greeted in America, congratulated the people of Scranton for collecting the money that made the trip possible, and thought the triumph would benefit eisteddfodau in North America and encourage Welsh-American choirs to compete against Welsh ones.[39] Indeed much column space was devoted to the 'pilgrimages' of Welsh-American visitors and contestants, and their supporters, to the various National Eisteddfodau held during these years.[40] The same applies to the events themselves, with lengthy reports being provided by special correspondents sent over by the paper. At home in North America two important organisations were inaugurated in the 1920s and given a great deal of coverage, the National Eisteddfod Association of America in 1925, and, even more momentous given its flourishing existence in present day

North America, the National Gymanfa Ganu. The latter was established at Niagara Falls, New York, in 1929, and revisited there the following three successive years. *Y Drych*'s correspondent in that place, Ellis Hughes, was a key member of the local organising committee, and became the National Gymanfa Association's first vice president and, later, its secretary.[41]

As in previous decades, much space was also devoted to politics and political issues, at home and abroad. Like most of his predecessors, and indeed his fellow countrymen and -women in general, editor Hughes was a committed Republican and strongly advocated the party's principles and ideas in his editorials. Political and other developments in Wales also received a great deal of comment, especially the fortunes of the

The Eisteddfod 'Pilgrims' Raise the Red Dragon: hoisting the Welsh flag on board the *SS Laconia* as it leaves New York bound for the 1929 National Eisteddfod of Wales at Liverpool. In the picture are Captain William Protheroe, First Officer Crattidge, Revd. R. T. Upton, D.D., Mr and Mrs M. E. Comerford, Muriel Comerford, Mr and Mrs W. J. Phillips, Janet Phillips, Gwladys Wilson, Martha Young Jones (raising the flag); Margaret Dyer, all from Scranton, and R. M. Maddocks.

From Y Drych, *1 August 1929.*

A WELCOME INVASION.
A boatload of Welsh-Americans arrive to-day for the Eisteddfod.

Cartoon from the *Western Mail*, 30 July 1928.

Reproduced by kind permission of the Western Mail.

nationalist party, Plaid Genedlaethol Cymru, formed in 1925, which enjoyed extensive support in editorials, letters and articles.[42] But *Y Drych* paid little attention to the hardship experienced in Wales during the 1926 miners' strike, only launching an appeal to assist children of mining families right at the end of the lock-out.[43] Nevertheless, it did eventually raise $2,500.[44] Two years later, however, shocked reports of the scale of misery, unemployment, poverty and hardship in mining communities in south Wales began to appear regularly, and at length. In response to the reports, Hugh Hughes launched a 'Drych Relief Fund' in January 1929 which, the paper explained, was intended to rectify the fact that Welsh people across the United States and Canada wanted to contribute money but had been prevented by the absence of an organisation to collect it.[45] This fund had amassed $1,500 by April 1929.[46] In addition, large sums were donated to similar funds established in various towns and cities in North America, and these were given much prominence in the paper between January and April 1929.[47] In 1930 *Y Drych* also organised a fund in aid of impoverished Welsh students.[48]

In June 1929, somewhat idiosyncratically perhaps, the paper decided to celebrate its seventy-eighth birthday in style, producing a double issue. Among the numerous items were congratulations from David Lloyd George; Hon. James J. Davis, U.S. Secretary of Labor; the Archdruid of Wales, Pedrog; various Welsh-language newspapers in Wales; and a host of Welsh-American and Utica businesses.[49] Self-congratulation was surely only to be expected, and an editorial proudly proclaimed that by the present time *Y Drych* 'has become more than a newspaper. It can be called an important institution. . . . It is it that keeps the Welsh family on this continent in touch with each other. Through it alone can any Welsh movement in America be conducted. Its arrival 78 years ago was important to the nation, but its continuation today is even more important.'[50] Despite the undeniable existence of unfavourable long-term trends, the late 1920s, with (as the paper itself boasted) their economic boom and unprecedented prosperity, were generally good years for the paper.[51] When the depression that had wrought such distress in Wales was visited upon the United States, it would be a different matter.

The 1930s: Depression and Decline

In late 1931 Hugh Hughes resigned as editor of *Y Drych* in order to take up the same post with the *Utica Daily Press*. He was succeeded by the assistant editor, Sallie Evans, following her return from Wales where she had been covering the Bangor National Eisteddfod for the paper. Her first issue as editor was 8 October 1931.[52] Her promotion, contribution to Welsh journalism, and services on behalf of the cause of women in journalism, were celebrated in articles in *Y Gymraes*, local Utica newspapers and the *Liverpool Echo*.[53] Yet hers was to be a relatively short, although eventful, editorship. In the summer of 1933 she resigned for family reasons; she had married in June 1932 and, now expecting her first child, was finding it difficult to continue in post.[54] *Y Drych*'s owners showered her with praise for her hard work and regrets at her leaving, and it is clear the departure of this talented individual was a major loss to the paper.[55] The new editor was John Foulkes Jones. While substantial biographical information is available on most of *Y Drych*'s editors, and for some almost voluminously so, Jones is perhaps the most shadowy figure of all who held that office. Born in Dinorwig, Caernarfonshire, and educated at Llanberis County School and Bangor University, he had emigrated first to Detroit. He served as an elder, secretary and occasional preacher and organist for the Welsh Church there, before moving to Utica in April 1932 when he first came into *Y Drych*'s employ.[56]

Before becoming editor, John F. Jones was office secretary and book-keeper but he was also charged with increasing the number of subscribers to *Y Drych*. This included going on 'missions' to various Welsh communities in the eastern states to publicise the paper and boost circulation.[57] Of course, subscription drives were hardly an innovation,

A rare photograph of John Foulkes Jones, editor of *Y Drych*, 1933-1945. He is fourth from left in the middle row, and to his left is one of *Y Drych*'s most celebrated writers, Sam Ellis. J. F. Jones's wife, Anne, stands far right in the front row. They are pictured here as members of the party welcoming W. R. Hughes, of Bangor, Pennsylvania, to Utica in July 1933. *From* Y Drych, *10 August 1933.*

nor were travelling agents to drum up support. As far as is known, Jones' most recent predecessor as a *Drych* salesman had been John T. Jones of Chicago in 1924.[58] However, John Foulkes Jones' appointment to this role reflects the fact that increasingly by 1932, the paper was adopting desperate measures to try and improve its precarious position. Indeed, both Sallie Evans and Jones' stints as editors were overshadowed by three sets of deteriorating circumstances: *Y Drych*'s financial position, the American economy and the international situation. All three ensured that the thirties were perhaps the hardest decade for the paper since the 1860s.

After 1929, triggered by the Wall Street Crash of October that year, the United States was plunged into an economic depression of unprecedented severity; in Donald McCoy's words, it was 'The Great American Trauma'.[59] In 1930 unemployment had risen to 4.3 million and three years later to nearly 13 million, a quarter of the workforce, and one historian has suggested that possibly one third of all those available for work were jobless.[60] Living standards and income also fell drastically, and all sectors of the country's life were affected. The worsening situation itself was commented on regularly in *Y Drych* in the first few years of the depression, with editorial articles expressing concern at the scale of unemployment and its effects, especially on children, and insisting that society had a duty to protect the future generations.[61] Also discussed was the political fall-out, as discontent at Republican President Herbert Hoover's ineffectual inactivity gave way to intense expectancy following the ascendancy of Franklin Roosevelt, a Democrat, to the White House after the November 1932 presidential election and the introduction of the 'New Deal'. Not surprisingly given its avowed Republicanism, *Y Drych*'s editorial stance initially expressed confidence in Hoover, but in time voices sympathetic to Roosevelt could be heard in the paper.[62] Although the paper still urged readers to vote for Hoover's re-election in 1932, editorials applauded Roosevelt's Inaugural Address and declared it was the country's duty and honour to support the National Recovery Administration, the main vehicle for introducing the measures to alleviate unemployment and distress.[63] Roosevelt's re-election in 1936 was viewed in a sympathetic light in a guest editorial by Sam Ellis[64] (who apparently had favoured the Democrat Woodrow Wilson over Charles Evans Hughes, the Republican candidate in the 1916 presidential election),[65] reflecting perhaps that the Welsh as an ethnic group were divided in their political allegiance in the 1930s and early 1940s. Roosevelt seems to have developed a significant and loyal Welsh following, whilst Thomas Dewey, the unsuccessful Republican candidate who challenged Roosevelt in the 1944 presidential election, is said to have complained that he did not get the Welsh vote.[66]

Nor was it only the economy that was declining after 1929 and into the 1930s. All the evidence available suggests that during this period *Y Drych* suffered a catastrophic fall in subscriptions. Although deaths of older subscribers played their part, in the severe financial climate of the 1930s many Welsh people were no longer able to subscribe to the paper, either stopping their subscriptions or leaving their debts unpaid. Throughout the 1930s pleas by editors and correspondents to readers to secure new subscribers became increasingly frequent and insistent, often exploiting the language of patriotism by declaring it was the patriotic duty of 'y wir Gymry' [the true Welsh] to do so.[67] In the early years of the depression *Y Drych* attempted to adapt to the new hostile environment by offering work as subscription agents to unemployed Welsh people all over North America in order to help boost the paper's circulation. It promised to pay good rates for each new subscriber recruited.[68] What success the scheme achieved is not known. The paper also urged (in English) those readers who could afford it to pay the subscriptions of people who 'at present, owing to financial condition and old age, are unable to continue subscribing . . . thus causing them a great deal of pain and loss of comfort in their loneliness. Quite often cases of this kind are brought to our attention'.[69]

But the most telling indicator of the paper's straitened circumstances is the drastic action the owners were forced to take in 1933. On 22 June of that year *Y Drych* became a four-page rather than an eight-page weekly.[70] It did not hesitate to identify America's economic predicament as the primary cause, explaining that the paper had been reduced 'because of the lack of financial support of many subscribers as a result of the present great depression'.[71] It appears that an eight-page fortnightly had been considered but the paper believed readers would prefer the four-page weekly. It resolved to return to eight pages once circumstances allowed and appealed for subscribers' help towards achieving this.[72] Subscription rates for 1934 were cut to $2, probably to compensate for the scaled-down version, and although this might also be taken as an indication that the financial crisis had eased a little, it also effectively squashed any possibility that the number of pages would be increased.[73]

Its own financial difficulties, emotive debates over whether it should be an English- or a Welsh-language newspaper (as we shall see in the next chapter) and a savage economic depression in the United States naturally absorbed much of the energies of *Y Drych*'s editors and writers during the 1930s. Nevertheless, despite its reduced size and focus, columns of the period testify to some concern for issues in Wales and, not surprisingly perhaps given their seriousness, international relations. Plaid Genedlaethol Cymru, the nationalist party in Wales, was only occasionally mentioned in the paper during the early 1930s[74] but in 1936 the paper's colours became unmistakable with the introduction of a weekly column devoted to the party, 'Colofn Y Blaid'.[75] Later that year the famous Pen-y-berth incident, when three of the party's leaders, Saunders Lewis, Lewis Valentine and D. J. Williams set fire to the bomb training school in the Llŷn Peninsula, and their subsequent trials and convictions, were extensively reported, sometimes taking up to a third of the four-page issues. With only a few exceptions, comment was supportive, supplemented by condemnation and anger when the three were found guilty.[76] The paper's coverage of the case reached its apogee in September 1937 when they were released, and on 23 September much of both front and back pages were devoted to the triumphant welcome given to 'Y Tri Gwron yng Nghaernarfon' [The Three Heroes in Caernarfon].[77] Perhaps hardly surprisingly, during the 1930s a significant and growing number of items addressed the worsening international situation, and the growth of dictatorships in Europe. As early as 1926 editorials had suggested that Mussolini was a danger to the rest of the world[78] but they concentrated their criticism on Nazi Germany after Hitler came to power in 1933.[79] Dictatorships, among which *Y Drych* included Stalinist Russia,[80] were condemned for two reasons: they were a threat to religious freedom and a danger to democratic freedom.

And as Europe moved towards war for the second time in 25 years, *Y Drych* would face yet another crisis, the severest it had experienced for nearly a century.

1939-45: Struggling to Stay Alive

By the end of the 1930s, years of declining income from subscriptions and advertising had made *Y Drych*'s position even more precarious, if not untenable. Rumours that the paper's demise was imminent began to circulate, only to be denied by the editor. Starting in 1937, the paper's continued existence became dependent on successful annual end-of-year appeals to subscribers to clear their debts.[81] In 1939 *Y Drych* moved even closer to the brink. The Utica Cymreigyddion Society passed resolutions urging the owners and the Welsh in America to do all in their power to save the paper. Echoing sentiments expressed a decade earlier when a correspondent suggested that without *Y Drych* the Welsh would be 'like a nation astray, having lost our identity, or [like] children without their mother, and chickens, without the hen',[82] the Cymreigyddion feared that the paper's death would mean 'the end of Welsh life in America as a unity'.[83] An appeal in *Y Drych* in November drew attention to the closure of the paper's rival, *The Druid*, in July of that year as an indication of the bleak future awaiting *Y Drych* if subscription fees remained unpaid, and reminded defaulters that there was only one month left in which to pay.[84] The tactic worked once more; into the office came hundreds of letters pledging support for the ailing newspaper 'in words, and in deeds'.[85] But relief was only temporary. In the final issue of 1940, amid further rumours that the end was near, the editor declared that the paper was economically unviable. Nevertheless, the owners had been so distressed by readers' fatalism that they wanted to continue publication, but a change of format was obligatory.[86]

Y Drych stayed alive but from now on it would be seen less regularly in the homes of its subscribers. In January 1941 it became a monthly, rather than a weekly, and although each issue returned to eight pages in length, it now adopted a tabloid rather than a broadsheet size.[87] This may have been another attempt to reduce costs, although some years later it was explained, disingenuously perhaps, as 'following the trend of the times in journalism' in order to be 'more convenient for readers'.[88] Subscriptions were reduced, to $1.50. The paper also introduced other changes, some of them compelled by the new monthly cycle, and these soon became apparent. The 'Blodau Coffa' tributes to deceased persons were replaced by a mere list of names of those who had died, discussions on religious matters all but disappeared, letters to the editor appeared far less frequently, and the paper became increasingly dominated by local and regional Welsh-American issues and reports. A content analysis reveals a dramatic increase in coverage of Welsh-American news, which now accounted for over 80 per cent of the paper's total content. After 1935 a decrease in the number of front page headlines can also be detected. The monthly cycle prevented emphasis on immediate national and international news. In short, the paper was becoming less varied in its content, and possibly less interesting.

It was hoped that in the paper's new format 'it would be our pleasure to publish it more frequently than once a month if we receive the co-operation of Welsh Americans to make that possible'[89] but to

A veteran reporter: John T. Jones (1861-1945), Chicago, originally from Mynytho, Caernarfonshire, who emigrated in 1888. An agent for *Y Drych* in the 1920s, by the time of his death in 1945 he had contributed to the paper for fifty-four years.

From Y Drych, *16 March 1939.*

date *Y Drych* has remained a monthly. Numerous letters published in January and February 1941 expressed approval of the new format whilst others regretted that it was no longer published weekly.[90] Veteran Chicago correspondent John T. Jones insisted that readers had to be realistic, and that a monthly was all they could really expect; nevertheless he felt 'a strange emptiness during the weeks between issues'.[91] Another John Jones, this time of Criccieth, Caernarfonshire, privately expressed his disappointment at seeing the paper become so small, when formerly it had provided a lot of reading. Such remarks were clearly directed at the lack of substance as well as that of size.[92] It is difficult to underestimate the impact of the change from a weekly to a monthly in

1941; inevitably *Y Drych* could not avoid playing less of a role in Welsh-American life simply because it appeared far less frequently. Perhaps it recognised this when it hoped that in its new guise the paper could be 'interesting to the Welsh of our country'.[93] Clearly the paper's ambitions had been considerably scaled down in the face of the undeniable fact that more and more Welsh Americans were either unwilling, or as several letters suggested, were too lethargic or apathetic to support it.[94]

The events of the Second World War were a backdrop to *Y Drych's* own troubles during the early 1940s and they also imposed their own difficulties and challenges. America's policy of non-intervention following the outbreak of war in Europe in September 1939 was initially supported by the paper,[95] but by June 1941 there had been a reversal in the editorial line. 'There are clear signs that up to now our country has not realised the size of its danger,' *Y Drych* declared. 'It is foolish to try to believe that the Atlantic and the Pacific will defend our country from the enemy's attacks. . . . Let us forget about the pocket and the purse for a time and foster in our midst the spirit that ensures help for Britain and safety for America.'[96] When the United States finally declared war on 11 December 1941, a brief *Y Drych* editorial declared that the time for talking and supporting were over: 'It is the privilege and duty of every Welshman in America to do what they can to help their adopted country.'[97]

During the second global conflict Welsh Americans once more came to the aid of their countrymen and women in the homeland. Since March 1940 the 'Llythyr o Gymru' [Letter from Wales] column had been keeping readers informed of war developments and their effects on Wales including evacuees, blackouts and life in air-raid shelters.[98] At the end of 1940 the American Welsh Festival Fund was launched to collect and send to Wales items such as blankets, bottles, clothing and kerosene stoves. Mobile Feeding Units and ambulances were also purchased and shipped across the Atlantic, and not surprisingly the fund's activities were given generous exposure in *Y Drych's* columns.[99] By 1941 financial stringency meant the paper carried few photographs but two that did appear neatly symbolise the Welsh-American relief effort. These were: in July 1941, Mobile Feeding Units purchased with Welsh-American donations shown lined up outside the National Museum of

'Young Welsh Models in Exhibit for Wales', New York, 17 October 1941. From *Y Drych*, 15 December, 1941. A shipment of over a thousand garments was sent as a Christmas gift to Wales in 1941, as a result of the efforts of the 'Hand-Knits for the Children in Wales Committee'. In that year the organisation had forty-one branches all over the United States. *Reproduced by kind permission of the National Library of Wales.*

Wales in Cardiff, and in November, a group of Welsh children in New York wearing garments hand-knitted by Welsh Americans.[100] The Welsh-American response to the Second World War resembled that towards the First, but the role of *Y Drych* in the two relief funds was very different. This time *Y Drych* played no organisational role, confining itself to promoting the fund's activities.

Y Drych's eschewing of an organisational role might be interpreted as further evidence of a trend that was becoming more and more apparent as the years of Depression gave way to the years of World War. The paper was moving from the centre to a more peripheral place in Welsh-American life. Wartime issues certainly give the impression of a paper that had lost direction and a voice. From April 1943 until early 1944 editorials were either reproduced from newspapers in Wales such as *Y Tyst* and *Y Faner* or written by guest writers, among them Hugh Hughes and Ellis Hughes. Editorials disappeared completely after March 1944, to be replaced by obituaries. Throughout his twelve-year editorship John F. Jones seems to have suffered from prolonged bouts of illness and this may be one of the reasons for the fading of the paper's editorial presence. And eventually Jones, too, faded without notice. In April 1945 it was tersely announced that Hugh Hughes was returning as editor, and in the absence of any testimony we can only speculate on the circumstances of Jones' departure from office. Little more is known about him beyond that he was an agent for the Jim G. Brock insurance company in Utica until 1949 then in Plattsburg, New York.[101] On reassuming his old position Hughes apparently had 'unmistakably promising' plans for the future of the paper but they would remain unfulfilled due to his unexpected death in July 1945 at the age of seventy-four. A tribute to him (in English), probably written by the new editor, Arthur M. Roberts, speaks volumes about not only the man himself but the condition of *Y Drych*: 'we could ill afford a loss so great when the only Welsh newspaper in America needed him so much.'[102]

In 1929 *Y Drych* acknowledged that it was 'facing circumstances which are unfavourable to growth and often this is a cause for worry about its future, but up to now it has been able to meet every transformation successfully, and it is hoped that this will be its fate in years to come'.[103] In 1945 it was still alive, but it had had to pay a price for survival. Between 1920 and 1945 a changing Welsh America had not only jeopardised the paper's future but also necessitated adaptations which reduced and restricted the role it could hope to play in Welsh-American life. In the 1920s, in its avowed quest to be more than a newspaper, the paper could legitimately claim that providing news was its most important function, but that it also sought to carry debates and discussions on religion, literature and science in order to provide something 'to the taste of every class of reader'.[104] Twenty-five years later no such claim could be made, and if it had, it would have been resoundingly hollow. The paper had shrunk in size, appeared less frequently and had narrowed its range of content; no longer could it seek to represent the world to Welsh-speaking Welsh Americans. For above all *Y Drych* had become a predominantly English-language publication not a Welsh-language one, a process and a transformation which compelled massive cultural and ethnic re-definition. And it is to this, perhaps the most fundamental change of all that *Y Drych* underwent during its one hundred and fifty-year history, that we must now turn.

CHAPTER 6

'Problem *Y Drych*': Which Language?

'Running Y Drych is not easy work, especially during this present period in the history of the Welsh in America', began an editorial entitled 'Problem Y Drych' [Y Drych's Problem] in June 1928.[1] It went on to print two recent letters to the paper, one in Welsh, the other in English, and both claimed to represent the views of several other individuals. One of the letters complained, in Welsh, that there was too much English in the paper, 'and some have told me they intend to give it up' if this continued.[2] The other letter asked for more English-language material to be included 'for the sake of the children' because 'the children don't trouble or bother themselves with the Welsh language'. The editor believed both points of view had the paper's best interests at heart.[3]

More and more after about 1920, *Y Drych* had to confront the fundamental issue of how long to remain exclusively, or at least predominantly, a Welsh-language paper and how much, if any, English-language material to include. It found itself having to balance what were seemingly two irreconcilable positions, between 'y diafol a'r dyfnfor' [the Devil and the Deep Blue Sea] as another correspondent once described it.[4] Its own ideology committed it to providing a Welsh-language paper for its core readership. Yet, as we saw in the previous chapter, due to ageing and the drying up of immigration, that constituency was shrinking rapidly, depriving the paper of subscribers, writers and even printers. The stark reality was that if *Y Drych* was to survive, then it needed also to appeal to the American-born generations, and their language was not Welsh, but American English. The process of native language loss among the Welsh in America had been proceeding throughout the nineteenth century but due to continued immigration, it was not until the end of the century that Welsh institutions began to feel the impact. *Y Drych* itself had remained unaffected. Now, in the 1920s, as the editorial referred to earlier explained:

English is breaking in everywhere these days, especially in this country. There is not a Welsh family in the country where English cannot be heard in the home. The number of our societies that are wholly Welsh are few. Likewise our churches. In every Welsh district the ruins of old Welsh chapels are memorials to the death of the language. Our Eisteddfodau are also rather English. Lately English has appeared in the Drych, as a result of the above changes.[5]

The predicament in which *Y Drych* found itself was a common one for the non-English-language American press during these years. As Sally Miller has remarked, during the period 'the combination of shrinking numbers of newcomers and the ageing of the first generation appeared to be a virtually insurmountable barrier' to the ethnic press. Further factors were the economic depression and the impact of the more aggressive, '100 per cent Amercanism' that prevailed during the First World War and its aftermath. These adverse circumstances took their toll and it has been estimated that the number of non-English-language newspapers in the United States fell from a peak of 1,323 in 1917 to 1,037 in 1930 and 698 in 1960.[6] For example, the number of Swedish publications in America more than halved between 1915 and 1932.[7] *Y Drych*'s quandary of whether, when and to what extent it ought to switch to English was also shared by other ethnic publications. In the face of adverse conditions, they adopted various devices such as publishing English-language pages or issues – becoming what Joshua Fishman and others have termed 'mixed publications'[8] – and even converting to English entirely.[9] As we shall see, *Y Drych* would go through each of these stages.

This chapter focuses on the paper's trajectory from a 'monoglot' Welsh newspaper to one that in the late 1940s was, as Emrys Jones has written, 'to all intents and purposes, an English newspaper which also contains a few articles and news items in Welsh'.[10] It will first examine the wider context of language shift among the Welsh in America in the first half of the twentieth century, and commentaries upon it. That shift was a complex phenomenon, one shaped by a combination of forces and factors – social, economic, cultural, demographic and generational. It was at the same time determined by influences operating *within* the Welsh ethnic group itself, and *external* pressures exerted by mainstream American society and the prevailing ideology.[11] The primary aim here is to explore contemporary perceptions of the situation as mediated through *Y Drych*. The chapter will then turn to how the paper itself responded to its 'problem'.

The absence of any reliable statistics regarding usage of Welsh in America makes it impossible to trace language shift with precision. Nevertheless, there is abundant qualitative evidence to confirm that it was retreating even further in the years after the First World War, and that the process accelerated in the 1930s and 1940s. By this time even areas where Welsh was being spoken among the second generation, such as Utica itself and some of the rural settlements in the West were experiencing language shift.[12] In *Y Drych* in February 1923 it was reported from an unidentified town in Ohio that large numbers of Welsh

A well-known *Drych* couple: Ellis and Margaret Hughes, Niagara Falls, New York, taken on the occasion of their silver wedding anniversary, 1929. Ellis was *Y Drych*'s local correspondent and an organiser of the first four National Gymanfaoedd Ganu in the city, 1929-33. Margaret Hughes dressed up in Welsh costume in order to meet David Lloyd George when he visited the city in 1923.   *From* Y Drych *19 December 1929.*

Americans there were graduating from schools and colleges, but they had 'forgotten' the language. Only the correspondent, his wife and children spoke Welsh there now.[13] Ellis Hughes of Niagara Falls (and previously of Canada), himself a *Drych* correspondent, stated in a Welsh-language letter in 1930 that Welsh was fast dying out in the churches in the United States and believed it was only a matter of time before it completely disappeared. This was a shame, he thought, but was only to be expected because immigration had virtually ceased.[14] Earlier the same year Hughes had stated that there were a number of Welsh Americans in Niagara Falls but the Welsh language was a 'dead letter' among them.[15] There were similar reports from Poultney, Vermont, and Seattle,[16] whilst Ifan Morris Powell, Milwaukee, informed the Welsh bard Carneddog in 1934 that 'the Welsh language is ending in this place. It has declined terribly here in the last ten years.' The old people were dying one by one, he wrote, the new generation had no knowledge of Welsh, and many Welsh Americans in Milwaukee could hardly discuss the weather and other general matters in Welsh let alone appreciate poetry and literature.[17]

As these commentaries suggest, there was much agreement on some of the central features of the crisis – the consequences of declining immigration, the ageing of the population, the impact on churches – especially as many commentators observed that other ethnic groups were in a similar situation.[18] Yet not surprisingly, perhaps, the 'language question' also gave rise to passionate debate, controversy and squabbling. This was not new, of course. As we have seen in an earlier chapter, the future of the Welsh language in the USA was a contentious issue. The extent to which, if at all, it should be preserved and included in religious services and Welsh cultural activities had been a feature of *Y Drych*'s columns from the beginning. In the 1920s and 1930s, however, *Y Drych*'s role as a platform for this debate was intensified. Following the demise of all other papers and magazines in that language, it was the *only* vehicle for Welsh-language debate and comment about the nature, extent, desirability and causes of language shift among the Welsh in the United States. And given its own important role in, and commitment towards, maintaining the Welsh language in America, the possible impact of cultural and linguistic change on *Y Drych* itself was inevitably locked into the discussions. The concern over the position of the Welsh language in America as filtered through *Y Drych* was inseparable from anxieties regarding the paper itself; commentators may have been addressing the general situation, but they also had *Y Drych* in mind.[19]

If there was general agreement on some aspects of the contemporary language situation, then were was much disagreement on others. A minority believed the Welsh language had a future in America,[20] and even in 1936 *Y Drych* itself was insisting, naively perhaps, that there were more than enough Welsh speakers in North America to justify the paper's existence, if only more of them subscribed.[21] Some commentators would be increasingly heartened by efforts in Wales to save the language there,[22] but to most the decline of the language in America, though regrettable and a cause for sadness, was nevertheless inevitable.[23] To some, it was even desirable. In a revealing illustration of the way individuals found themselves in major dilemmas and having to adopt seemingly contradictory strategies in the circumstances, in 1923 William Owen expressed the conviction that the Welsh language was dying, and that this was God's Will as America was destined to be one nation, with one language and one flag. Even so, he and his wife had led their whole lives in Welsh, and had brought up their children in a home where only Welsh was spoken.[24]

Some commentators complained bitterly that the Welsh were apathetic about the preservation of their native language and especially condemned those who believed there was no point in teaching their children Welsh because it would be of no benefit to them in their American lives.[25] Others justified their actions in this respect as appropriate on the grounds that they had come to America to improve their circumstances and those of their children: 'We came here not to keep the language alive, but to keep ourselves alive,' maintained John Howell Williams in 1923.[26] It was also alleged that Welsh people tended to forget their language as they rose up the socio-economic ladder, though this, too, was denied by other correspondents.[27] In January 1933 Sam Ellis opined that the 'Dic Sion Dafydd' spirit was far less prevalent in the country than the frequency of complaints against it in *Y Drych* would suggest. ('Dic Sion Dafydd' is a derisory appellation for people who turn their backs on the Welsh language and Welsh nationality.) More important were the 'economic order' and other influences, including the different cultural identities and national allegiances of the younger, American-born generation. He appealed to Welsh-speaking parents, who like himself were 'more Welsh people than Americans', to try to realise 'that the United States is as dear to our children as Wales is to us'.[28]

In his reply to Ellis, and perhaps proving Ellis' point that the language issue was partly shaped by tensions on both sides of the linguistic/generational divide, Tom Jones of Port Huron, Michigan, insisted that young Welsh Americans should cherish sufficient respect for their mother tongue. They should not 'attempt to push the old language over the threshold to oblivion forever, as many are trying to do', suggesting that in some quarters there may have been not just apathy but outright hostility towards the native tongue.[29] As Emrys Jones has pointed out in his valuable discussion of language change in the Welsh community in Utica, *Y Drych's* home city, the children of Welsh immigrants adopted new beliefs and values derived from their experiences of the school system and the street, and this was often accompanied by a rejection of parental attitudes.[30] The paper itself lamented in 1930 that young Welsh people were overly interested in football and baseball and longed for a means of redirecting their energies towards singing, recitation and poetry-writing competitions in eisteddfodau.[31]

It was within the framework of this multi-dimensional debate that *Y Drych* itself had to formulate and execute its response to the crisis. The remainder of this chapter examines how eventually *Y Drych* came to be an English-language rather than a Welsh-language newspaper. First, we need to establish the trajectory, rate and incidence of change before turning to changing editorial policies and responses.

As part of his study of cultural change among the Welsh in Utica, Emrys Jones conducted an analysis of the amount of Welsh and English language material in *Y Drych* during 1874, 1900, 1910, 1920, 1939 and 1948, calculated by measuring column inches. Because *Y Drych* carried many English-language advertisements, even when all its other content was entirely in Welsh, both total content and all other printed matter (excluding advertisements) were surveyed. Jones found that between 1910 and 1920 the percentage of column inches of material other than advertisements that were in English rose from effectively zero to 5 per cent. By 1930 it was 6.5 per cent. Much of the 1930 figure was accounted for by the local items written in English from the Scranton, Pennsylvania, area, testifying to a more rapid rate of decline in usage of the Welsh language among the Welsh there.[32] The increase between 1920 and 1930 was comparatively slight, Jones rightly concluded, but it heralded greater changes to come. There was a very rapid increase in the amount of English, to nearly 30 per cent in 1939, and to over 80 per cent in 1948 (the date at which Jones' analysis ended).[33]

A subsequent content analysis in which we have measured the ratio of Welsh- to English-language column inches every year between 1925 and 1950 confirms the overall trend identified by Jones. However, it refines his findings by demonstrating that the increase in English-language content during the 1930s and 1940s was more uneven than he believed. Between 1930 and 1950 the amount of English in the paper did not increase incrementally year by year; rather, it rose to nearly 30 per cent in 1932 and early 1933 but then, with one year's exception, fluctuated between 7 and 16 per cent until the end of the decade, then varied between 20 per cent and 30 per cent between 1939 and 1942 and around 50 per cent during 1943-45. Between 1945 and 1950 there is an unequivocal collapse of Welsh-language content from 50 per cent to less than 10 per cent. In other words, *Y Drych* was predominantly a Welsh-language newspaper until 1942, became an equal bilingual one during the last three years of the Second World War, and then a predominantly English-language organ by 1950.

The variations and fluctuations in the amount of English in the paper were partly influenced by the paper's policy at any particular time, and this needs to be understood if we are to appreciate fully *Y Drych*'s metamorphosis into an English-language paper. We do not know to what extent editors were solely responsible for determining strategy during this period; perhaps the wishes of owners should not be discounted even if the general impression is that the two Griffiths brothers preferred a hands-off approach to the running of the paper.[34] Before discussing editorial strategy, however, it is important first to stress the existence of other fundamental factors that were undermining the paper's ability to continue as a Welsh-language medium. The declining body of correspondents who could write in Welsh was one, as has been mentioned, and linked to it was declining literacy in that language. Concern about the standard of some Welsh-language material submitted to *Y Drych* was being expressed by editors from the second decade of the twentieth century onwards. In 1919 the paper claimed it was 'greatly burdened by very imperfect writings' and urged inexperienced Welsh-language writers to refrain from sending correspondence.[35] Indeed, it is not clear to what extent much of the Welsh-language copy that actually appeared in *Y Drych* from the 1920s to the 1940s was submitted in English and translated in the office. The question is posed by an editorial in March 1926 which informed readers that reports in English were being included as there was no time to translate them,[36] though the lack of any further relevant testimony precludes any conclusiveness on the matter. Further, the paper was also dependent on printers who understood Welsh sufficiently to be able to set the paper. Here again *Y Drych* experienced difficulties. In March 1924, for example, it was forced to apologise profusely – significantly to what it described as 'old readers' – that the Welsh setter's illness had necessitated the inclusion of a greater volume of English language material around that time.[37] These factors would continue to restrain the paper's room for manoeuvre as it sought to respond to its 'problem' during the years after 1920.

In the early 1920s *Y Drych* reaffirmed its commitment to remaining a Welsh-language newspaper and keeping English content to a minimum except for advertisements. On his retirement as editor in 1923 Index stated that he had done his best to 'hinder English from rushing into the columns of the DRYCH' although there had been many attempts 'to cross the Offa's Dyke . . . [he] had built to keep English out for a term, at least, until the Old Language had peace to die.'[38] It seems that for some years writers had been supplying English-language reports and poetry but Index had refused to print them, declaring in March 1918, 'we do not see our way clear to do so yet'.[39] In 1923 new editor Hugh Hughes announced that one of the aims of the paper would be 'to emphasise the importance of keeping the language alive'.[40] He returned to the issue in 14 June 1928 in his 'Y Drych's Problem' editorial, stating that the inclusion of English material in the paper was not *Y Drych*'s fault, but of the Welsh who had allowed that language into their homes and institutions. The paper could not hope to oppose English under these circumstances. However, it was committed to remaining a Welsh-language newspaper for as long as readers supported it and to keeping 'the best aspects of the national spirit alive'.[41] Even so, there was room for some English:

> If it appears we can promote these aims through allowing occasional English reports, we will not refuse to do so. We want to fight the English bogey on its own territory, by enriching and strengthening Welsh life. . . . In allowing the occasional item in English we will not be trying to turn

the Drych into English, rather the aim is to make the paper more of an
influence in the Welsh-American world. Let not our old friends fear. . . .
English will be not be allowed to appear except when it serves the Welsh
and the Welsh language.[42]

The findings of the annual content analysis bear out Hughes' intentions,
and the amount of English remained low until the unmistakable increase
in content in that language from late September 1932 to summer 1933.
English-language editorials were introduced, more articles in that
language were put on the front page, and titles of columns were
switched to English.[43] There are no editorial statements in the paper to
indicate a change in policy, although there is other evidence to suggest
this is the case. The inclusion of limerick competitions in both Welsh
and English and other lighter material around this time may have been
deliberately aimed at a younger audience, in both languages.[44] Further, it
seems the paper involved in its plans Sam Ellis of Utica, one of its
longest serving, prolific, and most respected and influential columnists
as well as a prize-winning prose writer much admired by none other
than that literary giant, Kate Roberts.[45] He revealed (in Welsh) in a
column in January 1933 that *Y Drych* was trying to create interest in the
paper among 'the younger generation, and by this means to extend its
life and usefulness. I do not know if it will succeed or not.'[46] The paper's
'authorities' had asked if he would occasionally write for the paper in
English (and indeed English articles by him would duly appear over the
next few months).[47] Despite admitting that he preferred to write in
Welsh, Ellis' declared reason for agreeing to the request was 'not a lack
of patriotism . . . rather a desire that the Drych is able to reach a number
of American-Welsh, who cannot enjoy the Welsh language'. He urged
stalwart Welsh to be patient; 'if we can expand the Drych's circulation
among the younger Welsh through including more English, then we
should be content with that.'[48]

The evidence available, then, suggests that in 1932-33 *Y Drych*
was making a deliberate attempt partly to reorient itself towards an
English-speaking audience. Nevertheless, it was only a brief phase,
which ended with the change to a four-page format in June 1933 and
an announcement (in English) that henceforth 'in its form "Y Drych"
will be almost entirely in Welsh'.[49] We can only speculate whether

Sam Ellis (1876-1960), author of *Ann y Foty yn Myn'd i'r Mor* and a perennial contributor to *Y Drych*. Pictured here with his wife Margaret (née Jones) and children David, Margaret and Sarah before the family embarked on a return visit to Wales in 1924.

From Y Drych, *5 June 1924.*

the decision to prioritise the paper's traditional Welsh-speaking constituency was a cause or a consequence of the decision to reduce it to four pages.

To one commentator writing in August 1933, *Y Drych*'s U-turn in its language policy in 1932-33 was proof that, because of its variety of readerships, it could not hope to please everybody. Somewhat caustically, and indeed enigmatically in places, Mrs O. J. Davies of Marywood, Illinois, summarised recent developments thus:

A fair attempt was made to try and meet everyone's taste. There was a comfortable corner where the bards could count their fingers to decide how smoothly the lines [of poetry] scanned, the bread of angels for those who had grown wings to rise to a higher world, and plenty of the bread of mankind for the people who like conversation and a cup of tea. A fair amount of young blood was also poured in, and the Drych looked as if the flush of new life was spreading on its cheeks. Some went to feel jealous because the magical boar forced its snout in and Anglicised the only publication to which the old Welsh [-speaking] man could tell his secrets, but by now it appears as if the boar has been shipped to Chicago [i.e. to the stockyards], for us to do the same [to it] as is done here to every other boar.[50]

What concerned Davies most was that as a result of the change of policy, and its shrinking to four pages, *Y Drych* had become so meagre in size and substance. It was, she remarked, a shame to see it looking like one of Pharaoh's cows, after being 'fattened for over eighty years on sustenance that came from the deepest souls of our nation and its highest minds'.[51] It had remained a Welsh-language newspaper at the expense of a greater range of material, attracting a new audience and a more secure future. She believed that the Welsh in America needed less 'national sentiment' (English in the original) and more zeal for the best things in life.

Yet notwithstanding the paper's protestations, *Y Drych*, as we have already seen, did not keep its 1933 promise to be 'entirely' Welsh, a fact which its critics were not slow to grasp. Private testimonies reveal that changes in its format and the increase in English-language material caused some complaint among more 'traditional' readers, even loss of subscribers. In December 1934, in a letter to the Welsh poet, Richard Griffith (Carneddog), Ifan Morris Powell of Milwaukee was scathing about the quality of the paper's journalism: 'I have not subscribed to the Drych for a year. . . . I hardly see it at all now. . . . There is too much English in it for no good reason. It was cut in half in order for it to be more of a Welsh paper. But English is gaining ground again with the other half. It will soon be swallowed by the English Behemoth. And then the end will come.'[52] And as the perspectives of both Davies and Powell revealed, the debate went on.

But in 1934, the complete absorption by the Behemoth was still more than ten years away and occasional editorials and reports continued to stress the centrality of the Welsh language to the Welsh identity. 'It is impossible for a true Welshman to forget his Welsh language even though he lives in completely American circles. If we are true Welsh people we should be able to speak the language of Wales . . . YOU ARE NOT A WELSHMAN WITHOUT THE WELSH LANGUAGE', the paper declared in 1935.[53] It could be argued, therefore, that ultimately *Y Drych* stubbornly decided to resist the tide for as long as it could, for as late as 1942, nearly 80 per cent of the paper was still in Welsh. That editorial factors were a significant influence on the timing of the language shift is further confirmed by what occurred following Hugh Hughes' death during his second, very brief, term as editor between April and June 1945. The August 1945 issue can perhaps be regarded as the point of no return in *Y Drych*'s linguistic transformation. Its first two pages were dominated by bilingual tributes to Hughes, while the remaining six pages were predominantly in English. Even the date of the paper was now in English not Welsh.[54] The new editor, Arthur M. Roberts, apparently had 'a good knowledge of Welsh' and was willing to 'keep the columns of the paper open to those who desire to write in either Welsh or English'.[55] But during his editorship the floodgates opened even further, aided – or perhaps compelled – by the virtual disappearance of Welsh-language correspondents. In 1949, according to Emrys Jones, all of the half a dozen correspondents who still contributed to the paper in Welsh were over seventy and most were over eighty.[56] In the same year, Owen J. Jones of Chicago was described (in English) as being one of the few correspondents who wrote in 'pure, grammatical Welsh'.[57] What in 1920 had been North America's only Welsh-language newspaper was now the only Welsh newspaper in North America.

In their study of the non-English-language American ethnic press between 1910 and 1960, Fishman, Hayden and Warshauer argue that 'mixed' papers (which contain material in both English and the mother tongue) are introduced when 'Americanization had progressed to a point where non-English publications alone could not suffice if American-born offspring were to be kept within the ethnic-religious fold. . . . It was and is an attempt to bridge the linguistic and cultural cleavage that often develops between immigrants to the United States and their children and grandchildren.' But this type of publication, though playing an important transitional role, has frequently been an unstable medium: 'As a result of financial rather than ideological considerations, English slowly but surely pushes the ethnic mother tongue out of the mixed publication. . . . [They] tend toward a shorter life span . . . and have frequently made a subsequent transition to all-English, or have been discontinued entirely.'[58]

Y Drych fits the general pattern outlined here, although in its case it is difficult to prove whether financial rather than ideological reasons were the primary agent of its final mutation into an 'all English' paper. Fishman *et al* do not disclose the amount of English content required to qualify for a 'mixed' publication so it is arguable at what point *Y Drych* could more accurately be described as a 'mixed' rather than a 'non-English' paper. But the key point is that that transitional phase was relatively brief, at most fifteen years. The dynamics behind the process of language shift in *Y Drych* in the 1930s and 1940s are complex. The paper was at the same time responding to a changing readership and to a changing perception of its cultural functions, redefining itself as the interpreter of an American-Welsh identity which was not dependent on, or perhaps did not even require, the Welsh language. Yet what is most striking is that the language shift ocurred so late in the day. While many had argued in the pages of *Y Drych* from as early as the 1860s onwards that English – American English – should be the principal language of the Welsh Americans,[59] its editors remained committed to printing the paper in Welsh, perhaps until it was no longer feasible or even possible to do so. Alternatively, it might be argued that the paper tried to ignore what was occurring in Welsh America during these years, until change was forced on it. Either way, fundamentally, it did not prove possible to solve '*Y Drych*'s problem'. As William R. Thomas pithily observed in his report from Mankato, Minnesota, on 15 February 1952,

> Being a "Drych" correspondent these days is not an easy task. If one writes in Welsh the few subscribers who can't read Welsh complain that they are entitled to consideration, while if one writes in English some of the older Welsh people accuse one of being a traitor!

While in principle being in favour of continuing the paper in Welsh, he painfully acknowledged that the shrinking pool of Welsh readers rendered impractical such dreams. Of greater importance was the task of preserving '*some* of our characteristic Welsh culture and traditions' (our italics) by finding 'recruits among the younger generation regardless of language'. Although, as we shall see in the next chapter, the Welsh language would not always be an absent guest at the paper's table, *yr hen iaith* [the old language] had effectively ceased to be the defining feature of its Welshness.

CHAPTER 7

Into the Second Century, *Y Drych* 1945-2001

Y Drych emerged at the end of the Second World War intact, but fragile and severely depleted. Now effectively an English-language newspaper overwhelmingly geared towards carrying news of various Welsh-American activities in North America, it was heavily dependent on the support of a small but faithful band of individuals, writers and subscribers. As we have seen in an earlier chapter, during its late nineteenth and early twentieth century heyday, *Y Drych* claimed to have a circulation of 12,000. In 1956, the paper disclosed that it had 2,500 subscribers, exactly half the figure it claimed in 1860.[1] There was not to be a dramatic late twentieth-century expansion as there had been a hundred years earlier. In recent times *Y Drych* has generally enjoyed a circulation of between 2,000 and 4,000, although as has always been the case in its history, it is seen and read by many more people (that 'pass along' readership that has so irked *Y Drych*'s editors, owners and occasionally writers).[2] Nevertheless, a succession of dedicated and committed editors and owners, fortified by a loyal core of subscribers, have emerged to keep the paper going even when it seemed, in 1960 especially, that the end had finally come.

The abiding concern to successive editors and owners after 1945 was to produce a paper that was recognised as serving the interests of its new core audience. Otherwise what was then the continent's only remaining Welsh publication could not hope to survive. *Y Drych*'s primary constituency was now a Welsh group which continued to organise a range of cultural activities throughout North America but expressed its ethnicity in English, not Welsh. It was also a mainly second- and later-generation Welsh audience. After the doldrums of the 1930s there was a revival in the emigration of Welsh people to the United States after 1945, but the numbers have been small and in the 1970s they averaged about 300 a year.[3] The number of foreign-born Welsh people in the United States fell from 30,060 in 1950 to 23,469 in

1960 and 17,014 in 1970. As we saw in an earlier chapter, by the latter year, foreign-born were only one-fifth as numerous as American-born Welsh.[4] But in the years between 1945 and 2001 the character of *Y Drych*'s primary audience, and the nature of its attachment to Wales and a sense of Welshness, would not ossify. From the 1970s onwards there would be unmistakable signs, especially among younger Welsh Americans, of a revival and an expansion of Welsh ethnic awareness, and of greater interest in Wales, the Welsh language and Welsh cultural activity in North America. One contemporary observer in the 1980s was sufficiently moved by the extent of Welsh activities in North America to declare that a 'Welsh fever' raged there.[5] One manifestation of this heightened interest had obvious consequences for *Y Drych*: in 1975 a new Welsh North American newspaper, *Ninnau* [We, also], was founded. No longer would *Y Drych* have the clear field it had enjoyed since 1939. All these developments ensured that in the years between 1945 and 2001 *Y Drych* was hardly bereft of new challenges to confront and overcome.

1945-60: the final Utica years

Following the death of Hugh Hughes in July 1945, Arthur M. Roberts was appointed editor.[6] His elevation to the editorial chair marked a new era in at least one key respect: he was *Y Drych*'s first American-born editor. If any person could be said to have grown up with the paper, it was Roberts. Born in Utica in 1892, Arthur was the son of Richard E. Roberts, book-keeper and mailing department supervisor for *Y Drych* during the late nineteenth century. Following the death of his mother and father in 1896 and 1898 respectively,[7] Arthur was officially adopted by his uncle, John C. Roberts, whose giant editorial presence had guided *Y Drych* between 1869 and 1911. 'Art' Roberts learned his trade as a printer, and had worked for *Y Drych* for a time earlier in life. Once described as 'one of the liveliest mortals living',[8] he was a much respected and liked Utica figure and one of the city's most prominent and active Welshmen, including serving as Utica Moriah Welsh Church's financial secretary for forty-two years. Roberts ran *Y Drych* in his own time, retaining his full-time duties as a commercial printer with the Williams Typesetting Company. In 1957 he was awarded the St David's Society of the state of New York's William R. Hopkins Medal for Outstanding Achievement for his contribution to Welsh-American journalism.[9]

A new editor and the upbeat post-war mood brought something of a new lease of life for *Y Drych* in the late 1940s and early 1950s. The paper claimed in 1949 that circulation had 'increased splendidly'.[10] Extra income was secured by an increase in subscription rates at the end of 1946, to the paper's pre-1941 price of $2 a year, in order to offset increased labour and printing costs.[11] More photographs began to be included and the paper expanded. In August 1946 the number of pages was increased to twelve and by March of the following year a further four pages were added, as it had been 'swamped' by reports of St David's Day celebrations and appreciations

Arthur M. Roberts (1892-1973), editor of *Y Drych*, 1945-1960 and owner, 1951-1960.
Reproduced by kind permission of his daughter-in-law, Marion K. Roberts, Yorkville, New York.

of radio programmes broadcast on 1 and 2 March.[12] Two years later, in March 1949, it was announced that the number of pages would be increased to twenty although in fact the actual size of issues fluctuated greatly between sixteen and twenty pages during the next decade.[13]

In part, the paper's apparent improvement in fortunes can be attributed to its switch to English, thereby making it accessible to a larger Welsh-American audience. More specifically, the continued link with the National Gymanfa Ganu Association and the establishing of a mutually beneficial relationship with the Women's Welsh Clubs of America helped stabilise the paper's existence. The influential Women's Welsh Clubs movement, which boasted thirty-four affiliated clubs in 1946, had been without a medium for keeping members informed of its activities since the demise of *The Druid* in 1939. Now it turned to

Mary Jones, later Hasenpflug, of Cleveland, Ohio, and originally from New Straitsville, Ohio. President of the Women's Welsh Clubs of America, 1911-1923, and that organisation's 'Drych Representative' in the late 1940s.

From The Druid, *1 June 1923.*

Y Drych, a move made feasible by the paper's switch to English. At its 1946 annual convention in Columbus the paper was made the official organ of the organisation. Also, the dynamic Mary Jones Hasenpflug of Cleveland was appointed as the 'Drych Representative' and chair of a committee charged with conducting a campaign to augment the paper's circulation. Hasenpflug had been the Women's Welsh Clubs of America's first national president.[14] At the organisation's 1947 annual convention held in New York City, with editor Arthur Roberts in attendance, Hasenpflug made a plea for 'one hundred per cent support' for *Y Drych* as 'the only means of keeping the Women's Welsh Clubs in contact with the Welsh people everywhere. Mr. Roberts has been very liberal in giving space to the clubs and unless our women become interested as subscribers we cannot expect this to continue.'[15] From the next fifteen years or so, *Y Drych* devoted one or two pages per issue entirely to enthusiastic and lively reports of the organisation's activities, and in the late 1940s, at least, was granting the clubs commissions on subscriptions.[16]

The new association with the Women's Welsh Clubs was fittingly symbolic of a more fundamental change in *Y Drych*, for it was during the late 1940s that a trend apparent during previous decades made its most forceful impact. This was the crucial shift in the gender of correspondents. From the late 1920s and early 1930s onwards, new female correspondents began writing for the paper, either in Welsh or English, sometimes replacing deceased or retired male reporters in certain communities. This development was urged and welcomed by at

One of the new group of women who began writing for *Y Drych* from the inter-war years onwards – Mrs Philip Davies, 'Meirionferch' (Christian and maiden name unknown), Detroit correspondent, and originally from Blaenau Ffestiniog.

From Y Drych, *1 May 1930.*

Another of the same group: Esther Evans, later Baran, who covered the Caernarfon National Eisteddfod of Wales in 1935 for the paper, and wrote Welsh news from Racine, Wisconsin.

From Y Drych, *20 June 1935.*

least one man.[17] Examples of the new breed are Mrs Philip Davies ('Meirionferch') of Detroit, who wrote Welsh-language reports, and later English-language ones, from that city from the late 1920s into the 1940s;[18] Daisy Williams of Waukesha, Wisconsin, an English-language correspondent for Milwaukee whose regular features and news columns after 1932 earned praise from 'younger folk' who read the paper;[19] and Esther M. Evans (later Baran) of Racine, Wisconsin. The latter is the daughter of *Y Drych*'s longstanding correspondent for that city, R. D. Evans, who first came to Racine in 1911 and began writing for the paper soon afterwards (and was still writing for it in 1949[20]). In 1935, whilst on her way to Wales, Esther Evans was asked by *Y Drych* editor John F. Jones to be the paper's reporter and representative at that year's National Eisteddfod of Wales at Caernarfon. She penned Welsh-language

Mary King Sarah (1885-1965): a *Drych* 'booster', as the paper called her in 1952.
From Y Drych, *15 Sept. 1959.*

accounts of that event and her subsequent travels in the British Isles, and in subsequent years occasionally wrote Racine news reports for *Y Drych*.[21]

The number of female writers in *Y Drych* continued to increase gradually during the 1940s, and accelerated further towards the end of that decade, so that by 1951 women were writing 60 per cent of the paper. The link with the Women's Welsh Clubs obviously contributed to this process, but it was by no means the sole explanation. A new generation of committed female writers was emerging, some of whom would continue to write regularly for the paper for many years to come.

Notable here was Eirwen Jones of Llandeilo, whose 'News Letter from Wales' and other items of Welsh news, especially reports of National Eisteddfodau in Wales, were a very prominent feature through to the 1980s.[22] She began writing for the paper regularly in July 1948 and one of her first acts was to write a supplement on the Bridgend National Eisteddfod of that year.[23] Other important regular writers of the period included Anna (Annie) E. Parry (later Watkins and Roberts) of Jim Thorpe, Pennsylvania, who wittily entitled her news columns from the Slatington area 'Musings of the Missing Rib',[24] and Enid Jones Beaupre, New York correspondent and also chairperson of the Radio Committee of the National Gymanfa Ganu Association during the late 1940s. The latter was a tireless supporter of *Y Drych*, constantly urging subscribers to boost circulation in order to ensure the paper's survival. The same was true of another regular columnist during the late 1940s and 1950s, the renowned singer Mary King Sarah (later Thomas) of Waukesha, Wisconsin, and originally from Talysarn, Caernarfonshire. She occasionally ended her columns with 'Cofiwch Y Drych' [Remember the Drych] and on 15 February 1953 told her readers, 'It is hard to resist the temptation of writing to the "Drych". It is like pouring our my heart to an old friend.'[25]

Contemporary commentators in the late 1940s were in no doubt that *Y Drych* was being revitalised. In June 1949 editor Arthur Roberts remarked in a letter that 'Our Welsh-American correspondents are increasing in number each month and I find it very difficult to find room for their effusions.'[26] A guest editorial by Ann Davies of Kansas after the 1948 Detroit Gymanfa Ganu reported that 'We all agree with Humphrey Jones, Toronto, that Y DRYCH is getting more interesting each month.'[27] Many of its writers were also concerned with a new agenda, or at least giving more prominence to an old issue, that of encouraging and promoting a much greater awareness of Wales and the Welsh-American ethnic group among people with Welsh heritage and in the country at large. Enid Beaupre initiated a campaign to get American national and local radio networks to play Welsh music on St David's Day, with a fair measure of success. 'There always has to be sufficient demand to back up program requests. And the public should be constantly familiarized with good Welsh music throughout the year. We don't have to imitate the groundhogs coming out that one day and hiding if we see a shadow,' she wrote in January 1947.[28] She and others frequently fumed that the Welsh were being 'soft pedalled' or ignored in the American and British press, and that it was difficult to promote Welsh goods in the United States. 'Americans picture Wales pretty much as a series of coal heaps, and the Welsh as very gloomy, dour, poverty-stricken, only breaking out into the singing of hymns occasionally, and addicted to the most bigoted forms of religion', she bewailed in 1949.[29] But the biggest complaint of the paper was the apathy of the Welsh in America themselves, and their perceived inability to organise as a coherent ethnic group and make themselves heard. 'We float along listlessly overlooking our God-given heritage', lamented an editorial written by David J. Davies in December 1950, and consequently the Welsh were 'a minor factor in the scheme of things.'[30] The role of promoting and defending Welsh interests and instilling pride in a Welsh heritage would remain one of *Y Drych*'s core purposes for the remainder of the twentieth century and beyond.

Given the scale of his commitment to the paper, it is more than fitting that when in April 1951 the long association between the Griffiths family and the paper finally came to an end, 'Art' Roberts became its owner and publisher. Charles W. and Thomas J. Griffiths Jnr told readers that they were disposing of their interest in the paper 'in order to perpetuate its existence' since, with both of them well into their seventies, they felt the guiding hand of a younger man was needed. Roberts was their chosen successor.[31] Had he not agreed, revealed Sam

Producing *Y Drych*, 1956.   *Reproduced by kind permission of the National Library of Wales.*

Ellis in the paper three months later, 'there was a possibility, even a probability, that the "Drych" would have "folded up", as they say, ere long'.[32] Arthur Roberts was the first but by no means the last dedicated saviour to step in at the last moment when the paper's future seemed doomed, as the coming years would show.

After Roberts became owner, the Drych Publishing Company was set up to publish the paper and it was printed by 'The Franklin Press', 305 Jay Street, Utica. Now in full control, Roberts inaugurated an 'up building program' that would re-establish the paper's pre-eminent position in Welsh-American homes. A key element was to attempt to reverse the massive decline in advertising revenue the paper had suffered during the previous twenty years, which had contributed greatly to its financial problems. Declaring advertisements to be 'the lifeblood of every publication, without it no newspaper could long survive from a financial standpoint', he urged subscribers to encourage their business associates to place adverts 'in its columns'.[33] Initially Roberts' efforts were successful with the number of advertisements per issue increasing from nine in January 1951 to fifty-eight later that year.

Yet although the paper kept going through the 1950s, the tide could be stemmed only for so long. An interview with Roberts in the Utica *Observer-Dispatch* in 1956 revealed how dependent the paper's continued appearance was on his time and effort – and his own money; it has been 'a losing venture for years', he said.[34] In 1959 correspondents referred to *Y Drych*'s 'present crisis', widespread fears about its future, and plans to help Arthur Roberts.[35] In April 1960 the front page headline starkly proclaimed: '"Y Drych" to terminate its 109 year career next month . . . May Issue to be final.' In the lead article Roberts explained that

> we have done our utmost to keep the only remaining Welsh publication in this country alive. We've worked night and day to preserve the publication, but time has run out. . . . Our circulation is deteriorating at a rapid rate, and the financial burden is becoming prohibitive.[36]

It was a 'heart-breaking conclusion', and he later revealed that 'earnings are far from adequate to provide us with even a modest living. . . . We've carried on in the past nine years in the hope that adequate help would be forthcoming, but this far it has not been offered.'[37] The final issue was postponed until June 1960 to enable 'an announcement from persons interested in the continuation of Y Drych' but by 2 June when Roberts went to press no successor had emerged. 'What of the future – ???', he wrote. This seemingly last appearance of *Y Drych*, which correspondent Helen Richards of Evanston, Illinois, evocatively described as a 'requiem for a newspaper', was full of letters from Wales and the United States. These paid tribute to Roberts' selfless sacrifices – made 'despite far too few subscribers, assistance or gratitude' – and expressed hopes that the paper might continue. They also blamed those believed to be responsible, especially 'wealthy Welsh Americans', and generally condemned Welsh Americans for not doing enough to save the paper and allowing it to die. Enid Beaupre insisted the paper was 'too important to neglect. However, I know too well that there are those who would welcome the paper's demise'. Helen Richards was disappointed that there was 'so much indifference' to *Y Drych* 'among the many so-called Welsh patriots in the United States'.[38]

Horace Breese Powell MBE (1897-1980), owner, editor and publisher of *Y Drych*, 1960-1980.

Reproduced from a line drawing by kind permission of Patricia Powell Viets.

But as in 1951, *Y Drych* was saved yet again, although it would mean saying goodbye to Utica after a century of being published there. In an act of what a very relieved Enid Beaupre described as 'courage and enterprise', the paper was purchased by Horace Breese Powell of Milwaukee.[39] A Mankato, Minnesota, correspondent was quick to draw a witty parallel to *Y Drych*'s move to Wisconsin: 'It took a long time for it to take Horace Greeley's advice ['Go West Young Man'] and it had to find another Horace to do it.'[40]

'A Little Chapel Has a Day With Its Memories', from *Y Drych*, September 1960. Olwen Morgan Welk of Ripon directing the singing at the annual Gymanfa Ganu Sunday in mid-August 1960 at Rock Hill in Kingston township near Dalton, Wisconsin. The chapel was dedicated as Salem church in 1851.

Before the paper was one hundred and fifty years old it too would move to Minnesota.

1960-2001 Revival in the Mid West

In moving to Wisconsin in mid-1960, *Y Drych* was making its home in a state that had a rich Welsh heritage dating back to the early decades of the nineteenth century.[41] The new editor, owner and publisher's own impeccable Welsh background testified to this. Horace Breese Powell was the grandson of Breese and Powell families who a hundred years earlier had come from the Abergavenny area to settle on neighbouring farms in Waukesha County, where Powell himself was born in 1897.[42] Following a career as a journalist and a religion editor of the *Milwaukee Journal*, and then running his own public relations company in Milwaukee, he bought *Y Drych* as a project for his retirement, having always had a deep regard for, and interest in, his Welsh roots.[43] 'Hap'

Powell would publish the paper for the next twenty years – 'the happiest period of his professional life' – and in 1972 was awarded the Member of the British Empire (Honorary Rank) medal 'in recognition of his outstanding services'.[44] Tributes to him after his death recalled that he 'regarded his readers as his relatives', to whom in turn he was 'like a member of the family', and under his guidance, *Y Drych* became a strong and unifying influence among the Welsh in North America once again.[45]

In the 1960s and 1970s *Y Drych*'s circulation increased significantly, rising steadily from 2,400 in 1960 to 2,750 in 1963, 2,910 in October 1970, and 3,500 in the same month in 1978.[46] In broad terms, he sought to continue the paper's traditional role, informing readers that *Y Drych* would 'strive to serve Welsh families everywhere and to create a closer feeling of fellowship and goodwill . . . *Y Drych* has been a medium and contact through which Welsh people on both sides of the Atlantic have kept in touch with each other and loved ones. The new editor promises to continue it as such, to maintain its interest in all things Welsh, and to strive to broaden the paper's influence for good.'[47]

Yet alongside the emphasis on overall continuity, Powell nonetheless put his own stamp on the paper. The number of pages was reduced to eight, but the size of the page was increased, with a tabloid format being adopted. Annual subscription remained at $3 – indeed it was kept at that level for a further seventeen years until it rose, very belatedly perhaps, to $5 in 1978 and $10 in 1979.[48] Among the most popular new features in the paper was Powell's own series on 'Stories of Famous Hymns', which would grace the overwhelming majority of issues during the 1960s and 1970s (and indeed the 1980s, for the next editor, Powell's daughter, Patricia Powell Viets, continued to print this feature). The face of *Y Drych* changed palpably as articles became much shorter, with fewer carrying by-lines. But the most immediately striking change – and it is one which has remained a characteristic of *Y Drych* to date – was the introduction of large, attractive photographic images as a central element in the paper's style and layout. From 1962 onwards full- or half- page-size photographs of contemporary Welsh views regularly appeared on the front page. These were provided by photographers such as E. Emrys Jones, of Colwyn Bay, Denbighshire. According to a feature on him in May 1982, he 'never tires of the Welsh landscape',

From Y Drych, *November 1962.*

and his photographs have continued to be among the most popular features of *Y Drych* right up to the present day.[49] Also very popular were ones taken by Geoffrey Charles, photographer for the Welsh newspaper, *Y Cymro*.[50] For example, a Geoffrey Charles photograph of daffodils in the Moelfre area appeared on page one on June 1971 and photographs of the Ogwen Valley and Aberaeron Harbour by E. Emrys Jones on July 1972.[51] Other prints were secured from newspapers, government bodies and agencies in Wales such as the BBC and the Wales Tourist Board.[52] In the early 1970s, Powell also ran a series of reproductions of paintings of Welsh scenes held by the National Museum of Wales, for example Augustus John's portrait of Dylan Thomas and Paul Sandby's depiction of 'Iron Forge between Dolgellau and Barmouth'.[53]

A survey of the issues that appeared in the 1960s and 1970s reveals that the content mostly comprised news, reviews of books and records, historical items, obituaries, short biographies of Welsh people in the news, and reports of societies and activities. There was a liberal quota of advertisements, anything from 35mm colour slides which enabled purchasers 'to enjoy the scenic beauty of your favorite districts' in

'The Real Gymanfa Ganu': Ann Davies Thomas of Salt Lake City leads informal singing after the formal sessions, Milwaukee National Gymanfa Ganu, 1958.

From Y Drych, *March 1970.*

Wales to tea towels on the themes of the Welsh language, Welsh T-shirts and Welsh Dragon Insignia.[54] Their extent and variety suggests that Welshness in America was becoming a far more commercial and marketable product during these years. Letters were rare in the paper's pages, however, as were editorials, an absence that had been increasingly becoming the norm over the previous twenty years. Powell consistently wrote articles for the paper but usually seems to have eschewed an overt editorial presence and comment on specific topics. Many of the features focused on events and groups in Wales: Powell's 'Keeping Up With the Joneses' column almost exclusively contained news of people in Wales, rather than news of the Welsh in North America.[55] Much emphasis was also placed on encouraging visits to Wales, with advertisements for charter flights, news from the Wales Tourist Board, and alluring feature articles such as the extended, and illustrated, 'Tourism Helps to Keep Wales Different' item in June 1972, or 'Mid Wales is Becoming Increasingly Attractive to Holiday-Seeking Visitors' in March 1974.[56] These trends, together with the large photographs of Welsh scenes and the frequent positioning of Eirwen Jones' Wales news column on the front page, suggest that Powell was more keen than the previous editor to give the homeland its due place. The overall impression during these years is of a newspaper that was more concerned with presenting popular, perhaps even uncontroversial and nostalgic, aspects of Wales to the Welsh in North America than it was with informing them of Welsh developments and activities on their own continent.

Though less prominent, the 'doings' of North America's Welsh were not completely absent in *Y Drych* in the 1960s and 1970s. There was still some space for reports of, for example, the annual conventions of the Women's Welsh Clubs of America, cultural events such as Utica's 'Welsh-American Weekend', and of course, the National Gymanfa Ganu and St David's Day celebrations, though far fewer in number – and briefer – than had been the case half a century previously.[57] Occasionally there were also obituaries of prominent or active Welsh-Americans, such as Mary T. Frankenfield of Ambler, Pennsylvania, one of the founders of the Philadelphia Women's Welsh Club and former president of the national organisation, 1942-44, who died aged 94 in 1973, or of much respected former *Y Drych* correspondent, Janet

Morgan Price of Scranton, Pennsylvania.[58] Occasionally there was reflection on the contemporary condition of the Welsh ethnic group in North America. In a thoughtful article entitled 'Maintaining Our Welsh Culture in the USA' in 1963, Anna May Jones traced her family's relationship with Welshness over six generations, beginning with emigrants from north Wales to Wisconsin in the 1840s through to the present time. She herself was fourth generation, and of the fifth and sixth generations she wrote:

> Mostly gone are the days of spoken Welsh in the home in the United States and also disappearing are the Welsh churches and communities. But there is an increasing interest in Welsh culture especially among people of Welsh descent. They just need a little exposure to Welsh culture, and encouragement to become actively interested. A lecture on Wales with color slides inspires the young and the old to want to see Wales, to attend a Gymanfa Ganu and an Eisteddfod, and to hear and learn some Welsh words. . . . Now the fifteen young ones of the present generation sometimes hear and recognise Welsh music, enjoy photographs of Wales, and realize they are Welsh on their Jones side. The time will come when they will explore Welsh culture and enjoy creative experiences relating to their heritage. The interest is there.[59]

The last three decades of the twentieth century would show only too well that the interest was there, and increasingly so. In some respects a new Welsh America was being born, with a strengthened institutional infrastructure to support it. The Welsh National Gymanfa Ganu Association (as the National Gymanfa Ganu Association became after 1971[60]) expanded: its annual gatherings thrived and it established scholarships and grants to support Welsh projects.[61] Welsh Associated Youth was formed at the Milwaukee Gymanfa Ganu in 1970.[62] In 1975, as we have seen, Arturo Roberts established *Ninnau*, 'Papur Bro Cymry Gogledd America/The North American Welsh Newspaper', with the aim of 'answering the need for a stronger link between the many Welsh communities in North America'.[63] In 1977 Cymdeithas Madog held the first of its annual crash courses in Welsh, 'Cwrs Cymraeg', at Green Mountain College, Poultney, Vermont, and was incorporated in Maryland three years later.[64] The National Welsh American Foundation was established in 1980 to nurture links with Wales, provide financial assistance, study grants and fellowships to individuals, organisations and events, and co-ordinate Welsh-American cultural and educational activities.[65] And in the 1990s would come the founding of the North American Association for the Study of Welsh Culture and History[66] and the establishing of Welsh Studies centres at the Madog Center, Rio Grande University, and at Green Mountain College. Numerous new Welsh societies and other organisations were also formed in various states and cities in Canada and the United States. For the first time in many years, the Welsh-American scene was once more displaying a variety and liveliness that augured well for a plentiful supply of good copy for *Y Drych*.

Horace Breese Powell, editor since 1960, would live to see only the first decade of this reawakening. He died in June 1980 whilst still running the paper. He had been in declining health since his wife's death in 1976, and during those last years publication had become uneven and he had been unable to answer correspondence. As Patricia Powell Viets, Powell's daughter recalled in 2000, on her father's death there was much concern about *Y Drych*'s continuance'.[67] But the 'Great Survivor' (as we might call the paper) would prevail yet again: Viets herself strode into the breach. Born in Milwaukee, and a graduate in Journalism from the University of Wisconsin – Madison, she was a freelance writer and critic, and had worked as a journalist and as Public Relations Director at St Norbert College, De Pere, Wisconsin.[68] Due to raising a family in Green Bay, Wisconsin, she had had very little contact with *Y Drych* during her father's editorship, but 'because of my journalistic background . . . it seemed right to keep publishing a newspaper that had meant so much to Welsh people in the United States and Canada for over 100 years – and I had the skills to do so.'[69]

Describing her efforts as 'picking up the reins of newspaper that had faltered but not halted',[70] Viets relaunched the paper at the 1980 Vancouver National Gymanfa Ganu. Her first issue, October 1980, received an overwhelmingly enthusiastic response, encouraging her to continue and convincing her 'that she could make the paper work'.[71] She declared her goal to be 'the kind of newspaper that will be of value and interest to Welsh people everywhere' and her intention was to introduce several new features. There was a new emphasis on readers' particip-

Patricia Powell Viets, owner, editor and publisher of *Y Drych*, 1980-1989. Photograph taken around the time she took over the paper.
Reproduced by kind permission of Patricia Powell Viets.

ation: a 'Letters to the Editor' column was reintroduced, 'because we Welsh are *always* articulate'. From the outset she intended 'to include more North American news than it has in the past', without sacrificing 'our usual coverage of everyday life in Wales'.[72]

The pages of *Y Drych* soon bore testimony to Viets' plans for the paper. The number of pages per issue expanded during the 1980s from initially twelve to around twenty and, by the end of the decade, around twenty-four.[73] Some familiar aspects of issues during the previous twenty years were retained by the new editor, for example Horace Breese Powell's 'Stories of Famous Hymns' whilst advertisements of Welsh goods and events remained a significant proportion of the paper's pages. However changes in content after 1980 testify that a redirection of emphasis away from Wales itself and back to the Welsh in North America was also taking place. Photographic content, with landscapes and portraits of ordinary and famous people in Wales, by E. Emrys Jones and others, continued to be prominent. But to these were now added far more images of Welsh North American cultural events, sometimes in special photographic features. Examples are: the Ontario Annual Gymanfa Ganu in April 1981, and the National Gymanfa Ganu at Toronto the following year and Baltimore in 1988, which included photographs of the Welsh Heritage Tour of Delta, York County, Pennsylvania.[74] News of Cymdeithas Madog's 'Cwrs Cymraeg' was well represented, together with other features on the growth of Welsh-language classes in North America, a development described in 1981 as 'steadily gaining ground'.[75] New monthly columns introduced in October and November 1981, respectively, were Basil Davies' 'Y Golofn Gymraeg' [The Welsh Column] with lessons for Welsh-language learners and 'In Search of Welsh Roots', a genealogical feature written by the late Marylou Wilkinson, who also organised popular 'Welsh Grandfather Hunt' family history research tours to Wales.[76] The column testified powerfully to the tremendous growth of interest among Welsh Americans in their families' history and their ancestral roots. In a subtle shift of role, in the second half of the twentieth century the paper was carrying requests for information on 'lost' ancestors in the same way as years earlier it had carried enquiries for any news on missing relatives.[77]

From 1980 onwards *Y Drych* also adopted a new layout. The first half of the paper was normally devoted to general news relating to the Welsh in North America and their national organisations, and to digests of news of Wales, reviews of books, and features on Welsh places, literature, history and contemporary issues. In December 1985, for example, there were articles recalling memories of 'New Year's in the Rhondda', topographical and historical features on Tintern Abbey and St Asaph, and discussions of the prospects of the coal industry in Wales.[78] Regular writers on Wales-based news and features included the evergreen Eirwen Jones, Lyn Evans and Patrick Soper (who supplied the 'Window on Wales' and 'A Glance in the Rear View Mirror' columns). For the first time on a regular basis, Welsh rugby was given its corner in *Y Drych* (perhaps to the consternation of late nineteenth-century writers for the paper had they known), supplied by 'Mab y Fro'. A cookery column, Audrey Collins' 'O Gornel y Gegin' [From the Kitchen Corner], was also introduced.[79] The final few pages of each issue were usually devoted to news from Welsh churches and local organisations in North America. Significantly, in the context of the importance attached to North American news, these items were incorporated under the old heading 'Keeping Up With the Joneses', which Horace Breese Powell had largely devoted to news of the Welsh in Wales.[80] As if further to emphasise *Y Drych*'s self-perception as a key network, a Calendar of Events was included every month.

Viets' vision reaped rewards. The paper recovered from the drop in circulation it experienced following the temporary halt in production as a result of Horace Breese Powell's death. The number of subscribers had fallen from 3,124 in 1980 to 1,324 in 1981, but had increased to 2,249 by 1985.[81] Subscription rates rose from $10 in 1980 to $12 in 1985 to $15 by 1988. In the mid-1980s the paper's quality, and Viets' efforts, received a glowing tribute from David Greenslade in his book, *Welsh Fever*. He praised its 'unmaudlin' content, 'excellent use of photographs', and the wealth of contacts it provided.[82] By 1989 Viets felt that with the paper doing very well and since she had achieved her overall goal of producing a top quality newspaper, it was time to move on to other projects: to continue her writing career and do more travelling with her husband, John, *Y Drych*'s business manager. In her valedictory address to her subscribers in May 1989, she revealed how in personal terms, her tenure had been inseparable from her own discovery of her Welsh roots: 'We began to understand what it was that kept these people so fiercely proud of their culture and so eager to preserve it for coming generations. We began to appreciate what a privilege it was to be part of this process.'[83] It was an experience more and more Welsh Americans were sharing during the last quarter of the twentieth century, as the large crowds and level of enthusiasm and passions at the annual Gymanfa Ganu alone vividly testified.

The new owner, editor, and publisher who purchased the paper in May 1989 was Mary Morris Mergenthal.[84] She has continued to run *Y Drych* since then, publishing it out of St. Paul Minnesota, with her husband, Jennings serving as business manager. Danny Proud was assistant editor until February 1995.[85] Raised on a farm in Lafayette, Minnesota, Mergenthal was no stranger to the paper. She had previously been one of its correspondents (one of several journalistic and editorial posts she has held), and had read it since she was a child. Her paternal grandparents, Griffith and Mary Ellen Morris, had taken out a subscription to *Y Drych* as soon as they arrived in Denver from north Wales in 1910, and her father, Griff Morris, continued the family tradition of taking the paper. A noted and prodigious choral conductor, Mergenthal has led several choirs and conducted a large number of cymanfaoedd canu throughout North America, including the 'National'. She is also a previous vice-president of Cymdeithas Madog and served as president of the St David's Society of Minnesota and the Minnesota Gymanfa Ganu Association. In 1995 she was awarded the Welsh Society

The name of this Welsh-American newspaper means "The Mirror."

It's the mirror in which you see other Welsh North Americans like yourself...

The mirror in which you read of their activities and they read of yours...

The newspaper that reports events and happenings in Wales.

The place where you can learn more about Wales and learn the Welsh language.

Subscribe today!

Buy a gift subscription for a friend here or in Wales.

Send $15 US / $18 Canadian to

Y Drych
Box 8089, St. Paul, MN 55108

An advertisement for *Y Drych* from the Program of the National Gymanfa Ganu, Victoria, British Columbia, 1990.   *From the Utica College Welsh Collection.*

Mary Morris Mergenthal, owner, editor and publisher of *Y Drych*, 1989 to the present day.
Reproduced by kind permission of Mary Morris Mergenthal.

of Philadelphia's prestigious Robert Morris award, the first woman to receive it.[86] Mergenthal bought *Y Drych* because 'it seems like an extension of something I have cared about for a long time' and 'it would provide me with a podium to discuss my interests, to read and write about that I love'.[87] Since taking over she has broadly maintained the previous balance between matters relating to Wales and those to the Welsh in North America. A typical contemporary issue carries at least four pages of 'Welsh News in the US' and 'Welsh News in Canada', whilst the number of pages varies between twenty and twenty-four, as previously. Subscriptions have risen from $15 in 1989 to $17.50 in 1991 and $20 in 1995.[88] A number of new features have been introduced over the past twelve years, whilst others have been continued from the previous ownership, for example, the cookery feature, the calendar of events and the genealogy column, provided first by the late Marylou Wilkinson (entitled 'Welsh Grandfather Hunt'), then after January 1998, Donelle Meyer's 'Searching For Welsh Connections'.[89] The photographs of E. Emrys Jones still feature prominently,[90] as do those of Ron Davies, Aberaeron, and Kathy De Witt, Porthyrhyd, Carmarthenshire. Since 1989 news of Wales has been provided by Lyn Evans and Patrick Soper in the early 1990s and more recently, Lyn Ebenezer, Lawrence Hourahane, Tudur Jones, Don John and the late Peter Jones.[91] Coverage of Welsh sport has been expanded to include news and features on cricket, football and so on by Lawrence Hourahane.[92] Two new regular features introduced in June-July 1989 were the late Martin Eckley's 'Dear Llewellyn' column, which answered readers' questions relating to Welsh culture, history, literature and other matters, and Lincoln Jones Hartford's 'Sweet Singers of Wales', which featured Welsh hymns.[93] One of the most popular of all the new items has been Tecwyn Vaughan Jones' 'Cymru'r Werin O Fis i Fis'/'Folk Wales From Month to Month', which first appeared regularly after September 1995.[94] In terms of its efforts to resurrect a Welsh institution which once thrived in North America but which has since all but disappeared, perhaps the most innovative newcomer has been the annual 'Eisteddfod by Mail'.[95]

Another Mergenthal initiative has been the reintroduction of editorials, following an absence from the paper of around half a century. Her first in June-July 1989 emphasised three themes. First, Welsh North Americans should look forward, not back: 'Our Welsh societies will not long survive if our attention is given chiefly to recalling how things used to be . . . either in Wales or North America'. Second, they should not be only introspective but needed to support each other, 'personally and corporately'. Above all *Y Drych* would do all it could to 'increase familiarity with and fluency in Cymraeg, the Welsh language . . . [and] encourage readers to respect, if not to speak, the language of Wales.'[96] Mergenthal has adhered unflinchingly to these guiding principles during her editorship, and they were reinforced in the first editorial of the new millennium (or the first of the penultimate year of the old millennium, depending on your point of view). Exactly five years earlier in 1995, a list of suggested New Year resolutions included memorizing a Welsh hymn (with one verse in Welsh), learning ten new Welsh verbs, writing to relatives or friends in Wales to solicit their views about the possibility of a parliament for Wales, encouraging Welsh societies to give scholarships to someone to attend an intensive Welsh course, helping to pay for someone to go to the National Gymanfa Ganu, and giving someone a gift subscription to *Y Drych*.[97]

Much space in the paper has been devoted to commentary on Welsh language issues in Wales and the history of the Welsh language movement, and to promoting, and reporting on, various Cwrs Cymraeg programmes in North America and learners' courses in Wales.[98] In December 2000, on the eve of its own twenty-first anniversary as an incorporated body, Cymdeithas Madog's Jenny Hubbard Young paid tribute to *Y Drych* for the support the paper had given the organisation.[99] Further, efforts to encourage the learning of Welsh through *Y Drych* itself have been intensified. In June-July 1989 two new learners' columns by Basil Davies were introduced and these have appeared continuously until very recently. 'Un Cam Ar Y Tro' [One Step at a Time], was aimed at beginners, with the earlier lessons being repeated alongside the later ones during the late 1990s for the benefit of a new wave of recruits. A more advanced column, 'Cam Bach Ymlaen' [A Little Step Forward], was geared towards students working to improve their language skills.[100] The increased awareness and promotion of the Welsh language in *Y Drych* from the 1980s onwards clearly distinguishes its pages from those of the 1950s to 1970s. Fishman's study of English language ethnic newspapers in the USA sheds light on this question and helps to identify some of the ways in which *Y Drych* resembles other papers of this kind. In analysing their attitudes, purposes, and plans, he found that many of them claimed 'language maintenance interests . . . These interests might be expressed via *content* (articles encouraging language maintenance, language instruction) or *activities* organised or supported by the publication – contents, schools, courses, camps, publication and sale of books.'[101] As will be immediately evident from contemporary issues, *Y Drych*'s columns fit readily into many of these categories.

Undoubtedly the revival of interest in the Welsh language as demonstrated in the pages of *Y Drych* reflects developments in Wales over the past forty years, with the emergence of campaigning for the language, the passing of Welsh Language Acts, the acquisition of Welsh-language television and radio channels, and the growth of Welsh-medium education. As it has done since 1851, *Y Drych* has also continued to keep a watchful eye on the political scene in Wales, especially the dramatic constitutional reconfigurations that occurred at the end of the 1990s with the establishing of the National Assembly and the holding of the first ever Assembly elections in 1999. A new column by Tudur Jones, 'Assembly Watch', has monitored developments and discussed key issues: for example, the February 2001 column debated: 'Can/will the Welsh language debate be conducted in Welsh?'[102] In terms of its own political sympathies, under Mergenthal *Y Drych*'s stance has been overtly supportive of self-government for Wales and of Plaid Cymru:

Harpist William Lovelace observes his student, Veronica Shreve, on the 170-year-old Erard harp following the Knoxville, Tennessee, Welsh Society's St David's Day Concert, 2001.

From Y Drych, *April, 2001. Reproduced by kind permission of the photographer, Billie R. McNamara.*

The Party of Wales, the Welsh Nationalist Party, a relationship that is perhaps symbolised best by Gwynfor Evans' writing of the guest editorial for the paper's one hundred and fiftieth anniversary issue in January 2001.[103] It is perhaps an indication of the paper's evolution during the twentieth century generally, and its current priorities in providing a platform for debate and news on contemporary Welsh politics, that little coverage of American politics can be found in its pages in comparison to that available on Wales. This is only one of several ways in which the content of today's *Y Drych* would surprise readers of a century ago.

From the 1980s onwards, then, a visible shift has occurred in *Y Drych*'s content and style, and its pages bear testimony to the changing concerns and composition of the Welsh ethnic group in North America. Its emphasis on keeping in touch with Welsh roots, and on keeping the Welsh in North America in contact with each other, is hardly new in terms of the paper's history. However, the introduction of columns such as Jeffrey Thomas' 'Wales on the Web' suggests an eagerness to grasp the new opportunities for networking that are now available.[104] But during the last twenty years or so, as well as looking forward, *Y Drych* has also still looked back into its own history in the same way as it has done since the late nineteenth century. Extracts from previous issues, translated by writers such as Alun Hughes, the late Phillips G. Davies and Martha Davies, have been printed in the 'As We Were' column,[105] whilst similarly the 'Glimpses in the Mirror' column has from September 1998 onwards tried to make previous pages of the paper accessible to non-Welsh-reading, modern-day members of 'Teulu'r Drych' [*Y Drych*'s Family]. And with the paper's continued publication there have come the times for marking important milestones. In March 1991, on the occasion of the paper's one hundred and fortieth anniversary, and then in February 1996 for its one hundred and forty-fifth birthday, Phillips G. Davies provided articles featuring the history of the paper. In January 2001 a special one hundred and fiftieth anniversary insert reproduced the paper's first-ever front page dated 2 January 1851 and several photographs from previous issues, as well as commentaries on its history and its relationship with Wales.[106]

But after the celebrations are over, it is back to business as usual. An editorial in February 2001 urged Welsh North Americans, as St David's

Day approached, to 'Find a way to pass along your priorities – language, hymnody, cawl cennin, or bara brith – to someone you had not thought to share them with before, not as novelties, but as a matter of survival.'[107] To which list of 'priorities' surely we must add *Y Drych* itself.

Y Garn mountain and Rhyd Ddu village, Snowdonia, taken by E. Emrys Jones, Colwyn Bay, the man who 'never tires of the Welsh landscape'. His photographs have been a familiar sight in *Y Drych*'s pages for over forty years. This one appeared in *Y Drych* in December 2000.   *Reproduced by kind permission of E. Emrys Jones.*

Conclusion

B iographies often end with the deaths of their subjects, followed by a consideration of their posthumous legacies. This one does not. At the time of writing, *Y Drych* remains an important player in the field of Welsh self-expression in America. Like *Ninnau*, it continues to develop long-established lines of communication between the Welsh on both sides of the Atlantic. Yet, looking back over its long journey from the bustling streets of downtown Manhattan in 1850, through its century in Utica to its most recent manifestation in St Paul, we cannot help but notice that *Y Drych* was constantly changing, even when it appeared to be staying the same. A successful newspaper cannot ever stay still, or pause in its relentless search for the new. So it was with *Y Drych*. Its editors and correspondents were, and had to be, acutely sensitive to the multi-layered, sometimes contradictory, but ever-changing needs and expectations of its readership. If new immigrants looked to it for help and guidance, so did those who had already put down strong roots. Successive generations searched for different forms of knowledge and amusement, and they did so, as the editors eventually acknowledged, in different languages. But this study has argued, and has tried to demonstrate, that *Y Drych* did not 'mirror' the Welsh in America in any simple or linear way. Its responses to changes in its readership, and to the public and private worlds that they inhabited, were often stubbornly conservative, insisting on a number of enduring and defining characteristics of Welsh national identity that included a powerful combination of language, religious faith and modes of personal conduct. In that respect, *Y Drych* did not so much reflect the Welsh as offer them a form of leadership, an image of themselves and a sense of who they were and might in the future become. What emanates most strongly from the pages of *Y Drych* over the period of its long life is its *idealism*.

It is also, of course, a richly endowed source of information on virtually all imaginable areas of Welsh life in America and elsewhere – a veritable 'corph o hanes' [body of history] as one admirer described the paper in 1929.[1] For that reason alone it deserves far more critical scrutiny than it has received in the past. We hope that by writing this book in English, the paper's contents and potential, in particular during its first hundred years, may become more generally appreciated and that, as a consequence, all those interested in the history of the Welsh will wish to consult it. But in addition to the information it so lavishly contains on the public activities and the private emotions of the Welsh in America, we can learn a great deal also from a closer study of the ways in which that information was communicated. Further research is urgently needed on such important areas as its poetry columns, serialised novels, the rhetoric of nationality and the language of ethnic politics in its news coverage, letters and editorial columns, and its relationship to the Welsh commercial sector, including its own industry, printing. A study of what it reveals about the changing forms and idioms of the Welsh language over a hundred-year period might also prove to be particularly rewarding. Did a specifically *American* form of Welsh emerge at this time? And if not, why not? *Y Drych* is a vital laboratory for all manner of investigations of this kind.

In addition to its rich possibilities as a source of information on the history of the Welsh, it also makes a valuable, and possibly a critical, contribution to the broader debate on the role played by the periodical press in the process of integrating new migrants to the United States. Given that *Y Drych* is one of the oldest continuously running ethnic newspapers in North America, it is strange, to say the least, that its involvement in this process has not received more serious historical attention. The historian Rudolph Vecoli has rightly both lamented the lack of research on immigrant print culture and criticised existing studies for being 'fixated' on the role of journalism in 'assimilating' its readers into the civic structures and cultural environment of the 'host' community.[2] Much of the controversy on the immigrant press in the Americas has centred on whether it accelerated the assimilation of minorities, or whether it acted as a brake to that complex and contested process. While *Y Drych* did not, and could not, write the script for that highly subjective and individualised drama of displacement and integration, it was, as far as many of the Welsh were concerned, one of its leading actors and, as is often the way with leading actors, it also made strenuous attempts to influence its direction. It may be said to have exerted different effects on different groups of readers, but the overall impression given by the paper's editorial policies and style is a deeply ambivalent one. While it urged its immigrant readers to integrate themselves into the civil society of their new country, and to take advantage of its economic opportunities, it also sent out powerful messages to remind all its readers that they were still Welsh, and that the greatest of all the opportunities offered by the United States was their ability to remain Welsh, in language, faith and culture. What a reading of *Y Drych* suggests above all else is that the people who used this newspaper as one of their means of living a Welsh life in America, be they editors, writers or readers, were searching for ways of becoming Americans on their own cultural terms.

As this book has constantly endeavoured to show, the story of *Y Drych* is as much about flesh and blood as it is about ink and paper. Behind the communication medium lies a very human history of Welsh migration and settlement. To a considerable extent, the length of its lifespan as a newspaper can be attributed to the loyalty of its readers and advertisers. But its survival was also crucially dependent on the long-term commitment of a handful of strong-willed individuals. These people, especially its publishers, editors, leader writers and leading correspondents (and all too often they were one and the same person) created on the pages of *Y Drych* a virtual Welsh world that connected private and public lives in an almost infinite variety of ways. By offering its 'Welsh reflections' on the *hiraeth* and the hope of its readers, *Y Drych* wove itself like a silver thread through a hundred and fifty years of the history of the Welsh in America.

Notes

INTRODUCTION
[1] Jones remained the publisher and proprietor of the *New York Times* until 1891.

CHAPTER 1
[1] Accounts, of varying length, of the paper's history can be found in Paul Demund Evans, 'The Welsh in Oneida County, New York' (unpublished MA thesis, Cornell University, 1914), pp. 107-109; Deian Rhys Hopkin, 'Welsh Immigrants to the United States and their Press, 1840-1930' in Christine Harzig and Dirk Hoerder (eds.), *The Press of Labor Migrants in Europe and North America 1880s to 1930s* (Bremen, 1985), pp. 349-367, which includes a content analysis; E. G. Hartmann, *Americans from Wales* (Boston, 1967), pp. 128-129; T. M. Jones, *Llenyddiaeth Fy Ngwlad sef Hanes y Newyddiadaur a'r Cylchgrawn Cymreig yn Nghymru, America, ac Awstralia* (Holywell, 1893), pp. 205-206; Idwal Lewis, 'Welsh Newspapers and Journals in the United States', *National Library of Wales Journal*, 2 (Summer 1942), pp. 124-130; Bob Owen, 'Welsh American Newspapers and Periodicals', *National Library of Wales Journal*, 6 (Winter, 1950), pp. 373-384; Daniel E. Wager, *Oneida County and its People* (Utica, 1896).
[2] The Welsh press in the United States is generally an under-researched subject. For details, see Evans, 'The Welsh in Oneida County', pp. 88-119; Hartmann, pp. 127-136; Jones, *Llenyddiaeth Fy Ngwlad*, pp. 203-217; Lewis, 'Welsh Newspapers and Journals'; Owen, 'Welsh-American newspapers'; Robert D. Thomas, *Hanes Cymry America* (Utica, 1872), Dosran C, pp. 47-51, 63-65 [an English language version of this is available, trans. Phillips G. Davies, *Hanes Cymry America: A History of the Welsh in America* (Lanham, Md. and London, 1983)]. For a useful interpretive study, see Hopkin, 'Welsh Immigrants to the United States and their Press'.
[3] Ruth Vasey, 'The Media' in Mick Gidley (ed.), *Modern American Culture. An introduction* (London and New York, 1993), p. 214.
[4] For further details on Rowlands, see Evans, 'The Welsh in Oneida County', pp. 90-92.
[5] For biog. details of John Morgan Jones (1818-1912), see *Y Drych*, 4 Jan. 1912; *Cambrian* (Cincinnati and Utica), Vol. 22 No. 4 (15 Feb. 1912) p. 14; *Utica Herald Dispatch*, 1 Jan. 1912; *Utica Daily Press,* 2 Jan. 1912; National Library of Wales [hereafter NLW] MS 9262A Henry Blackwell, 'A Dictionary of Welsh Biography', pp. 374-376.
[6] Alexander Jones, *The Cymry of '76; or Welshmen and their descendants of the American Revolution. An Address* (New York, 1855), p. 130.
[7] NLW MS 9262A, Blackwell, 'Dictionary', pp. 374-376.
[8] *Utica Morning Herald*, 26 Apr. 1886; *Utica Daily Press*, 2 Jan. 1912, 13 Feb. 1923. Mary Griffiths (d.1886) emigrated from Caernarfonshire to Steuben, N.Y., with her

parents in the 1820s. Sarah Maria Jones, later Merrill, was born in New York City in 1838 and died in New Hartford, N.Y., in 1923.

[9] *Y Drych*, 2 Jan. 1851.

[10] *Y Drych*, 9 Jan.–8 Feb., 8 Mar. 1851.

[11] *Y Drych*, 16 Jan., 29 Mar. 1851.

[12] *Y Drych*, 8 Mar. 1851.

[13] See, e.g., *Y Drych*, 15 Feb. 1851.

[14] '. . . yn mhob teulu Cymreig yn yr ardal, oddieithr ychydig o eithriadau'. *Y Drych*, 29 Mar. 1851.

[15] *Y Drych*, 29 Mar. 1851.

[16] '. . . chwe diwrnod a dwy noson – weithiau rhan o dair a phedair noson yn yr wythnos'. *Y Drych*, 20 Dec. 1851.

[17] See, e.g., *Y Drych*, 4 Oct., 1 Nov. 1851.

[18] Advertisements like these were very common in newspapers of the time, especially those that had an immigrant readership. See Virginia Beveridge, 'Popular Journalism and Working Class Attitudes 1854-1886' (unpublished Ph.D. thesis, University of London, 1979), chap. 5.

[19] 'Mae yn llawn bryd i'r Cymry yn yr America feddiannu cyhoeddiad wythnosol yn iaith eu gwlad enedigol: . . . Mae gan yr Ellmyn a'r Ffrangcod eu papyrau yn eu gwahanol ieithoedd, a chan y Gwyddelod amryw yn cael eu golygu gan gydwladwyr iddynt, a phaham na allai hil Gomer gynnal un hefyd?' *Y Drych*, 9 Jan. 1851.

[20] '. . . cyfnod newydd yn hanes ein cenedl.' *Y Drych*, 29 Mar. 1851.

[21] 'Nis gall helyntion America fod yn ddibwys yn y wlad hon, tra y mae cynifer o filoedd o'n cydgenedl yno, a miloedd yn debyg o'u dilyn cyn hir. Gwna hyn ryw gyfrwng gohebiaeth rhwng y ddwy wlad yn angenrheidiol, ac addawa y "Drych" y bydd iddo wneyd yr angen i fynu.' *Y Drych*, 1 Mar. 1851.

[22] *Y Drych*, 5 Dec. 1851.

[23] *Y Drych*, 9 Jan. 1851.

[24] *New York Morning Star*, 29 Nov. 1850.

[25] *Williamsburgh Daily Gazette*, 2 Dec. 1850.

[26] *Y Drych*, 9 Jan. 1851.

[27] '. . . gan fod cymaint o bobl yn y wlad yn analluog i ddarllen Saesonaeg, ac o ganlyniad y maent yn amddifad o wybodaeth ymarferol'. *Y Drych*, 4 Oct. 1851.

[28] *Y Drych*, 17 May 1851.

[29] *Y Drych*, 9 Jan. 1851.

[30] *Y Drych*, 5 Apr., 24 May, 4 Oct. 1851.

[31] *Y Drych*, 12 Apr., 4 Oct. 1851.

[32] *Y Drych*, 3 Feb., 8 Mar. 1851.

[33] *Y Drych*, 19 Apr., 3, 10 May, 16 Aug., 13 Sept., 29 Nov. 1851.

[34] 'Ein bod ni, er yn Dramoriaid trwy enedigaeth, yn Americiaid a Gweriniaid mewn teimlad; ac wedi gwneud gwlad Washington yn dir mabwysiedig; ac yn gwerthfawrogi y Rhyddid a'r Cyfleusderau a ganiateir i ni idd eu mwynhau.' *Y Drych*, 19 Apr. 1851.

[35] '. . . ni fyddai yn gyson â'n hegwyddorion i adeiladu cofgolofn i'r caethfeistr llywyddol cyntaf a fu yn ein gwlad'. *Y Drych*, 19 Apr. 1851.

³⁶ *Y Drych*, 2 Jan. 1851.

³⁷ *Y Drych*, 16 Aug., 27 Sept., 26 Oct., 27 Dec. 1851.

³⁸ *Y Cyfaill o'r Hen Wlad*, Vol. 19 No. 1 (Jan. 1856), p. 41.

³⁹ '. . . pan nad oes newmawr byth grybwylliad am yr enwad mewn modd ffafriol yn y cyhoeddiadau *misol*'. *Y Drych*, 5 Dec. 1851.

⁴⁰ '. . . i wneud i fynu eu diffyg mor bell ag y mae yn cydweddu a natur ein cyhoeddiad'. *Y Drych*, 5 Dec. 1851.

⁴¹ See Daniel Williams, 'The Welsh Atlantic: mapping the contexts of Welsh-American Literature' in Marc Shell (ed.), *American Babel, or, the other languages of the United States* (Cambridge, Mass., 2002), forthcoming. For a revealing treatment of a Welsh-language novel written by a *Y Drych* writer and published by the paper (though not serialised in it), R. R. Williams' *Dafydd Morgan* (1897), see Melinda G. Gray, 'Language and Belonging: A Welsh-Language Novel in Late-Nineteenth Century America' in Werner Sollors (ed.), *Multilingual America: Transnationalism, Ethnicity, and the Languages of American Literature* (New York, 1998), pp. 91-102.

⁴² 'Yr ydym wedi cyhoeddi y Newyddiadur Wythnosol Cymreig cyntaf a gyhoeddywd yr ochr hyn i'r Werydd am ystod blwyddyn'. *Y Drych*, 20 Dec. 1851.

CHAPTER 2

¹ '. . . llawer o *ups and downs*'. *Baner ac Amserau Cymru*, 2 Apr. 1862.

² NLW MS 9262A Blackwell, 'Dictionary', p. 375; *Baner ac Amserau Cymru*, 2 Apr. 1862; *Y Drych*, 24 Mar. 1921.

³ Thomas, *Hanes Cymry America*, Dosran C, p. 47.

⁴ *Y Drych a'r Gwyliedydd*, 21 Jun. 1855, 6 Jan., 1 Mar., 20 Dec. 1856.

⁵ For biog. details of William B. Jones (1815-1887), see *Cambrian*, Vol. 8 No. 1 (Jan. 1888), pp. 1-2; R. Hughes, *Enwogion Mon 1850-1912* (Dolgellau, 1913), p. 66.

⁶ See, e.g., *Y Drych*, 13 July 1882.

⁷ For biog. details of Daniel L. Jones (1807-1898), see NLW MS 9261A Blackwell, 'Dictionary', pp. 462-465; *Cambrian*, Vol. 17 No. 2 (Feb. 1897), p. 73, Vol. 18 No. 3 (Mar. 1898), p. 139.

⁸ *Y Drych*, 30 Nov. 1905.

⁹ *Baner ac Amserau Cymru*, 2 Apr. 1862; *Y Drych a'r Gwyliedydd*, 22 Feb. 1855, 8 Jan. 1856; *Y Gwyliedydd Americanaidd*, 4 Jan. 1855; Evans, 'The Welsh in Oneida County', p. 112; Thomas, *Hanes Cymry America*, Dosran C, p. 48.

¹⁰ *Y Drych a'r Gwyliedydd*, 22 Feb. 1855.

¹¹ Ellis left in May 1856 to run a school in Slate Hill, York County, Pa. *Y Drych*, 3, 10 May 1856.

¹² NLW MS 9262A Blackwell, 'Dictionary', p. 408.

¹³ *Y Drych a'r Gwyliedydd*, 28 Mar., 4 Apr. 1857.

¹⁴ *Y Drych a'r Gwyliedydd*, 22 Feb. 1855; *Y Drych*, 13 Mar. 1858.

¹⁵ *Baner ac Amserau Cymru*, 2 Apr. 1862.

¹⁶ *Y Drych*, 13 Mar. 1858, 11 June 1859.

¹⁷ For biog. details of Morgan A. Ellis (1832-1901), see *Dictionary of Welsh*

Biography down to 1940 (London, 1959) [hereafter *DWB*], p. 210; *Cambrian,* Vol. 21 No. 8 (Aug. 1901), pp. 377-378; *Y Cyfaill,* Vol. 64 No. 767 (July 1901), pp. 287-288; *Y Drych,* 22 Oct. 1903.

[18] For biog. details of Gwyneddfardd (1825-?), see NLW MS 19216C Revd Tudur Lloyd Frimston, 'Y Cymry a ymfudasant ac a Godasant i Enwogrwydd yn America a'r Trefedigaethau Prydeinig' [c.1893], pp. 183-184. See also *Y Drych,* 10 Jan. 1863; Evans, 'The Welsh in Oneida County', p. 108.

[19] For biog. details of John William Jones (1827-1884), see *DWB,* pp. 489-490; NLW MS 9262A Blackwell, 'Dictionary', pp. 407-409; *Cymru,* Dec. 1905, pp. 274-276; *Y Drych,* 16 Oct. 1884; *Y Geninen,* Apr. 1886, pp. 131-133; *Utica Daily Press,* 9 Oct. 1884; *Utica Morning Herald,* 9 Oct. 1884; *Western Mail,* 1 Nov. 1884.

[20] '. . . yn gryf ysgubellog ac unochrog; ond yn wir alluog.' *Y Drych,* 30 Nov. 1905.

[21] *Baner ac Amserau Cymru,* 2 Apr. 1862.

[22] 'Fe fydd traul cyhoeddiad y *Drych a'r Gwyliedydd* am y flwyddyn 1855 dros *bum' mil o ddoleri* ($5,000), heb son am yn agos i *ddwy fil o ddoleri* ($2,000) am Danysgrifrestr (*Subscription list*) y ddau Newyddiadur, am yr hon y talasom yn nghorff y flwyddyn 1855 dros *bymtheg cant o ddoleri* ($1,500); ac . . . ni dderbyniasom meddwn namyn *tair mil o ddoleri* ($3,000). Gwelir fel hyn, fod yn annichonadwy dwyn allan Newyddiadur cyffelyb i'r *Drych a'r Gwyliedydd* am ddolar y flwyddyn heb golledion mawr'. *Y Drych a'r Gwyliedydd,* 5 Jan. 1856.

[23] '. . . fel y gallo pawb wybod yn uniongyrchol fod eu taliadau wedi dyfod i law yn ddyogel'. *Y Drych a'r Gwyliedydd,* 18 Oct. 1855, 5 Jan. 1856.

[24] *Y Drych a'r Gwyliedydd,* 29 Nov. 1855, 5, 12 Jan., 23 Feb., 26 Apr., 7 May 1856.

[25] 'Ei ffurf a'i arwedd *bresenol* a'm boddha yn fawr. Wrth ei gymeryd i fyny yr ydys ar unwaith yn cael ein taro â'r drychfeddwl – Wel, dyma "bapyr newydd" a gafael go dda ynddo. Mae ei wisg a'i *drimmings* yn *respectable.* Teilynga, ddigon siwr, safle ar fwrdd y boneddwr Cymreig, yn mhlith newyddiaduron Seisonig, megys y "*New York Recorder,*" y "*Tribune,*" yr "*Observer,*" &c., &c. Ei ddullwedd a'i gynwysiad ydynt ar y cyfan yn ddyddorol, adeiladol, a difyrus.' *Y Drych a'r Gwyliedydd,* 12 Jan. 1856.

[26] 'Newyddiadur Cenedlaethol at Wasanaeth Cenedl y Cymry yn y Talaethau Unedig'. *Y Drych,* 12 May 1860.

[27] For details, see NLW MS 9262A Blackwell, 'A Dictionary of Welsh Biography', pp. 374-376; Evans, 'The Welsh in Oneida County', pp. 109-112; Thomas, *Hanes Cymry America,* Dosran C, pp. 47-48.

[28] *Y Drych,* 16 Oct. 1884. For the quarrels between John Morgan Jones and *Y Drych,* see *Y Drych a'r Gwyliedydd,* 21 June 1855, 1 Mar., 28 June, 18, 25 Oct., 26 Dec. 1856; Evans, 'The Welsh in Oneida County', p. 110.

[29] *Y Drych a'r Gwyliedydd,* 28 June, 18 Oct. 1856.

[30] '. . . gelyniaeth annghymodlawn a bythol, a thorai allan yn barhaus mewn ysgrifen fitriolaidd a chigyddol'. *Y Drych,* 30 Nov. 1905.

[31] *Utica Daily Press,* 2 Jan. 1912. John Morgan Jones made his home in Utica around this time, although he was to travel extensively as a publisher and seller of Welsh books and other works. On his death in 1912 at the age of 96 he was described by *The*

Cambrian as 'one of oldest and most esteemed Welsh residents of Utica'. Vol. 22 No. 4 (15 February 1912), p. 14.

³² *Y Drych a'r Gwyliedydd*, 22 Feb. 1855.

³³ *Y Drych a'r Gwyliedydd*, 26 July, 22 Aug., 6, 20, 27 Sept. 1856.

³⁴ *Y Drych a'r Gwyliedydd*, 1 Nov. 1856.

³⁵ See, e.g., *Y Drych a'r Gwyliedydd*, 26 July, 2 Aug., 18 Oct. 1856.

³⁶ *Y Drych a'r Gwyliedydd*, 16 Aug. – 4 Oct. 1856.

³⁷ *Y Drych*, 24 Mar. 1921.

³⁸ 'Mae Utica y lle mwyaf manteisiol i gyhoeddi papyr wythnosol, canys mae y ddinas yn nganol gwlad o Gymry, ac yn fwy canolbarthol i'r Cymry yn gyffredinol.' *Y Cyfaill o'r Hen Wlad*, Vol. 23 Nos. 271, 275 (July, Nov. 1860).

³⁹ '. . . buasai yn myned i sefyll ar ei ben, neu waeddi *boo hoo* ar benau'r heolydd, yn hytrach na chroeshoelio ei hun gyda gwaith mor ddielw a diddiolch.' *Baner ac Amserau Cymru*, 2 Apr. 1862.

⁴⁰ '. . . uchel-deyrnfradwyr, llofruddion a lladron'. *Yr Herald Cymraeg*, 8 Feb. 1862.

⁴¹ *Y Drych*, 4 Apr. 1863.

⁴² *Y Seren Orllewinol*, July 1861, May 1863; *Yr Herald Cymraeg* (quoting a report taken from *Y Drych*) 9 Aug. 1862. For fuller discussion of these crucial years in the history of the Welsh in America, see Huw Griffiths' forthcoming University of Wales Ph.D. thesis on the Welsh and the American Civil War.

⁴³ *Yr Herald Cymraeg*, 8 Feb., 2 Aug. 1862.

⁴⁴ *Yr Herald Cymraeg*, 15 Feb. 1862.

⁴⁵ *Y Drych*, 31 Jan., 14, 21, 28 Feb. 1863.

⁴⁶ 'Prin y credwyf fod fy nghydgenedl, er ei holl anwybodaeth o wir natur y gwrthryfel a'r canlyniadau anferth sydd yn dibynu arno, yn barod i droi yn fradwr i'w hegwyddorion gwaed-brynedig, drwy amddiffyn yr encilwyr caethwasiol yn eu hymdrech i ddinystrio ein gwlad ac i sefydlu ymerodraeth gaeth ar ei hadfeilion.' *Y Drych*, 14 Feb. 1863.

⁴⁷ *Y Drych a'r Gwyliedydd*, 27 Dec. 1855.

⁴⁸ 'Yn y fan gwisga y dynion haiarn gymeriad y plentyn tyner, a gwelir hwynt yn chwilied, mewn pryder, am frawd, neu gyfaill yn mysg y meirwon a'r clwyfedigion a orweddent yn eu gwaed. Tynant y naill oddiar gefn y llall tra y cura y galon gan brudd-der, a thra y treigla y deigryn gloyw yn ddistaw dros y rudd. O ddifrifoldeb! O bryder! O ddifrod ar fywyd! Ow Ryfel!' *Y Drych*, 10 Jan. 1863.

⁴⁹ *Y Gwladgarwr*, 18 Feb. 1865.

⁵⁰ NLW MS 9262A Blackwell, 'Dictionary', p. 408; *Y Drych*, 24 Mar. 1921.

⁵¹ For biog. details of John Mather Jones (1826-1874), see NLW MS 9262A Blackwell, 'Dictionary', pp. 378-379; *Y Drych*, 24 Dec. 1874; *Utica Observer*, 21 Dec. 1874; *Utica Morning Herald and Daily Gazette*, 22 Dec. 1874.

⁵² For details of the Kansas scheme see, e.g., *Y Drych*, 24 Mar. 1870, 12 Jan. 1871 (advertisements), 20 Jan. 1870, 20 Jan. 1881. For John Mather Jones' own writings on it, see 1 Sept., 10 Nov. 1870. See also *Baner ac Amserau Cymru*, 25 Aug., 22 Dec. 1869; Phillips G. Davies, 'The Welsh in Kansas: Settlement, Contributions and Assimilation', *Welsh History Review*, Vol. 14 No. 3 (1989), pp. 380-398.

[53] *Y Drych a'r Gwyliedydd*, 1 Feb. 1856. For S. R. and Brynffynnon, see Wilbur S. Shepperson, *Samuel Roberts: a Welsh Colonizer in Civil War Tennessee* (Knoxville, 1961); Glanmor Williams, *Samuel Roberts, Llanbrynmair* (Cardiff, 1950). For a study which discusses various Welsh colonizing schemes in the context of nationalism and constructions of Welshness, see Anne Kelly Knowles, 'Migration, Nationalism, and the Construction of Welsh Identity' in Guntram H. Herb and David H. Kaplan (eds.), *Nested Identities: Nationalism, Territory, and Scale* (New York, 1999), pp. 289-315.

[54] For some of *Y Drych*'s accusations see, e.g., *Y Drych a'r Gwyliedydd*, 23 Feb., 19 Apr., 24 May, 19 July, 9 Aug. 1856, 19 Sept. 1857.

[55] *Y Drych a'r Gwyliedydd*, 19 July 1856.

[56] NLW Gee MSS, X Misc X6, press cutting, S. R., 'Y Gogledd a'r De', *Y Drych*, 11 May 1861.

[57] Samuel Roberts, *Pregethau a Darlithiau* (Utica, 1865), p. 174.

[58] NLW MSS 9511D T. J. Griffiths to Samuel Roberts, 23 Mar. 1877. See also NLW MS 3265 T. J. Griffiths to Samuel Roberts, 22 Feb. 1881, Samuel Roberts to T. J. Griffiths, 21 Jan. 1882.

[59] '. . . yn waeth bradwr, ac yn fwy selog caethbleidiwr na'r Deheuwyr eu hunain'. Samuel Roberts, *Hunan-Amddiffyniad S.R.: yn ngwyneb y camddarlunio fu arno drwy adeg cynddaredd, y rhyfel cartrefol yn America* (Conway, 1882, first pub. 1867) p. 14, p. 155 (the latter taken from *Y Drych,* 26 Oct. 1865, of which there appear to be no extant copies).

[60] See, e.g., 23 Nov. 1865.

[61] J. W. Jones and T. B. Morris, *Hanes Y Gwrthryfel Mawr Yn Y Talaethau Unedig* (Utica, 1866).

[62] 'HANES yr oeddid y gallai Cenedl y Cymry ymddybynu arno, a'r oes a ddaw gyfeirio ato fel awdurdod ddilys'. Jones and Morris, *Hanes Y Gwrthryfel Mawr*, p. 3.

[63] *Y Drych*, 9 Nov. 1865. According to Blackwell, Welsh people lost interest in the work, so only the first volume was produced. NLW MS 9262A Blackwell, 'Dictionary', p. 408.

[64] ' . . . [c]rach-feddygon y Drych roddi *strychnine* rhyfel i wrthweithio effeithiau *arsenic* caethiwed o'r cyfansoddiad'. Roberts, *Hunan-Amddiffyniad*, p. 18.

[65] 'yn tori eu gair, yn rhwygo eu cyfamod, yn mathru dan draed *holl honour* eu hymrwymiadau, ac yn troseddu rheolau pob rhyddymresymiad, a deddfau swyddfa pob cyhoeddiad o'r unrhyw enw.' Roberts, *Hunan-Amddiffyniad*, p. 140. In 1883 John C. Roberts maintained in a letter that *Y Drych* had always given fair play to S. R. and published his side. NLW MS 3265D John C. Roberts to Revd John Davies, Spring Green, Wis., 7 May 1883.

[66] 'Ni bu caethfeistri poethwylltaf y De erioed yn fwy cynddeiriog am gam-ddarlunio ac erlid unrhyw *anti-slavery* man, nag y bu undebwyr y Drych am erlid S.R. oblegyd ei fod yn *anti-war* man.' Roberts, *Hunan-Amddiffyniad*, p. 153.

[67] *Y Drych*, 27 Jan. 1881. See also 3 July, 16, 30 Oct., 20 Nov. 1879.

[68] See, e.g., *Y Drych a'r Gwyliedydd*, 26 Apr., 3 May, 5 July, 13, 20 Sept., 1 Nov. 1856, 28 Feb., 16 May, 8 Aug. 1857; *Y Drych*, 24 Jan., 7, 21 Feb., 7 Mar., 4, 11, 25 Apr. 1863, 4, 11 Feb., 4 Mar. 1875. See also Gareth Alban Davies, 'Wales, Patagonia and the

printed word: the missionary role of the press', *Llafur*, vol. 6 no. 4, 1995, pp. 44-49. For the Welsh Colony in Patagonia, see Robert Owen Jones, 'The Welsh Language in Patagonia' in Geraint H. Jenkins (ed.), *Language and Community in the Nineteenth Century* (Cardiff, 1998), pp. 287-316; Glyn Williams, *The Desert and the Dream: a Study of Welsh Colonization in Chubut, 1865-1915* (Cardiff, 1975). See also Knowles, 'Migration, Nationalism, and the Construction of Welsh Identity'.

[69] See, e.g., *Y Drych*, 11 Dec. 1902, 22 Jan., 16, 23 Apr., 14 May 1903. See also Lewis H. Thomas, 'From the Prairie to the Pampas: The Welsh Migration of 1902', *Saskatchewan History*, Vol. 24 No. 1 (Winter, 1971), reprint by the St. David's Society of New York (no date).

[70] *Y Drych a'r Gwyliedydd*, 12 Apr. 1856 – 4 Apr. 1857. For illustrations see, e.g., 1 Nov. 1856. See also Bill Linnard, 'Ar Drywydd y Cewri ym Mhatagonia', *Y Casglwr*, 69 (Summer, 2000), p. 3.

[71] NLW MS 4616B W. S. Jones, Scranton (editor of *Baner America*) to Revd D. S. Davies, 19 April 1872; *Y Drych*, 8 Aug. 1872.

[72] *Y Drych*, 12 Jan. 1871, 11 July – 5 Sept. 1872.

[73] *Y Drych*, 24 Mar. 1921; Evans, 'The Welsh in Oneida County', p. 108.

[74] *Y Drych*, 12 May 1860.

[75] *Y Drych*, 1 Dec. 1860; *Y Drych* advertisement in *Y Cyfaill o'r Hen Wlad*, Vol. 23 No. 273 (Sept. 1860).

[76] Thomas, *Hanes Cymry America*, Dosran C, p. 63.

[77] *Y Drych*, 9 July 1868. The phrase is taken from the English-language notice to advertisers first introduced in this issue.

[78] *Y Drych*, 24 Dec. 1868. Lewis' title was printed in English in the paper's English-language guidance for advertisers.

[79] *Y Drych*, 4 Apr. 1872.

[80] '. . . yn obeithiol ac anogaethol'. *Y Drych*, 6 Jan. 1870.

CHAPTER 3

[1] For a recent discussion of 'old' and 'new' immigration, see James P. Shenton, 'Ethnicity and Immigration' in Eric Foner (ed.), *The New American History* (Philadelphia, 1990), pp. 256-258.

[2] Sally M. Miller (ed.), *The Ethnic Press in the United States: A Historical Analysis and Handbook* (Westport, Conn., 1987) p. xiii. See also Robert E. Park, *The Immigrant Press and Its Control* (New York, 1922); Vasey, 'The Media', pp. 215-216.

[3] U. S. Bureau of the Census, *Historical Statistics of the United States from Colonial Times to 1957* (Washington, D.C., 1960), p. 66; John Williams, *Digest of Welsh Historical Statistics*, 2 vols (Cardiff, 1985), Vol. 1, p. 76. These figures almost certainly exclude emigrants from Monmouthshire. See David Williams, 'Some Figures Relating to Emigration from Wales', *Bulletin of the Board of Celtic Studies*, 7 (1935), pp. 396-415, 399-400.

[4] Thomas, *Hanes Cymry America*, Dosran C, pp. 5-20; Daniel Jenkins Williams, *The Welsh of Columbus, Ohio: A Study of Adaptation and Assimilation* (Oshkosh, Wis.,

1913). See also the discussion on this topic in William D. Jones, 'The Welsh Language and Welsh Identity in a Pennsylvanian Community' in Jenkins, *Language and Community*, pp. 261-286, 261-263.

⁵ William D. Jones, *Wales in America: Scranton and the Welsh, 1860-1920* (Cardiff, 1993), p. xx.

⁶ For biog. details of Thomas J. Griffiths (1835-1924), see NLW MS 9258A Blackwell, 'Dictionary', pp. 403-408; Cardiff University, Salisbury MSS 218, Bob Owen 'Bywgraffiadau Cymry Americanaidd' (unpublished typescript, 1960), pp. 41-42; *Y Drych*, 4 Mar. 1921, 7, 14 Feb. 1924; *Utica Daily Press*, 7 Feb. 1924; *Utica Observer-Dispatch*, 7 Feb. 1924. See also D. H. E. Roberts, 'Welsh Publishing in the United States of America' in Philip Henry Jones and Eiluned Rees (eds.), *A Nation and its Books: A History of the Book in Wales* (Aberystwyth, 1998), pp. 253-264, 256-257.

⁷ Griffiths is alleged to have once said 'I don't read or speak Welsh, and it saves people complaining to me'. NLW MS 9258A Blackwell, 'Dictionary', p. 407, also cited in Roberts, 'Welsh Publishing in the US', p. 257.

⁸ NLW MSS 9511D T. J. Griffiths to Samuel Roberts, 23 Mar. 1877; Roberts, 'Welsh Publishing in the US', pp. 256-257.

⁹ Evans, 'The Welsh in Oneida County', pp. 115-116.

¹⁰ Advertisement for T. J. Griffiths, *Y Drych*, 25 Apr. 1867, 20 Jan. 1870, also cited in Roberts, 'Welsh Publishing in the US', p. 257.

¹¹ NLW MS 9258A Blackwell, 'Dictionary', pp. 407-408.

¹² For histories of the Welsh in Utica and Oneida County, see Evans, 'The Welsh in Oneida County'; Erasmus W. Jones, 'The Early Welsh Settlers of Oneida County', *Transactions of the Oneida Historical Society at Utica*, 5 (1889-1892), pp. 60-67; Pamela Kneller, 'Welsh Immigrant Women as wage earners in Utica, New York, 1860-70', *Llafur*, Vol. 5 No. 4 (1991), pp. 71-78; Allen Noble, *An Ethnic Geography of Early Utica, New York: Time, Space and Community* (Lewiston, N.Y. and Lampeter, 1999), pp. 15-29; Howard Thomas, 'The Welsh Came to Remsen', *New York History*, Vol. 30 (1949), pp. 33-42; Jay G. Williams III, *Memory Stones. A History of Welsh-Americans in Central New York and their churches* (Fleischmanns, N.Y., 1993), pp. 26, 108-109, and the numerous works by David Maldwyn Ellis, son of one of *Y Drych*'s most respected and prolific contributors in the first half of the twentieth century, Sam Ellis. David Maldwyn Ellis, 'The Welsh in Oneida County in New York State', *Transactions of the Honourable Society of Cymmrodorion*, 1961 Pt. 1, pp. 115-124; idem, 'The Assimilation of the Welsh in Central New York', *New York History*, Vol. 53 (July 1972), pp. 299-333; idem, 'The Assimilation of the Welsh in Central New York', *Welsh History Review*, Vol. 6 No. 2 (1973), pp. 424-50; idem, 'The Welsh in Utica', *Transactions of the Honourable Society of Cymmrodorion*, 1981, pp. 127-135; idem., 'Cwm Rhondda: The Welsh in Utica' in James S. Pula (ed.), *Ethnic Utica* (Utica, 1994), pp. 217-228.

¹³ *Aberdare Times*, 15 Oct. 1864. The observer was Henry Hughes, formerly of Aberdare, who at the time was working in T. J. Griffiths' office but not on *Y Drych*. He reported that all the office staff were Welsh.

¹⁴ Williams, *Memory Stones*, pp. 26, 108-109.

¹⁵ Ellis, 'The Assimilation of the Welsh in Central New York', *New York History*, pp.

306-313. See also Remsen-Steuben Historical Society, Remsen, N.Y., Hugh Hughes file, Hugh Hughes, 'The Welsh in Utica, N.Y.' (unpub. MSS, undated).

[16] Evans, 'The Welsh in Oneida County', pp. 82-84.

[17] *Y Drych*, 24 Mar. 1921; Wager, *Oneida County and its People*, p. 359.

[18] For biog. details of John C. Roberts (1840-1911), see NLW MS 9272A Blackwell, 'Dictionary', p. 138; *Y Drych*, 9, 30 Nov. 1911, 19 May 1921; *Cambrian*, Vol. 25 No. 7 (July 1905), pp. 312-313, Vol. 31 No. 22 (15 Nov. 1911), pp. 15-16, Vol. 32 No. 3 (1 Feb. 1912), p. 15; *Utica Daily Press*, 6 Nov. 1911; *Utica Herald-Dispatch*, 6 Nov. 1911.

[19] *Y Drych*, 17 Apr. 1884, 30 June 1898.

[20] '. . .i raddau uchel yn ddyladwy i'w ddiwydrwydd, ei ffyddlondeb, ei chwaeth dda, a'i ymroddiad diflino'. *Y Drych*, 9 Nov. 1911.

[21] NLW MS 9258A Blackwell, 'Dictionary', p. 407.

[22] For biog. details of G. H. Humphrey (1844-1906), see *Y Drych*, 22 Nov. 1906; *Cambrian*, Vol. 26 No. 11 (Nov. 1906), pp. 503-507; *Utica Daily Press*, 17 Nov. 1906; *Utica Herald-Dispatch*, 15 Nov. 1906; Hugh Hughes, *Pryddestau Er Cof am Griffith H. Humphrey, Utica, N.Y.: Gyda Sylwadau ar ei Fywyd* (Utica, 1908).

[23] Undated *Utica Herald* report cited in Ebeneser Edwards (William Penn), *Facts about Welsh Factors: Welshmen as Factors in the Foundation and Development of the U.S. Republic* (Utica, 1899), pp. 421-422.

[24] For biog. details of Benjamin F. Lewis (1832-1897), see NLW MS 9264A Blackwell, 'Dictionary', pp. 77-81; *Cambrian*, 1897, pp. 297-300; *Y Drych*, 7 June 1897, *Utica Daily Press*, 4 June 1897; *Utica Herald-Dispatch*, 4 June 1897.

[25] For biog. details of Dafydd Rhys Williams (1851-1931), see *DWB*, p. 1029; *Druid*, 1 Apr. 1931; *Y Drych*, 24 Mar. 1921, 10 May 1928, 19, 26 Mar. 1931; D. Craionog Lewis, *Hanes Plwyf Defynog* (Merthyr, 1911), pp. 182-183.

[26] For biog. details of R. Morris Williams (1884-1950), see *Y Drych*, 15 Sept. 1950; *Utica Daily Press*, 12 Sept. 1950.

[27] *Y Drych*, 24 Mar. 1921.

[28] '. . . ymddangosai pob peth yno yn drefnus a bywiog – T. J. Griffiths yn siriol a gweithgar yn arolygu y cwbl; J. W. Jones a J. C. Roberts yn trefnu a dethol pethau cyfaddas i'w harddangos yn y DRYCH, er budd y genedl Gymreig trwy y Talaethau; a Richard E. Roberts yn gofalu am un o adranau mwyaf pwysig y Swyddfa, sef y cyfrifon. Ac wrth gwrs yr oedd yno amryw o Gymry eraill o dalentau llenyddol yn hyrwyddo gwaith y Swyddfa.' *Y Drych*, 17 Apr. 1884.

[29] *Y Drych*, 26 Apr., 3 May 1900.

[30] '. . . gweled degau o lythyrau yn bwrlymu i mewn yn wastadol, a phob gohebydd yn gofyn am le yn y nesaf. . . . Yr oedd R. M. o'r golwg bron mewn gohebiaethau a dim golwg o'r ddesc.' *Y Drych*, 20 Aug. 1914.

[31] *Y Drych*, 15 Mar. 1877; Wager, p. 359.

[32] Jones, *Wales in America*, esp. pp. 88-89.

[33] *Y Drych*, 31 Jan. 1884.

[34] *Y Drych*, 8 May 1890.

[35] *Y Drych*, 8 Feb. 1894. *Y Columbia*'s Chicago office on Monroe Street was retained by *Y Drych* at least until August 1894.

[36] For quarrels with *Y Wasg*, e.g., see Y *Drych*, 5 Aug. 1875.

[37] Jones, *Wales in America*, p. 155; William D. Davies, *America a Gweledigaethau Bywyd* (Scranton, 1895), p. 357. To make matters worse, perhaps, a *Y Drych* correspondent was refused entry to one session at the eisteddfod because the committee had neglected to give him a pass. Jones, *Wales in America*, p. 171.

[38] ' . . . . cydnabyddir er's blynyddau lawer mai prin yr oedd gan Y DRYCH gystadleuydd yn eangder ei gylchrediad, helaethrwydd ei newyddion, a chymeriad ei lenyddiaeth'. *Y Drych*, 8 May 1890.

[39] ' . . . Cymreig o ran iaith a theimlad'. *Y Drych*, 8 Feb. 1894.

[40] ' . . . yn ddigon lluosog yn y wlad hon i gynal dau bapyr wythnosol'. *Y Drych*, 8 Feb. 1894.

[41] *Baner ac Amserau Cymru*, 16 Jan. 1895. There appear to be no extant copies of *Yr Adlais* (published 1894-95). The report in *Baner ac Amserau Cymru* contains hints that before the take-over *Y Columbia* had halved its price to a dollar in order to undercut *Y Drych*.

[42] Wager, *Oneida County*, p. 359.

[43] *Y Drych*, 30 Jan. 1879.

[44] *Y Drych*, 5 Apr. 1877, 15 May 1890, 8 Feb. 1894.

[45] *Y Drych*, 26 Jan., 10 Aug., 14 Sept. 1893.

[46] *Y Drych*, 18 May 1893. Both the photograph and the article that accompanied it first appeared in the Wales-published newspaper *Seren Cymru* [The Star of Wales].

[47] *Y Drych*, 9 Jan. 1851, 13 Nov. 1930, *Y Drych a'r Gwyliedydd*, 20 Sept. 1856.

[48] 'DAVID R. JONES, mab i'r diweddar Meredith Jones, Arthog, Meirionydd. Ymfudodd i'r wlad hon tua 18 mlynedd yn ol. O Dakota y clywyd oddiwrtho ddiweddaf. Teimlaf yn hynod ddiolchgar am air oddiwrtho ef neu rywun sydd yn gwybod am dano. Ei frawd – JOHN M. JONES, Box 389 Granville, N.Y.' *Y Drych*, 20 Aug. 1891.

[49] See, e.g., 11 July 1895, 2 Apr. 1903, 16 Feb. 1911.

[50] *Y Drych*, 3 Sept., 1 Oct. 1908; *Cambrian*, Vol. 28 No. 10 (Oct. 1908), p. 453.

[51] *Y Drych*, 11 June 1859, 6 Apr. 1882, 15, 22 Dec. 1887, 12 Jan. 1888, 8 Feb., 29 Mar. 1923.

[52] 'yn ddystawach na hyny am wyr a gwragedd i lawer o Gymry ar gael, ond yn ymddwyn fel rhai ar goll'. *Y Drych*, 24 Mar. 1921.

[53] *Y Drych*, 8 Dec. 1904 – 12 Jan. 1905.

[54] ' . . . yn sicr dylai darllenwyr y DRYCH cael eu hanrhegu a'r un danteithion meddyliol a dyddorol.' See, e.g., *Y Drych*, 31 Jan. 1884.

[55] *Y Drych*, 1 May 1884.

[56] See, e.g., 11 June 1859, 13, 20 Jan., 3 Feb. 1881, 31 Jan. 1884. See also 8 Jan. 1885 for a suggestion that his travel writings be collected in a book.

[57] *Y Drych*, 1 Jan. 1876 – 4 Mar. 1880 passim; William O. Thomas, *Dwywaith o Amgylch y Byd; sef Hanes Teithiau yn Ewrop, Asia, Affrica, America, ac Australasia, yn ystod Pum Mlynedd o Amser* (Utica, 1882).

[58] See, e.g., *Y Drych*, 17 Apr. 1884, 24 July 1890, 1 Aug. 1895; William D. Davies, *Llwybrau Bywyd; neu, Haner Can Mlynedd o Oes* (Utica, 1889); idem, *America*. See

also NLW MS 3191C Letters from W. D. Davies to Daniel Davies, Ton [Rhondda], 1 Jan. 1883, 12 Mar. 1885.

[59] *Cambrian*, Vol. 3 No. 2 (Mar.-Apr. 1883), p. 153.

[60] *Y Drych*, 1 Sept. 1898.

[61] *Y Drych*, 1, 15 Sept. 1898.

[62] *Y Drych*, 22 Mar. 1888.

[63] *Y Drych*, 10 Nov. 1887.

[64] *Y Drych*, 15 Sept. 1887.

[65] *Y Drych*, 1, 8, 15, 22, 29 Sept. 1898.

[66] *Y Drych*, 1 Sept. 1898.

[67] *Y Drych*, 21 Feb. 1884.

[68] *Y Drych*, 6, 13, 20, 27 June 1889, 26 Apr., 3 May 1906.

[69] *Y Drych*, 22 May, 5 June 1902; *Cambrian*, Vol. 22 No. 6 (June 1902), p. 292.

[70] For a wider discussion of the reaction to the First World War among the Welsh in America, see Jones, *Wales in America*, pp. 197-199.

[71] See, e.g., *Y Drych*, 10 Dec. 1914, 24 June 1915, 14 Dec. 1916.

[72] *Y Drych*, 13 Aug. 1914.

[73] *Y Drych*, 13 Aug. 1914 – 16 Jan. 1919. Following this, until 4 Sept. 1919, the paper ran a weekly column 'Rhyfel a Heddwch' [War and Peace], which reported news of the Peace Conferences.

[74] *Y Drych*, 10 Sept. 1914.

[75] *Y Drych*, 3, 17, 24 Sept. 1914.

[76] *Y Drych*, 27 Aug., 22, 29 Oct., 10 Dec. 1914, 28 Dec. 1916.

[77] *Y Drych*, 3 Sept. 1914.

[78] 'Byddai yn warth oesol i Gymru adael i Lloegr, Ysgotland a'r Werddon amddiffyn Prydain a'i gwareiddiad.' *Y Drych*, 24 Sept. 1914.

[79] *Y Drych*, 4 Feb. 1915, 8 June, 26 Oct. 1916, 14 Nov. 1918.

[80] *Y Drych*, 1, 15 Oct. 1914.

[81] '. . . pe buasai bob eglwys Gymreig yn y Talaethau ac yn Canada i wneyd casgliad arbenig bob Sabboth. . . . Ni all unrhyw Gymro o'r iawn ryw adael i gyfleusdra fel hwn gael ei droi ymaith. Gadewch i ni drethu ein hunain am swm neillduol bob wythnos tra y bydd y miloedd o'n cydgenedl ar faes y frwydr.' *Y Drych*, 1 Oct. 1914.

[82] *Y Drych*, 10 Dec. 1914, 14 Jan. 1915. It appears that various kinds of collections in America to aid Wales continued throughout the war. For details of funds organised by T. Owen Charles, editor of *The Druid*, see Jones, *Wales in America*, p. 197.

[83] See, e.g., *Y Drych*, 16 May 1918. See also 8 Mar. 1917.

[84] *Y Drych*, 12 Apr. 1917.

[85] *Y Drych*, 1 June 1916, 'Y Gwr Bach Mawr o'n cenedl fach ni'. 19 Dec. 1918, 27 Oct. 1921.

[86] 'Mae sylwadau golygyddol y "Drych" ar Lloyd George fel ser dysglaer yn y ffurfafen yn saethu goleuni i bob cyfeiriad.' *Y Drych*, 8 Feb. 1917.

[87] '. . . y mae genym ni fwy na Bil yn Daff'. *Y Drych*, 25 Jan. 1917.

[88] *Y Drych*, 14 Nov. 1918.

[89] *Y Drych*, 23 Jan. 1919; see also Jones, *Wales in America*, p. 196.

[90] '. . . wnaiff les i'ch cyrff a'ch heneidiau'. *Y Drych*, 20 Mar. 1919.

[91] See Aled Gruffydd Jones, *Press, Politics and Society: A History of Journalism in Wales* (Cardiff, 1993); NLW E. Morgan Humphreys Papers, A/3720, W. Owen Williams, Wilkesbarre, Pa., to Humphreys, 8 Feb. 1932.

[92] See, e.g., items from *Y Drych* reprinted in Y *Gwladgarwr*, 21 Feb. 1863, 18 Feb. 1865, 15 Oct. 1880.

[93] Jones, *Press, Politics and Society*, pp. 24, 101.

[94] *Y Cenhadwr Americanaidd*, Vol. 60 No. 12 (1899) p. 367.

[95] See, e.g., *Baner ac Amserau Cymru*, 19 Sept. 1860, 17 June 1871, 3 Nov. 1881, 1 Jan. 1903.

[96] *Baner ac Amserau Cymru*, 8 June 1870.

[97] *Y Drych*, 6 Feb. 1919.

[98] *Y Drych*, 20 Nov. 1919.

CHAPTER 4

[1] *Cambrian*, Vol. 31 No. 22 (15 Nov. 1911), p. 16.

[2] NLW MS 2834B, f. 47 Account of a Tour of the USA by David Samwel, 1889; Jones, *Wales in America*, p. 109.

[3] *Y Drych*, 2 Jan. 1851.

[4] 'Yn unol a deddf anysgrifenedig ond anhyblyg, ni all dyn fod yn Gymro heb fedru Cymraeg. Gall ei wythienau fod yn llawn o'r 'gwaed coch cyfa' puraf yn y byd; oni fedr ei dafod barablu yr hen iaith, nid yw ond ysgymun yn ein plith. . . . I olwg allanol, yr iaith sydd yn profi cenedl y Cymro, ac y mae yn rhy ddiweddar ar y dydd i newid y rheol. . . . Pan gyll Cymro ei Gymraeg, nid yw Gymro mwyach yng ngolwg cyffredinol-rwydd ei gydgenedl. Mae y peth yn reddf yn y natur bellach, ac nis gellir ei ddiwreddio. . . . [B]yddant yn sicr o ymgolli ac ymdoddi yn y genedl Americanaidd pan gollir y Gymraeg. Unig obaith cadw yn fyw gymeriad a neillduolrwydd Cymreig yn America yw glynu wrth yr iaith. Bydded ddoeth, bydded annoeth, y mae bywyd Cymreig America yn guddiedig yn yr iaith.' *Y Drych*, 10 Aug. 1893.

[5] For context, see Samuel L. Baily, 'The Role of Two Newspapers and the Assimilation of the Italians in Buenos Aires and Sao Paulo, 1893-1913', *International Migration Review*, Vol. 12 No. 3 (Fall 1978), pp. 321-340; Joshua A. Fishman et. al., *Language Loyalty in the United States: The Maintenance and Perpetuation of Non-English Mother Tongues by American Ethnic and Religious Groups* (The Hague, 1966); Robert F. Harney, 'The Ethnic Press in Ontario', *Polyphony*, 4 (Spring/Summer 1982), pp. 3-14; Miller, *Ethnic Press*; Rudolph J. Vecoli, 'The Italian Immigrant Press and the Construction of Social Reality, 1850-1920' in James P. Danky and Wayne A. Wiegand (eds.), *Print Culture in a Diverse America* (Urbana and Chicago, 1998), pp. 17-33.

[6] *Y Drych*, 19 May, 28 July, 18 Aug., 1, 15 Sept., 20 Oct. 1898.

[7] See, e.g., *Y Drych*, 2 Jan. 1908; John William Jones, *Yr Athrawydd Parod: sef hyfforddydd anffaeledig i ddarllen ac ysgrifenu Cymraeg yn nghyda rheolau barddonaieth Gymreig ac elfenau rhifyddiaeth* (Utica, 1860). See also advertisements and notices for the latter in *Y Drych*, e.g., 1 Dec. 1860, 9, 23 Nov. 1865.

⁸ J. C. Roberts, *Y Trysor Teuluaidd* (Utica, 1877). See also advertisements in *Y Drych*, e.g., 6 Dec. 1877.

⁹ Two useful recent discussions of the attitudes of the Welsh press in America towards this subject are Hywel Teifi Edwards, *Eisteddfod Ffair Y Byd Chicago, 1893* (Llandysul, 1990), esp. pp. 34-61, and Hopkin, 'Welsh Immigrants to the United States and their Press'.

¹⁰ 'Pregethir, siaredir a darllenir yr Omeraeg yn y wlad hon am rai oesoedd.' *Y Drych*, 28 July 1898.

¹¹ '. . . yn aflwydd tu hwnt i ddychymyg. . . . Mae heddwch a llwyddiant gwladol a chrefyddol y wlad hon yn gofyn fod rhyw un iaith i lyncu yr holl ieithoedd eraill, ac i hyn y daw er gwaethaf pob cri ac ymdrech i'r gwrthwyneb. Mae yr ymdrech i geisio tragwyddoli yr iaith Gymraeg yn y wlad hon mor ofer a'r ymdrech i yru yn ol lanw y mor ag ysgubell.' *Y Drych*, 18 Nov. 1909, also cited in Hopkin, 'Welsh Immigrants to the United States and their Press', p. 361.

¹² '. . . miloedd o bethau gwerth eu gwybod'. *Y Trysor Teuluaidd*, passim (the quote is an extract from the full title).

¹³ See, e.g., 11 June 1859 (for Welsh servant girls in Birmingham, Pa.), 4 Sept. 1890 (an apprentice in a dry goods store and window dresser in Youngstown, Ohio), 29 Mar. 1923 (Welsh farmhands in South Dakota), 25 Aug. 1932 (Welsh slate quarrymen, splitters and dressers in Georgia).

¹⁴ *Y Drych*, 9 Jan. 1868, 26 May 1881. See also, e.g., letter from Minneapolis pointing out shortage of carpenters in the city. *Y Drych*, 4 Sept. 1890.

¹⁵ *Y Drych*, 4 Oct., 1872, 22 Jan. 1874. See also, e.g., 1 Mar. 1855.

¹⁶ See, e.g., *Y Drych*, 31 Oct. 1872, 22 Jan. 1874, 4 Feb. 1881, 4 Sept. 1890.

¹⁷ *Y Drych*, 7 Aug. 1884.

¹⁸ See Miller, *Ethnic Press*, xv-xvi; Vecoli, 'The Italian Immigrant Press', pp. 17-18.

¹⁹ *Y Drych*, 28 Jan., 29 Apr. 1909.

²⁰ 'Y "Drych" yw fy unig gyfaill Cymreig ar ol marwolaeth fy mhriod, John A. Jones, 14 mlynedd yn ol. Yr oedd yn dderbyniwr o'r "Drych" cyn ymadael a Carbondale, Pa., am Nebraska, yn 1858. Daethym inau yma yn 1860, a dyoddefasom lawer o galedi mewn gwlad newydd . . . Prynasom haner section o dir ac yr wyf yn byw ar un rhan o hono, a fy mab ar y llall. Go debyg ar ol fy nydd i, yr atelir y "Drych" gan nad yw fy mhlant yn medru darllen nac ysgrifenu y Gymraeg. Credaf fy mod gyda'r hynaf o dderbynwyr y "Drych," ac y mae yn ddyddanwch mawr i mi.' *Y Drych*, 18 Jan. 1912. For an English-language report of her letter, see *Cambrian*, Vol. 22 No. 4 (15 Feb. 1912) p. 15. For a later, similar case, see *Y Drych*, 24 Jan. 1929.

²¹ *Y Drych*, 1 Feb. 1912.

²² Ellen Jones (nee Owens) died on 16 Mar. 1916. Born in Cardigan in 1835, she came to the USA as a child with her parents. *Y Drych*, 27 Apr. 1916.

²³ *Y Drych*, 28 Sept. 1899.

²⁴ 'Yn ngholofn y marwolaethau yn y "Drych" yn aml y cyfarfyddir y sylw . . . fod yr ymadawedig yn hoff iawn o'r Beibl a'r "Drych;" yr hyn, yn ddiau, sydd yn glod nid bychan i'r newyddiadur. Y mae bod yn gydymaith i'r Beibl yn barch mawr. Nid ydym wrth hyn yn golygu fod y "Drych" yn gydradd a'r Beibl, eithr ei fod fel dysgybl yn

dilyn blaenoriaeth yr Hen Lyfr ac yn hoff o athrawiaeth a moes yr Ysgrythurau. Peth rhagorol arall yn nglyn a'r "Drych" yw ei fod yn Gristion heb fod yn enwadol, yn debyg i fel ydyw y Beibl ei hun. . . . Mae yn rhy fawrfrydig i fod yn eiddo i blaid na enwad. Ceir y Bedyddiwr[,] y Weslead, yr Annibynwr a'r Trefnydd Calfinaidd yn y hoffi fel y maent yn hoffi eu Beibl.' *Y Drych*, 28 Sept. 1899.

[25] See the reports by 'Awstin' in the *Western Mail* during this period. For accounts of the 1904-05 Religious Revival in Wales, see Eifion Evans, *The Welsh Revival of 1904*, 3rd edition (Bridgend, 1987); Basil Hall, 'The Welsh Revival of 1904-05: A Critique', in C. J. Cuming and Derek Baker (eds.), *Popular Belief and Practice* (Cambridge, 1972), pp. 291-301; C. R. W. Williams, 'The Welsh Religious Revival of 1904-05', *British Journal of Sociology* Vol. 8 (1952); and in Carmarthenshire, Russell Davies, *Secret Sins: Sex, Violence and Society in Carmarthenshire 1870 – 1920* (Cardiff, 1996), chap. 5.

[26] 'Dyma broffwyd eto wedi codi o fynwes cymdeithas, fel Ioan Fedyddiwr, a'i allu yn ddirgelwch, a'i ddylanwad yn anesboniadwy.' *Y Drych*, 8 Dec. 1904.

[27] In this respect *Y Drych* resembled the general reaction of the Welsh-American press to the revival. See *Cambrian*, Vol. 15 No. 2 (Feb. 1905), pp. 47, 48, 49; *Y Cyfaill*, Vol. 68 No. 805 (Feb. 1905), pp. 85-88, No. 806 (Mar. 1905), pp. 122-123, No. 810 (Dec. 1905), p. 511.

[28] ' . . . nid dywygiad yn cyffroi y teimlad yn unig, eithr yn gwellhau y galon'. *Y Drych*, 15 Dec. 1904.

[29] *Y Drych*, 12 Jan. 1905.

[30] *Y Drych*, 26 Jan. 1905. These included Wilkesbarre, Pa., Lansford, Pa., Hyde Park, Pa., Providence, Pa., Johnstown, Pa., Chicago, Ill., Granville, N.Y., Utica, N.Y., Rome, N.Y., Waterville, N.Y., Remsen, N.Y., Fair Haven, Vt., and New York City. See also *Y Cyfaill*, Vol. 68 No. 806 (Mar. 1905), pp. 125-28.

[31] 'Teimlwn yn ddiolchgar am gymaint o hanes y diwygiad. Mae y ffeithiau rhyfedd gyflwyna y "Drych" o'n blaen wedi gwresogi llawer calon yn barod, yn toddi allan fateriolaeth oer . . . Mae'r wythnos weddi yn barod wedi myned yn wythnosau gweddi mewn llawer man. *Y Drych*, 9 Feb. 1905.

[32] *Y Drych*, 23 Mar. 1916. The column was still appearing in the 1930s.

[33] ' . . . cludo newyddion i eithafion unig yn mhellderau cyfandiroedd anferth . . . cludo llawer o Efengyl. Mae y "Drych" yn bregethwr a gweinidog i aml i hen Gymro a Chymraes ydynt mor bell o gyfleusderau fel na chaent bregeth o gwbl oni bae am y "Drych". *Y Drych*, 24 Mar. 1921.

[34] *Y Drych*, 23 Mar. 1916, 24 Mar. 1921.

[35] ' . . . nis gallaf feddwl am Gymry heb feddwl am Dduw . . . gobeithiwn na welir y dydd pryd na bydd rhyw gongl fach i Iesu Grist yn y Drych'. *Y Drych*, 11 Apr. 1935.

[36] *Y Drych*, 5, 12, 19 Jan. 1893. These included Bellevue (Scranton), Lansford, Mahanoy City, Moriah Church in Nanticoke, and Shamokin, Pa; Sardis Church, Chicago; Delphos, Ohio; Oskaloosa, Ia.; Fair Haven, Vt.; and Utica and Middle Granville, N.Y.

[37] 'Wrth gadw yr Eisteddfod i ni ein hunain, trengu wna, ond wrth ei throi yn efengyl

i'r cenedloedd daw yn fuddiol o for i for ac o'r afon hyd derfynau y ddaear. Y ffordd i'w bytholi (am oesau o leiaf) yw ei chydio a'r Ser a'r Brithresi, a'i rhoi dan nawdd arbenig 'Newythr Sam . . . . Gwell iddi fyw yn sirioldeb yr Americaniaid na marw mewn dinodedd ac o ystyfnigrwydd Cymreig.' *Y Drych*, 12 Jan. 1899.

[38] *Y Drych*, 22 July, 5 Aug., 16 Sept., 1909.

[39] *Y Drych*, 3 Aug. 1893.

[40] *Y Drych*, 20 Jan., 17 Feb. 1898.

[41] *Y Drych*, 26 May 1898.

[42] *Y Drych*, 20 Apr. 1893.

[43] For biog. details of George T. Matthews (1847-1932), see *Druid*, 15 Feb. 1932; *Y Drych*, 12 Feb. 1891, 4 July, 15 Aug. 1929, 4 Apr. 1932.

[44] *Y Drych*, 4 July 1929.

[45] See, e.g., 27 Nov. 1884.

[46] 'Crist Ger Bron Pilot'. See, e.g., *Y Drych*, 9, 16, 23, 30 Jan. 1890.

[47] ' . . . ysbrydoliaeth i fywyd gwell'. See, e.g., *Y Drych*, 26 Feb. 1903.

[48] See, e.g., *Y Drych*, 29 Dec. 1904.

[49] *Y Drych*, 21 Dec. 1905.

[50] *Y Drych*, 12 Feb. 1891.

[51] For the latter, see, e.g., *Y Drych a'r Gwyliedydd,* 16 May 1857.

[52] *Y Drych*, 4 Oct. 1894.

[53] 'Paham yr ymddiriedwch i ddyeithriaid pan y mae Cymro ieuanc o gymeriad da, hollol adnabyddus i bawb yma yn barod i'ch gwasanaethu?' *Y Drych*, 5 May 1881.

[54] 'Dylai y Cymry sydd yn dyfod i America i ymgartrefu gymeryd y cyfle cyntaf i ymddinaseiddio, fel ag i allu cymeryd rhan weithredol yn y llywodraeth, trwy bleidleisio a dylanwadu ar ei chymdeithas a'i gwleidyddiaeth. Wrth wneyd hyn, ni raid i ni golli dim o'n cariad at yr Hen Wlad, ei hiaith a'i deifion.' *Y Drych*, 5 Oct. 1893.

[55] ' . . . trefnu ffyrdd a moddau i ochelyd yr hyn sydd yn ein bygwth – darparu cynllun a fydd yn effeithiol i gadw America yn Americanaidd.' *Y Drych*, 29 Mar. 1888.

[56] 'Ofer ac ynfyd fyddai dadleu dros i'r holl lwythau a chenedloedd o fewn ein Gweriniaeth i ymdoddi i'w gilydd. Ai priodol fyddai i hil Gomer ymgymysgu a'r Negro du a'r Indiad coch, neu a'r Dago gwaedlyd?' *Y Drych*, 4 July 1895.

[57] ' . . . truenus o gymysglyd . . . Babel o genedloedd ac anialwch o grefyddau, a syniadau a phaganiaethau.' *Y Drych*, 8 Mar. 1917.

[58] *Y Drych*, 28 Apr. 1892.

[59] *Y Drych*, 10 Nov. 1870.

[60] *Y Drych*, 16 Mar. 1893.

[61] ' . . . yn falch o fod yn frodor o Sir Feirionydd, ond yr wyf lawer balchach o fod yn ddinesydd o'r Talaethau Unedig'. *Y Drych*, 19 Mar. 1896.

[62] ' . . . afiechyd oedd wedi cymeryd gafael yn ein cyfansoddiad moesol'. *Y Drych*, 8 Oct. 1896.

[63] 'Wedi dod i awyr glir annibyniaeth America y gwelsom yn ddigon eglur arwyddion y clefyd parlysol.' *Y Drych*, 8 Oct. 1896.

[64] 'EISIAU GWRAIG! – Dymunaf agor gohebiaeth â merch ieuanc neu gwraig weddw ieuanc; dim gwrthwynebiad fod ganddi un plentyn ieuanc. Rhaid iddi fod o

gymeriad da ac yn proffesu crefydd. Y bwriad yw gwneyd dau yn un i gario yn mlaen ffarm yn y Gorllewin, a gwneyd cartref yn gysur. Dim twyll na chwareu.' *Y Drych*, 22 Dec. 1887.

[65] *Y Drych*, 13 July 1893 onwards.

[66] 'Ffaith ddiymwad yw fod y merched yn cynrychioli yr ochr oreu i wareiddiad; ac yn sicr byddai eu presenoldeb yn mhob cyngor dinasol a chenedlaethol yn debyg o effeithio yn rasol ar eu penderfyniadau.' *Y Drych*, 24 Aug. 1899. James P. Shenton has argued that 'the presence of women was essential to the Americanizing of the immigrants'. Shenton, 'Ethnicity and Immigration', p. 257.

[67] *Y Drych*, 5 Jan. 1893.

[68] For biog. details, see *Cambrian*, Vol. 22 No. 12 (Dec. 1902), pp. 419-21; *Y Drych*, 3 Mar. 1881, 24 Oct. 1907, 2 Mar. 1911. It seems Roberts returned to Wales permanently in 1911 due to her failing eyesight. So complete was her subsequent disappearance from public life that a search of relevant primary sources has failed to uncover the date or place of her death.

[69] *Y Drych*, 4 Nov. 1909.

[70] See, e.g., *Y Drych*, 11 July 1878, 1 Jan. 1880 (both on the status of women), 1 Nov. 1883 (on Wales' moral and religious condition), 16 Oct. 1884 (on women preachers), 17 Jan. 1895 (on the Women's Christian Temperance Union), 30 Oct. 1902 (on Astronomy), 8 Dec. 1904 (her experiences and impressions of the Religious Revival in Wales) and 30 Jan. 1908 (on the Hague Peace Conference).

[71] '. . . [gan fod] y maes o amddiffyn iawnderau y rhyw fenywaidd yn y wlad hon yn mhlith y Cymry yn cael ei adael bron yn hollol i mi. Yr wyf yn penderfynu mawrhau y fraint hon, er fod llawer chwaer yn codi ei ffroen mewn diystyrwch arnaf am wneyd – i'r rhai a maddeuaf yn rhwydd, fel y gwnaf i blentyn am gamsyniadau angenrheidiol ei natur blentynaidd.' *Y Drych*, 4 Jan. 1894.

[72] See, e.g., 1 Dec. 1879, 3 Apr. 1884, 18 Jan., 18 Mar. 1894.

[73] *Y Drych*, 17 Apr. 1884, 18 Jan., 8 Mar. 1894.

[74] '. . . yn cynwys ychydig o blaid ei rhyw, yn erbyn llawer sydd yn treio ein cadw yn y gwter er dyddiau Adda.' *Y Drych*, 15 Aug. 1907.

[75] *Y Drych*, 18 Jan. 1894, 24 Aug. 1899.

[76] '. . . ymddirywiad ac yn berygl enbydus i gymdeithas, sef y duedd amlwg sydd yn merched yr oes i esgeuluso a dirmygu y swydd a berthyna iddynt yn arbenig, sef cadw ty.' *Y Drych*, 24 Aug. 1899. See also editorial, 4 July 1895.

[77] *Y Drych*, 25 Apr. 1895.

[78] Vecoli, 'The Italian Immigrant Press', p. 28.

CHAPTER 5

[1] Miller, *Ethnic Press*, pp. xiii, xvi.

[2] Williams, 'Some Figures Relating to Emigration from Wales', pp. 408- 411; Rowland T. Berthoff, *British Immigrants in Industrial America* (Cambridge, Mass., 1953), p. 5.

[3] Williams, 'Some Figures Relating to Emigration from Wales', p. 407; *Historical*

Statistics of the United States, p. 66; Williams, *Digest of Welsh Historical Statistics*, vol. 1, p. 76.

[4] Rowland Berthoff, 'Welsh' in Stephan Thernstrom, (ed.), *Harvard Encyclopedia of American Ethnic Groups* (Cambridge, Mass., 1980), pp. 1011-1017, 1013; Williams, 'Some Figures Relating to Emigration from Wales', p. 407.

[5] See, e.g., *Y Drych*, 21 Nov. 1929, 25 July 1935.

[6] *Y Drych*, 24 Mar. 1921.

[7] Utica City Directories; *Y Drych*, 14 Sept. 1922; *Utica Observer-Dispatch*, 9 Sept. 1922.

[8] David M. Ellis, *The Upper Mohawk Country: An Illustrated History of Greater Utica* (Woodland Hills, Calif., 1982). In recent years the building has retained its links with publishing and printing, with the *Utica Herald-Dispatch* and *The Sunday Tribune* being published there. See also photograph on p. 19.

[9] *Y Drych*, 14 Apr. 1951.

[10] *Y Drych*, 29 June, 3 Aug. 1922.

[11] *Y Drych*, 19 Sept. 1929.

[12] *Y Drych*, 15 Aug. 1929, 17 July 1930.

[13] *Y Drych*, 20 Nov. 1930.

[14] *Y Drych*, 1, 8, 15 Feb. 1934.

[15] *Y Drych*, 10 May 1923.

[16] *Y Drych*, 19 Apr. 1923, 9, 26 Mar. 1931.

[17] *Y Drych*, 7 Feb. 1924; *Daily Sentinel* [Rome, N.Y.], 7 Feb. 1924; *Utica Daily Press*, 7 Feb. 1924; *Utica Observer-Dispatch*, 7 Feb. 1924.

[18] *Y Drych*, 15 Apr. 1951.

[19] *Y Drych*, 18, 25 Dec. 1924, 27 June 1929; *Daily Sentinel*, 13 Dec. 1924; *Utica Daily Press*, 13 Dec. 1924; *Utica Observer-Dispatch*, 13 Dec. 1924.

[20] *Y Drych*, 27 June 1929.

[21] For biog. details of Hughes (1870-1945), see *Y Drych*, 10 May 1923, Apr., July, Aug. 1945; *Utica Daily Press*, 30 June 1945; *Utica Observer-Dispatch*, 30 June 1945.

[22] Hughes, *Pryddestau Er Cof am Griffith H. Humphrey*.

[23] *Utica Observer-Dispatch*, 4 Feb. 1945.

[24] *Y Drych*, 13 Sept. 1923. For biog. details of Sallie Evans Surridge (1901-1990), see *Y Drych*, 4 June 1931, 30 June 1932, 13 July 1933, June–July 1990; *Y Gymraes*, Vol. 36 No. 6 (June 1932) pp. 121-123; *Liverpool Echo*, 17 Nov. 1931; *Utica Observer-Dispatch*, 26 Apr. 1931, 26 Apr. 1990.

[25] Tape recording of Sallie Evans Surridge interviewed by her family in the 1982, kindly made available to the authors by her daughter, Judith Heuser.

[26] Jacob Werthman died in a car accident in 1933. He was involved in printing *Y Drych* for 43 years, though his obituary did not disclose in what capacity. *Y Drych*, 15 June 1933.

[27] *Y Drych*, 6 Sept. 1928, 10 Dec. 1931, 28 Sept., 5 Oct. 1933. NLW John W. Jones Papers, E. Hughes to Mr and Mrs E. Williams, 2 Feb. 1930.

[28] *Y Drych*, 21, 28 Apr. 1921.

[29] *Y Drych*, 18 Dec. 1924, 11 Dec. 1930.

[30] *Y Drych*, 30 Apr. 1930.

[31] E.g., letter from Revd J. F. Humphreys, Ithaca, *Y Drych*, 13 Sept. 1923.

[32] *Y Drych*, 23 May 1929.

[33] 'Nid yw mwyafrif yr oes bresenol yn gofalu am lithiau golygyddol meithion, nac am ddadleuon ar bynciau crefyddol ac athronyddol, a llai fyth am gwerylau personol . . . Edrychir yn awr am lithiau byrion a newyddion – (newyddion, sylwch) am y byd a'r bywyd Cymreig yn y Talaethau.' *Y Drych*, 27 June 1929.

[34] *Y Drych*, 9 Oct. 1930.

[35] *Y Drych*, 4 July 1929.

[36] *Y Drych*, 4 Oct. – 15 Nov. 1923; Jones, *Wales in America*, pp. 192-193, 243-44; Thomas Jones, *Lloyd George* (London, 1951), pp. 204-206. See also the accounts of Lloyd George's visit to Niagara Falls by Ellis Hughes, the local *Y Drych* correspondent, and his wife Margaret, NLW John W. Jones Papers, 2543, 2544, E. and M. Hughes to E. Williams (Glyn Myfyr), 23 Oct. 1923; and NLW MS 23265D Megan Lloyd George, Notes on visit to United States and Canada, 1923.

[37] *Y Drych*, 14, 21, 28 Feb., 13, 20 Mar. 1924. See also NLW T. I. Ellis Papers, Class A A359, undated press cutting from *Y Drych* re the Women's Peace Mission.

[38] *Baner ac Amserau* Cymru, 14 Aug. 1928; *Y Drych*, 16 Aug. 1928; *Druid*, 15 Aug. 1928; *Western Mail*, 10 Aug. 1928.

[39] *Y Drych*, 16 Aug. 1928.

[40] See, e.g., *Y Drych*, 4 Aug. 1927, 23 Aug. 1928, 7, 21, 28 Aug. 1930. An editorial on 30 Aug. 1928 commented on the increasing numbers of Welsh Americans who were visiting National Eisteddfodau in Wales during those years.

[41] *Y Drych*, 22 Aug., 5 Sept. 1929, 7, 14, 28 Aug., 4, 11, 25 Sept. 1930, 13, 20 Aug., 3, 17 Sept. 1931, 25 Aug., 22 Sept. 1932. See also *Y Drych* Special Gymanfa Edition, 2 Sept. 1999.

[42] *Y Drych*, 8 Apr., 14 Oct. 1926, 1 Sept., 29 Dec. 1927, 4 Apr. 1929.

[43] *Y Drych*, 11, 25 Nov. 1926.

[44] *Y Drych*, 24 Mar. 1927.

[45] *Y Drych*, 24 Jan. 1929; *Utica Daily Press*, 22 Jan. 1929.

[46] *Y Drych*, 4 Apr. 1929.

[47] See, e.g., *Y Drych*, 14 Mar. 1929.

[48] *Y Drych*, 11 Sept. 1930.

[49] *Y Drych*, 27 June 1929. It appears *Y Drych* celebrated its birthday in June because during these years many of the paper's staff and writers believed it had first been published in June not January 1851. By now many of the pioneers who had been associated with it since the mid-nineteenth century had passed away and the paper's library of previous issues had been destroyed in the 1924 fire.

[50] ' . . . wedi dyfod yn fwy na newyddiadur. Gellir ei alw yn sefydliad pwysig. . . . Efe sydd yn cadw y teulu Cymreig ar y cyfandir hwn mewn adnabyddiaeth a'u gilydd. Trwyddo ef yn unig y gellir cario yn mlaen unrhyw fudiad Cymreig yn yr America. Yr oedd ei ddyfodiad 78 mlynedd yn ol yn bwysig i'r genedl, ond y mae ei barhad heddyw

yn fwy pwysig.' *Y Drych*, 27 June 1929. For similar sentiments, see editorial article, 4 Feb. 1926.

[51] *Y Drych*, 19 Aug. 1926.

[52] *Y Drych*, 4 June, 6, 13, 27 Aug., 24 Sept. 1931; Information provided by her daughter, Judith Heuser. Strangely, around this time there appears to be no reference in the paper that Evans had taken over as editor.

[53] *Y Gymraes*, Vol. 36 No. 6 (June 1932) pp. 121-123.

[54] Tape recording of Sallie Evans Surridge interviewed by her family in the 1982.

[55] *Y Drych*, 13 July 1933.

[56] *Y Drych*, 14, 28 Apr., 20 July 1933, 13 Aug., 19 Nov. 1936.

[57] *Y Drych*. 25 Aug., 8 Sept. 1932.

[58] *Y Drych*, 26 June 1924.

[59] Donald R. McCoy, *Coming of Age: The United States during the 1920s and 1930s* (Harmondsworth, 1973).

[60] Anthony J. Badger, *The New Deal: The Depression Years, 1933-1940* (London, 1989), p. 18.

[61] *Y Drych*, 16 Jan., 13 Mar. 1930, 2 Mar. 1933.

[62] *Y Drych*, 30 July 1930, 6, 27 Oct., 17 Nov. 1932.

[63] *Y Drych*, 3 Nov. 1932, 9 Mar., 3 Aug. 1933. For the N.R.A., see Badger, *The New Deal*, pp. 73-94.

[64] *Y Drych*, 12 Nov. 1936.

[65] Margaret Ellis Blabey, David Maldwyn Ellis and Sarah Ellis Ward, 'Growing up Welsh', *Ninnau*, Vol. 11 Nos. 3–5 (1 Jan.–1 Mar. 1986), Vol. 11 No. 3, p. 24.

[66] *Y Drych*, May 1945; *Utica Observer-Dispatch*, 4 Feb. 1945. For articles that link Roosevelt with the 'Welsh liberal democratic movement', see Sam Ellis, 'Sosialaeth', *Y Drych*, 14 Mar. 1940, and 'Roosevelt from a Welsh Viewpoint', *Y Drych*, 15 June 1945.

[67] See, e.g., *Y Drych*, 22 Jan. 1931, 10 Jan., 16 May, 28 Nov. 1935, 9 Jan. 1936; Utica College, Welsh Collection, Utica Eisteddfod Programme, 31 Dec. 1929–1 Jan. 1930, advertisement for *Y Drych*.

[68] *Y Drych*, 6, 13, 20 Nov. 1930, 1 Oct. 1931.

[69] *Y Drych*, 27 Oct. 1932.

[70] *Y Drych*, 15 June 1933.

[71] ' . . . oherwydd diffyg cefnogaeth ariannol llawer o'r derbynwyr a achosir gan y dirwasgiad mawr presennol'. *Y Drych*, 6 July 1933. See also 15 June 1933 for an English-language version of this announcement.

[72] *Y Drych*, 6 July 1933.

[73] *Y Drych*, 26 Oct. 1933.

[74] See, e.g., a supportive editorial article in *Y Drych*, 30 Mar. 1933.

[75] See *Y Drych*, 27 Feb. 1936 onwards. The columns were penned by 'Cenedlaetholwr' [Nationalist], who explained in the first one that s/he had been invited by the editor to write them after having complained that the paper had misrepresented the party's policies.

[76] *Y Drych*, 1, 8, 15 Oct., 5 Nov., 10 Dec. 1936, 4, 11, 18, 25 Feb. 1937. For Penyberth, see Dafydd Jenkins, *Nation on Trial, Penyberth, 1936* (Cardiff, 1996).

[77] *Y Drych*, 2, 16, 23 Sept. 1937. From 21 Apr. 1938 onwards *Y Drych* printed a series of articles in which Valentine described his gaol experiences.

[78] *Y Drych*, 4, 26 Nov. 1926.

[79] *Y Drych*, 6 Apr., 7 Dec. 1933, 28 June, 12 July, 18 Oct. 1934, 28 Mar., 6 June, 8 Aug. 1935, 10 June 1937.

[80] *Y Drych*, 19 July 1934, 29 Aug. 1935, 28 Sept. 1939.

[81] *Y Drych*, 25 Nov. 1937, 1, 29 Dec. 1938, 30 Nov., 21, 28 Dec. 1939.

[82] '. . . fel cenedl ar ddisperod, wedi colli ein hunaniaeth, neu blant heb eu mam, a chywion ieir, heb yr iar'. *Y Drych*, 24 Jan. 1929.

[83] '. . . [d]diwedd y bywyd Cymreig yn America fel uned'. *Y Drych*, 21 Dec. 1939.

[84] *Y Drych*, 30 Nov. 1939.

[85] '. . . mewn geiriau, ac mewn gweithred'. *Y Drych*, 28 Dec. 1939.

[86] *Y Drych*, 26 Dec. 1940.

[87] *Y Drych*, 15 Jan. 1941.

[88] *Y Drych*, 15 Apr. 1951.

[89] 'Pleser gennym fydd ei gyhoeddi yn amlach na bob mis os ceir cydweithrediad Cymry America i wneud hynny'n bosibl.' *Y Drych*, 26 Dec. 1940.

[90] *Y Drych*, 15 Jan., 15 Feb. 1941.

[91] '. . . rhyw wagle rhyfedd yr wythnosau cydrhwng y rhifynnau'. *Y Drych*, 15 Feb. 1941.

[92] NLW Carneddog Papers, G806, John T. Jones, Criccieth, to Carneddog, 17 Mar. 1941.

[93] '. . . yn ddiddorol i Gymry'n gwlad'. *Y Drych*, 15 Jan. 1941.

[94] *Y Drych*, 15 Jan. 1941.

[95] *Y Drych*, 8 Feb., 11 July 1940.

[96] 'Ceir arwyddion amlwg nad yw'n gwlad wedi sylweddoli hyd yn hyn faint ei pherygl. . . . Ffol ydyw ceisio credu y gwarchoda'r Werydd a'r Tawelfor ein gwlad rhag ymosodiadau'r gelyn. . . . Anghofier y boced a'r pwrs am gyfnod a meithrinier yr ysbryd hwnnw yn ein plith a sicrha help i Brydain a diogelwch i America.' *Y Drych*, 15 June 1941.

[97] 'Dyletswydd a braint pob Cymro yn America ydyw gwneud a eill i helpu ei wlad fabwysiedig.' *Y Drych*, 15 Dec. 1941.

[98] *Y Drych*, 21 Mar. 1940 onwards.

[99] See, e.g., *Y Drych*, 15 Jan., 15 Feb, 15 July 1941.

[100] *Y Drych*, 15 July, 15 Nov. 1941.

[101] *Y Drych*, 15 Apr. 1945; Polk and Co.'s *Utica City Directories*, 1947, 1950.

[102] *Y Drych*, 15 July 1945.

[103] . . . yn gwynebu amgylchiadau sydd yn anffafriol i gynydd ac yn aml bydd hyn yn achos o bryder am ei ddyfodol, ond hyd yn hyn y mae wedi gallu cyfarfod pob cyfnewidiad yn llwyddianus, a gobeithir mai dyma fydd ei hanes yn y blynyddoedd i ddyfod.' *Y Drych*, 23 May 1929.

[104] *Y Drych*, 28 Jan. 1936.

CHAPTER 6

¹ 'Nid gwaith hawdd ydyw rhedeg y Drych, yn neillduol yn y cyfnod presenol yn hanes Cymry yr America.' *Y Drych*, 14 June 1928.

² '. . . ac fe ddywedodd rhai wrthyf eu bod am ei roddi fyny os y bydd cymaint o Saesneg yn cael ymddangos ar ei dudalenau.' *Y Drych*, 14 June 1928.

³ *Y Drych*, 14 June 1928.

⁴ *Y Drych*, 2 Aug. 1928.

⁵ 'Y mae y Saesneg yn tori i mewn yn mhob man y dyddiau hyn, yn neillduol yn y wlad hon. Nid oes teulu Cymreig yn y wlad nad yw yr "iaith fain" i'w chlywed ar yr aelwyd. Ychydig yw nifer ein cymdeithasau sydd yn hollol Gymreig. Felly ein heglwysi. Yn mhob ardal Gymreig gwelir adfeilion hen gapelau Cymreig megis cof-golofnau i dranc yr iaith. Y mae ein Heisteddfodau hefyd yn lle Seisnigaidd. Yn ddiweddar y mae y Saesneg wedi ymddangos ar faes y Drych a hyny mewn canlyniad i'r cyfnewidiadau uchod.' *Y Drych*, 14 June 1928.

⁶ Miller, *Ethnic Press*, pp. xiii, xvi, xvii.

⁷ Ulf Beijbom, 'The Swedish Press' in Miller, *Ethnic Press*, pp. 379-392, 385.

⁸ Joshua A. Fishman, Robert G. Hayden and Mary E. Warshauer, 'The Non-English and Ethnic Group Press, 1910-1960' in Fishman et. al., *Language Loyalty in the United States*, pp. 51-74.

⁹ Miller, p. xvi.

¹⁰ Emrys Jones, 'Some aspects of cultural change in an American Welsh community', *Transactions of the Honourable Society of Cymmrodorion* (1952), pp. 15-41, 21.

¹¹ For studies of language shift among the Welsh in America, see Jones, 'Some aspects of cultural change in an American Welsh community', p. 21; Jones, 'The Welsh Language and Welsh Identity in a Pennsylvanian Community'; Williams, 'The Welsh of Columbus', esp. pp. 105-136.

¹² *Y Drych*, 19 Jan. 1933; Phillips G. Davies, 'The Welsh Settlements in Minnesota: The Evidence of the Churches in Blue Earth and Le Sueur Counties', *Welsh History Review*, Vol. 13 No. 2 (1986) pp. 139-54; Ellis, 'The Assimilation of the Welsh in Central New York', *New York History* and *Welsh History Review*; idem, 'Cwm Rhondda: The Welsh in Utica'; Jones, 'Some aspects of cultural change in an American Welsh community'; Anne Kelly Knowles, *Calvinists Incorporated: Welsh Immigrants in Ohio's Industrial Frontier* (Chicago, 1996), pp. 221-224; idem, 'Religious Identity as Ethnic Identity: the Welsh in Waukesha County' in R. C. Ostergren and T. R. Vale (eds.), *Wisconsin Land and Life* (Madison, Wis., 1997), pp. 282-299.

¹³ *Y Drych*, 8 Feb. 1923.

¹⁴ NLW John W. Jones Papers, 2547, E. Hughes to E. Williams (Glyn Myfyr), 1 Dec. [1930?].

¹⁵ NLW John W. Jones Papers, 2546, E. Hughes to Mr and Mrs E. Williams, 2 Feb. 1930.

¹⁶ NLW Carneddog Papers, G809 John W. Jones (Ioan Eryri), Poulteney, Vt., to R. E. Jones, 18 March 1927; G1964 Thomas Charles Williams, Seattle, Wash., to Carneddog, 5 Dec. 1937. Williams was *Y Drych*'s Seattle correspondent.

¹⁷ ' . . . darfod y mae'r iaith Gymraeg yn y lle hwn. Y mae wedi darfod yn drybeilig y

deng mlynedd diweddaf yma.' NLW Carneddog Papers G1331, Ifan Morris Powell to Carneddog, 11 Dec 1934. For similar opinions see G1320, Powell to Carneddog, 4 Mar. 1927.

[18] *Y Drych*, 22 Mar. 1923, 19 Jan. 1933.

[19] For a good example of concern for the future of *Y Drych* because of the detrimental influences discussed here, see letter by 'Un yn Caru Ei Iaith' [One who Loves His Language], *Y Drych*, 25 Apr. 1929.

[20] See, e.g., *Y Drych*, 24 Mar. 1921, 12 Apr. 1923.

[21] *Y Drych*, 9 Jan. 1936. Similarly, see also letter by Robert D. Roberts, 15 Jan. 1941.

[22] See, e.g., *Y Drych*, 26 Apr. 1923, 2 Aug. 1928, 16 May 1935.

[23] See, e.g., *Y Drych*, 21 June, 2 Aug. 1928.

[24] *Y Drych*, 26 Apr. 1923.

[25] *Y Drych*, 22 Mar., 12 Apr. 1923, 16 May 1935.

[26] '. . . nid wedi dod yma yr oeddym i gadw yr iaith yn fyw, ond i gadw ein hunain yn fyw'. *Y Drych*, 22 Mar. 1923.

[27] *Y Drych*, 22 Mar., 12 Apr. 1923.

[28] '. . . yn fwy o Gymry nag o Americaniaid . . . fod yr Unol Dalaethau mor anwyl i'n plant ag yw Cymru i ni.' *Y Drych*, 19 Jan. 1933.

[29] '. . . ymdrechu gwthio yr hen iaith dros y trothwy i ebargofiant am byth, fel y mae llawer yn ceisio gwneyd'. *Y Drych*, 6 Apr. 1933.

[30] Jones, 'Some aspects of cultural change in an American Welsh community', pp. 27-28.

[31] *Y Drych*, 20 Nov. 1930.

[32] Jones, 'Some aspects of cultural change in an American Welsh community', p. 21. See also Jones, 'The Welsh Language and Welsh Identity in a Pennsylvanian Community'.

[33] Jones, 'Some aspects of cultural change in an American Welsh community', p. 19.

[34] *Y Drych*, 15 July 1951.

[35] 'Yr ydym yn cael ein beichio yn ddirfawr gan ysgrifau anmherffaith iawn'. *Y Drych*, 13 Feb. 1919.

[36] *Y Drych*, 18 Mar. 1926.

[37] *Y Drych*, 6 Mar. 1924.

[38] '. . . rhagod y Seisneg rhag rhuthro i fewn i golofnau y DRYCH'; '. . . i groesi y Clawdd Offa ag oedd y cyn-olygydd wedi ei godi i gadw y Seisneg allan am dymor, o leiaf, hyd y cai yr Hen Iaith dawelwch i farw.' *Y Drych*, 10 May 1923.

[39] '. . . ni welwn ein ffordd yn glir eto i wneyd hyny'. *Y Drych*, 28 Mar. 1918. See also 31 Oct. 1912, 27 July 1916, 10 July 1919, and for a letter urging him to print English-language material around this time, see 10 June 1920.

[40] '. . . i bwysleisio y pwysigrwydd o gadw yr iaith yn fyw'. *Y Drych*, 10 May 1923. According to one source, the introduction of English into *Y Drych* had been a Hugh Hughes innovation and it had brought wails of anguish from older subscribers. The content analysis does not bear out the first contention but there is plenty of supportive evidence for the second. *Utica Observer-Dispatch*, 4 Feb. 1945.

[41] ' . . . cadw yr ysbryd cenedlaethol yn fyw yn ei agweddau goreu'. *Y Drych*, 14 June 1928.

[42] 'Os gwelir y gellir hyrwyddo yr amcanion hyn trwy ganiatau gohebiaeth Seisnig yn achlysurol, ni wrthodir gwneyd hyny. Yr ydym am ymladd y bwgan Seisnigaidd ar ei dir ei hun, gan gyfoethogi a nerthu y bywyd Cymreig. . . . Nid ceisio troi y Drych yn Saesneg wneir trwy ganiatau ambell i ysgrif yn yr iaith fain, eithr yr amcan ydyw gwneyd y papyr yn fwy o ddylanwad yn y byd Americanaidd Cymreig. Na fydded i'n hen gyfeillion ofni. . . . Ni chaiff y Saesneg ymddangos ond pan y gwasanaetha y Cymry a'r Gymraeg.' *Y Drych*, 14 June 1928.

[43] See, e.g., *Y Drych*, 22, 29 Sept., 13 Oct. 1932.

[44] These were first introduced in English on 10 Nov. 1932 and in Welsh on 17 Nov. 1932.

[45] Sam Ellis (1876-1960) was born near Llanfyllin, Montgomeryshire, and after a period as a milk dealer in Pontypridd, emigrated to New York State in 1898. He eventually became a store-keeper in Utica and his wife Margaret Jones (m. 1908) worked in one of the mills in the city for a time. His collection of stories *Ann y Foty yn Myn'd i'r Mor ac Ystraeon Eraill* (Utica, 1913) draws on his Montgomeryshire childhood (see also advertisement for this in *Y Drych*, e.g., 1 Oct. 1914). For biog. details, see *Y Drych*, Nov. 1960, and the recollections of his children, Margaret Ellis Blabey, David Maldwyn Ellis (historian of the Welsh in Utica and Oneida County), and Sarah Ellis Ward, 'Growing up Welsh' [Part 1], *Ninnau*, Vol. 11 No. 3 (1 Jan. 1986), p. 24. For Sam Ellis' columns, and opinions on them, see, e.g., *Y Drych*, 20 Jan. 1921, 5 June 1924, 26 Sept. 1929, 20 Feb. 1930, 23 June 1932. He continued writing for the paper in both Welsh and English until the 1950s.

[46] ' . . . y to ieuanc, a thrwy hyny estyn ei oes a'i ddefnyddioldeb. Nis gwn a lwyddir i wneyd hyny ai peidio.' *Y Drych*, 19 Jan. 1933.

[47] See, e.g., *Y Drych*, 20 Mar. 1933.

[48] ' . . . nid diffyg cenedlgarwch . . . eithr awydd am i'r Drych allu cyraedd nifer o'r Cymry-Americanaidd, na allant fwynhau'r Gymraeg.' 'Os gallwn eangu cylchrededd y Drych yn mhlith yr ieuenctyd drwy gyhoeddi mwy o Saesneg ynddo, dylem foddloni i'r drefn.' *Y Drych*, 19 Jan. 1933.

[49] *Y Drych*, 15 June 1933.

[50] 'Gwnaed ymdrech deg i geisio cyfarfod a chwaeth pawb. Cafwyd congl glud i'r beirdd cyfrif eu bysedd i benderfynu pa mor llyfn y rhedai'r llinellau, bara angylion ar gyfer rhai sydd wedi magu adenydd i esgyn i fyd uwch, a digon o fara dynion i'r bobl sydd hoff ganddynt ymgom a 'paned te. Rhoddwyd hefyd gryn dipyn o waed ieuanc i mewn, ac edrychai y Drych fel pe bai gwrid bywyd newydd yn dod i'w ruddiau. Aeth rhai i deimlo yn eiddigeddus am i'r twrch trwyth wthio'i drwyn i mewn a Seisnigeiddio yr unig gyhoeddiad y gallai'r hen Gymro ddweud ei gyfrinion wrtho, ond erbyn hyn ymddengys fel pe bai'r twrch wedi ei shipio i Chicago, inni wneud yr un peth ag a wneir yma a phob twrch arall.' *Y Drych*, 3 Aug. 1933.

[51] ' . . . a besgwyd am dros bedwar ugain mlynedd ar ymborth enaid dyfnaf, a meddwl uchaf ein cenedl.' *Y Drych*, 3 Aug. 1933.

[52] 'Nid wyf yn cael y Drych ers blwyddyn . . . . Anaml iawn y byddaf yn ei weled o gwbwl. . . . Y mae gormod o Saesneg o ddim rheswm ynddo. Torrwyd ef yn ei hanner er mwyn iddo fod yn newyddiadur mwy Cymreig. Ond y mae y Saesneg yn ennill tir eto gyda'r hanner arall. Fei llyncir oll yn y man gan y Behemoth Seisnig. Ac yna y daw y diwedd.' NLW Carneddog Papers, G1331, Ifan Morris Powell to Carneddog, 11 Dec. 1934.

[53] 'Amhosibl i wir Gymro yw anghofio ei Gymraeg er iddo fyw mewn cylch hollol Americanaidd. Os ydym wir Gymry dylem fedru siarad iaith Cymru . . . NID CYMRO HEB GYMRAEG'. *Y Drych*, 16 May 1935

[54] *Y Drych*, 15 Aug. 1945.

[55] *Y Drych*, 15 July 1951.

[56] Jones, 'Some aspects of cultural change in an American Welsh community', p. 21.

[57] *Y Drych*, 15 Feb. 1951.

[58] Fishman, 'The Non-English and Ethnic Group Press, 1910-1960', pp. 62-63.

[59] See, e.g., *Y Drych*, 23 Nov. 1865, 14, 21 May 1868.

CHAPTER 7

[1] *Y Drych*, 15 Dec. 1956.

[2] Fishman et. al., 'The Non-English and Ethnic Group Press, 1910-1960', p. 61.

[3] Berthoff, 'Welsh', p. 1013.

[4] *Historical Statistics of the United States*, p. 66; Williams, *Digest of Welsh Historical Statistics*, vol. 1, p. 76; Berthoff, 'Welsh', p. 1013.

[5] David Greenslade, *Welsh Fever: Welsh Activities in the United States and Canada Today* (Cowbridge, 1986).

[6] For biog. details of Arthur M. Roberts (1892-1973), see NLW Huw T. Edwards Papers, A1/41 Arthur M. Roberts to Huw T. Edwards, 27 June 1949; *Y Drych*, 15 Aug. 1945, 15 Apr. 1951, May-June 1960, Aug. 1973; *Utica Daily Press*, 7 Mar., 1945, 22 May 1973; *Utica Observer-Dispatch*, 18 Nov. 1956, 22 May 1973.

[7] *Y Drych*, 30 June 1898.

[8] *Y Drych*, 15 July 1951.

[9] *Y Drych*, 15 May 1951, 15 Mar. 1957, May–June 1960.

[10] *Y Drych*, 15 Mar. 1949.

[11] *Y Drych*, 15 Oct., 15 Dec. 1946.

[12] *Y Drych*, 15 Aug. 1946, 15 Mar. 1947.

[13] *Y Drych*, 15 Mar. 1949.

[14] *Y Drych*, 15 July 1946. For the Women's Welsh Clubs of America, see *Druid*, 1 Nov. 1919, 1 June 1924, and for Hasenpflug, see also *Druid*, 1 July 1923; *Y Drych*, 15 Oct. 1947.

[15] *Y Drych*, 15 July 1947.

[16] See, e.g., 15 June, 15 July 1947, 15 Oct. 1949, 15 Sept., 15 Oct. 1959.

[17] Ioan Euron, Slatington, Pa., *Y Drych*, 10 June 1920, 19 Sept. 1929.

[18] Meirionferch was originally from Blaenau Ffestininog, and was an active worker in Welsh circles in the city, including being a deacon in the Welsh church. *Y Drych*, 13 Jan. 1927, 1 May 1930, 15 Apr. 1943, 15 Apr. 1947, 15 Oct. 1949.

¹⁹ *Y Drych*, 6 Apr. 1933, 15 Oct. 1954. Daisy Williams (maiden name unknown), who died in 1954 aged 69, was originally from Redfield, S.D., and wrote under the name of Mrs Griff Williams. For examples of her writings, see 3 Nov. 1932, 5 Jan. 1933, 22 Feb. 1940 (news), 25 July 1935 (on the Welsh language) and 5 Sept. 1935 (interview with the Asian missionary Dr Harriet Davies, herself a contributor to *Y Drych* and a subscriber who regarded the paper as 'a friend which comes to her regularly wherever she is').

²⁰ *Y Drych*, 29 Sept. 1927, 14 July 1932, 15 Sept. 1949. For a feature article on R. D. Evans, see 23 July 1925.

²¹ *Y Drych*, 20 June 1935; Private letter, Esther Baran to *Y Drych*, October 1998. For Caernarfon Eisteddfod reports etc., see *Y Drych*, 25 July, 22 Aug., 3, 24 Oct. 1935. For Racine reports see 18 Jan., 11 Apr. 1940, 15 Sept. 1959, July 1961, March 1964.

²² See, e.g., *Y Drych*, 15 Jan. 1949, 15 Jan. 1951, Oct. 1973, Mar. 1986. For a feature on Jones herself, see 15 Dec. 1948.

²³ *Y Drych*, 15 June, 15 Oct. 1948.

²⁴ A native of Slatington, Parry died in 1962. She had been a poet, vocalist and writer for local newspapers as well as for *Y Drych* and *The Cambrian*. *Y Drych*, June 1962. For examples of columns see 19, 26 Mar. 1935, 10 Aug. 1939, 11 Apr. 1940, 15 Sept. 1949, 15 Sept. 1959.

²⁵ *Y Drych*, 15 Apr. 1951. Beaupre seems to have begun writing for the paper on an occasional basis in 1940, and from around 1945 through to the 1960s her columns appeared every month, almost without fail. *Y Drych*, 25 Apr. 1940, Sept. 1965. For Mary King Sarah (1885-1965), see *Y Drych*, 18 Nov. 1909, 15 Feb. 1952, 15 Sept. 1959, Dec. 1965. For her columns, see, e.g., 15 July 1949, 15 Oct. 1951, 15 Oct. 1957, 15 Nov. 1959.

²⁶ NLW Huw T. Edwards Papers, A1/41 Arthur M. Roberts to Huw T. Edwards, 27 June 1949.

²⁷ *Y Drych*, 15 Oct. 1948.

²⁸ *Y Drych*, 15 Jan., 15 Feb., 15 Mar. 1947.

²⁹ *Y Drych*, 15 Nov. 1949.

³⁰ *Y Drych*, 15 Dec. 1950.

³¹ *Y Drych*, 15 Apr. 1951.

³² *Y Drych*, 15 July 1951.

³³ *Y Drych*, 15 May 1951.

³⁴ *Utica Observer-Dispatch*, 18 Nov. 1956, reprinted in *Y Drych*, 15 Dec. 1956.

³⁵ *Y Drych*, 15 Aug., 15 Oct. 1959.

³⁶ *Y Drych*, 15 Apr. 1960.

³⁷ *Y Drych*, May-June 1960.

³⁸ *Y Drych*, May-June 1960.

³⁹ *Y Drych*, June 1960.

⁴⁰ *Y Drych*, July 1960.

⁴¹ Phillips G. Davies, *The Welsh in Wisconsin* (Madison, Wis., 1982); Knowles, 'Religious Identity as Ethnic Identity'; Daniel Jenkins Williams, *The Welsh Community of Waukesha County* (Columbus, Ohio, 1926).

⁴² For biog. details of Horace Breese Powell (1897-1980), see *Y Drych*, July 1960, Oct. 1980.

[43] Letter from Patricia Powell Viets, Powell's daughter and herself editor and owner of *Y Drych*, 1980-89, to the authors, 3 Sept. 2000.

[44] *Y Drych,* Feb. 1972, Oct. 1980.

[45] *Y Drych,* Oct. 1980; Letter, Patricia Powell Viets to the authors, 3 Sept. 2000.

[46] *Y Drych*, Nov. 1960, Oct. 1963, Nov. 1970, Jan.-Mar. 1979.

[47] *Y Drych*, July 1960.

[48] *Y Drych*, Jan. 1978, July-Aug.-Sept.-Oct. 1978, Jan.-Mar. 1979. Subscriptions had been raised from $2 to $3 at the end of 1952. *Y Drych*, 15 Nov. 1952.

[49] *Y Drych*, Jan.-Feb. 1980, May 1982.

[50] *Y Drych*, June 1971.

[51] *Y Drych*, June 1971, July 1972.

[52] See, e.g., *Y Drych*, Apr. 1974, Nov. 1975.

[53] *Y Drych*, Nov. 1971 – May 1972.

[54] See, e.g., *Y Drych*, May 1972, Aug. 1977.

[55] See e.g., Jan. 1969, Nov. 1971.

[56] *Y Drych*, May, June 1972, Mar. 1974, Apr. 1975.

[57] See e.g., *Y Drych*, Apr. 1970, Mar., July 1972, July 1973.

[58] *Y Drych*, June, Sept. 1973.

[59] Y Drych, Nov. 1963.

[60] *Y Drych*, Oct. 1971.

[61] See, e.g., *Y Drych,* Sept. 1989.

[62] *Y Drych*, Oct. 1972, Mar. 1989.

[63] *Ninnau*, 1 Dec. 1980; Greenslade, *Welsh Fever*, pp. 104-105, 209-210.

[64] *Y Drych*, Jan., June-July 1989, Dec. 2000. See also Greenslade, *Welsh Fever*, esp. pp. 167-169.

[65] See, e.g., *Y Drych*, Aug. 1989, Mar. 2001.

[66] *Y Drych*, Apr. 1995.

[67] Letter, Patricia Powell Viets to the authors, 3 Sept. 2000.

[68] For biog. details of Patricia Powell Viets, see *Y Drych*, Oct. 1980; Greenslade, *Welsh Fever*, passim.

[69] Letter, Patricia Powell Viets to the authors, 3 Sept. 2000.

[70] *Y Drych*, May 1989.

[71] Letter, Patricia Powell Viets to the authors, 3 Sept. 2000; *Y Drych*, May 1989; Greenslade, *Welsh Fever*, pp. 97-98.

[72] *Y Drych*, Oct. 1980.

[73] See, e.g., *Y Drych*, Apr., June 1981, Sept., Dec. 1985, Oct. 1988.

[74] *Y Drych*, June 1981, Oct. 1982, Oct. 1988.

[75] *Y Drych*, Nov. 1981 (report on Welsh classes in Seattle and Waukesha, Wis.).

[76] *Y Drych*, Oct., Nov., 1981.

[77] See, e.g., Feb. 1974.

[78] *Y Drych*, Dec. 1985.

[79] See, e.g., Feb. 1989.

[80] See, e.g., Sept. 1985, Oct. 1988.

[81] *Y Drych*, Dec. 1980, Dec. 1981, Dec. 1982, Dec. 1985.

[82] Greenslade, *Welsh Fever*, pp. 96-98, 112-113.

[83] *Y Drych*, May 1989; Letter, Patricia Powell Viets to the authors, 3 Sept. 2000.

[84] *Y Drych*, May 1989, Feb. 1995. *Minnesota Women's Press*, 9 Aug. 1995, provided by Mary Morris Mergenthal.

[85] *Y Drych*, Feb. 1995.

[86] *Y Drych*, May 1989, Feb. 1995. *Minnesota Women's Press*, 9 Aug. 1995.

[87] *Y Drych*, May 1989; *Minnesota Women's Press*, 9 Aug. 1995.

[88] *Y Drych*, May 1991, Sept. 1995.

[89] *Y Drych*, June-July 1991, Feb. 1992, Jan. 1998.

[90] See e.g., May 1991 (photo and text feature on the 'Seven Wonders of North Wales'), Dec. 2000.

[91] See, e.g., Apr. 1990, May 1991, May 1996, May 1997, Feb. 2000.

[92] See, e.g., May 1996, Nov. 1999.

[93] *Y Drych*, June-July 1989.

[94] See, e.g., May 1991, May 1996, May 1997, Jan. 2001.

[95] See, e.g., Sept., Dec. 1990, Nov. 1999.

[96] *Y Drych*, June-July 1989.

[97] *Y Drych*, Jan. 1995, Jan 2000.

[98] See, e.g., *Y Drych*, April, Dec. 1990, Aug., Sept. 1992, Sept., 1994, Dec. 2000.

[99] *Y Drych*, Dec. 2000. See also congratulatory message, Jan. 2001.

[100] *Y* Drych, June-July 1989, and see, e.g., May 1990, Jan. 1991, Sept. 1995, May 1997.

[101] Fishman , 'The Non-English and Ethnic Group Press, 1910-1960', p. 71.

[102] *Y Drych*, Feb. 2001.

[103] See, e.g., May 1991, Nov. 1995, Aug. 2000, Jan. 2001.

[104] First introduced May 1998, and see also accompanying comment by the editor. For other examples of the column, see *Y Drych*, May, Nov. 1999.

[105] See, e.g., *Y Drych*, Apr. 1981, Sept., Dec. 1985, Feb., Mar. 1986, Jan., Feb. 1987, June–July 1990, Aug. 1994.

[106] *Y Drych*, Mar. 1991, Feb. 1996, Jan. 2001.

[107] *Y Drych*, Feb. 2001.

CONCLUSION

[1] *Y Drych*, 27 June 1929.

[2] Vecoli, 'The Italian Immigrant Press', pp. 18-19.

Bibliography

Note: The Primary Sources section includes material consulted but not necessarily used in the text. Secondary Sources are works cited in the text only.

Primary Sources

Manuscript and other collections including files of *Y Drych* containing copies not available in other repositories

United States of America
American Antiquarian Society Library, Worcester, Massachusetts:
Copies of *Y Drych*, 23 July 1853, 28 Mar. 1858, 28 Dec. 1865, 25 Mar. 1869

Huntington Library, San Marino, California:
Copy of *Y Drych*, 1 Dec. 1860

New York State Historical Association Research Library, Cooperstown, New York:
Copies of *Y Drych*, 11 June 1859, 9, 23 Nov. 1865; *Y Drych a'r Gwyliedydd*, 22 Feb., 1 Mar., 21 June, 18 Oct., 22, 29 Nov. 1855, 1 Mar. 1856

Oneida County Historical Society, Utica, New York:
Photographic sources

Remsen-Steuben Historical Society, Remsen, New York:
Newspapers, press cuttings, photographs and other primary sources relating to the Welsh in Central New York
Y Drych file
Hugh Hughes papers, including 'The Welsh in Utica, N.Y.' (unpub. MSS, undated)

Utica College of Syracuse University, Utica, New York:
Welsh Collection incl. Welsh imprints of Central New York; files of Welsh-American newspapers and periodicals incl. *Y Drych*, 12 May 1860, not available elsewhere; Utica Eisteddfod and National Gymanfa Ganu programmes.

Utica Public Library, New York:
Photographic sources

Note: Extended files of *Y Drych* from the nineteenth century are also held at the Balch Institute for Ethnic Studies, Philadelphia, and Harvard University

Wales
Bangor University:
Files of *Y Drych*

Cardiff Central Library:
Files of *Y Drych*

Cardiff University:
Sal. MSS 218 Bob Owen, 'Bywgraffiadau Cymry Americanaidd' (unpublished typescript, 1960)

National Library of Wales, Aberystwyth:
Brythonydd Papers, 15836E, Cuttings from *Baner America*, *Y Drych*, *Y Wasg*, 1872-81, compiled by Cynfelin.
Carneddog Papers, G196, Letter, John 'Cwmcloch' [Evans], Negunda, Nebraska, to Carneddog, 15 Dec. 1902
Carneddog Papers, G777, Letter, John Elias Jones, Milwaukee to Carneddog, 30 Aug. 1928
Carneddog Papers, G806, Letter, John T. Jones, Criccieth, to Carneddog, 17 Mar. 1941
Carneddog Papers, G809, Letter, John W. Jones (Ioan Eryri), Poultney, Vt., to R. E. Jones, 18 Mar. 1927
Carneddog Papers, G1173, Letter, William Morris, Stockport, to Carneddog, 16 Oct. 1929
Carneddog Papers, G1331, Letters, Ifan Morris Powell to Carneddog, 4 Mar. 1927, 11 Dec. 1934
Carneddog Papers, G1372, Letter, Ieuan Fardd (Daniel E. Richards) to Carneddog, 7 Jan. 1938
Carneddog Papers, G1964, Letter, Thomas Charles Williams, Seattle, Wash., to Carneddog, 5 Dec. 1937
Cwrtmawr Papers, 1A, MS 50E Cuttings from *Y Drych*
Cwrtmawr Papers, 1A, MS 73C Letter, John W. Jones to Ebenezer Thomas (Eben Fardd) 2 Feb. 1856
Cwrtmawr Papers, 1C, MS 202B Cuttings from *Y Drych*
Cwrtmawr Papers, 3, MS555B, MS564, Extract from *Y Drych*
Cwrtmawr Papers, 3, MS731C, 739C, 752C, 753B, 815C, Cuttings from *Y Drych* compiled by John Jones
Huw T. Edwards Papers, A1/41, Letter, Arthur M. Roberts to Huw T. Edwards, 27 June 1949; A1/538, Letter, Eirwen Jones to Huw T. Edwards, 24 July [1959]
T. I. Ellis Papers, A359, Press cuttings, 1924, many from *Y Drych*, relating to the Women's Peace Memorial
Gee MSS, X Misc X6, press cutting, S.R., 'Y Gogledd a'r De', *Y Drych*, 11 May 1861
E. Morgan Humphreys Papers, A/3720, Letter, W. Owen Williams, Wilkesbarre, to E. Morgan Humphreys, 8 Feb. 1932
John W. Jones Papers, 2543-2548, Letters, E. and M. Hughes to E. Williams (Glyn Myfyr), 1923-1930
Kitty Idwal Jones Papers, MS 38, Miscellaneous issues of *Y Drych*, 1930-2
Bob Owen Papers, 3/13, Selections from *Y Drych a'r Gwyliedydd*, 1856
Bob Owen Papers, 23/7, 10; 24/4, 6-9, 11-12, Cuttings from *Y Drych*
Bob Owen Papers, 31/21, Notes from *Y Drych a'r Gwyliedydd*, 3 Jan.-Dec. 1857 and from *Y Drych*, Jan 1899-1900
MS 2834B f. 47. Account of a Tour of the USA by David Samwel, 1889

MS 3191C Letters, W. D. Davies to Daniel Davies, Ton [Rhondda], 1 Jan. 1883, 12 Mar. 1885

MS 3265, Letters, T. J. Griffiths to Samuel Roberts, 22 Feb. 1881, Samuel Roberts to T. J. Griffiths, 21 Jan. 1882, John C. Roberts to Revd John Davies, Spring Green, Wis., 7 May 1883

MS 4616B Letter, W. S. Jones, Scranton (editor of Baner America), to Revd D. S. Davies, 19 Apr. 1872

MS 9251-77A Henry Blackwell, 'A Dictionary of Welsh Biography'

MS 9511D Letter, T. J. Griffiths to Samuel Roberts, 23 Mar. 1877

MS 19216C Revd Tudur Lloyd Frimston, Y Cymry a Ymfudasant ac a Godasant i Enwogrwydd yn America a'r Trefedigaethau Prydeinig' [c.1893]

MS 20472C Megan Lloyd George, Notes on a Visit to the United States and Canada, 1923

England
British Newspaper Library, Colindale
Y Drych, 13 Mar. 1858

Newspapers and Periodicals:
Aberdare Times
Baner ac Amserau Cymru
The Cambrian
Y Cenhadwr Americanaidd
Y Columbia
Y Cyfaill o'r Hen Wlad
Cymru
Daily Sentinel [Rome, N.Y.]
The Druid
Y Drych
Y Drych a'r Gwyliedydd
Y Geninen
Y Gwladgarwr
Y Gwyliedydd Americanaidd
Yr Herald Cymraeg
New York Morning Star
Y Seren Orllewinol
Utica Daily Press
Utica Herald Dispatch
Utica Morning Herald
Utica Morning Herald and Daily Gazette
Utica Observer
Utica Observer-Dispatch
Y Wasg

Western Mail
Williamsburgh Daily Gazette

Miscellaneous Material / Private Correspondence to Y Drych */ the authors:*
Esther Evans Baran
Phillips G. Davies
David B. Evans
David W. 'Buddy' Evans
Laurie Jones Fox
William A. Hastie
Judith Heuser, including tape recording of her mother, Sallie Evans Surridge, interviewed by her family in the 1982.
Dorine S. Jones Jenkins
Mary Morris Mergenthal
Marian K. Roberts
Alun Trevor
Patricia Powell Viets

Reference Works
Blackwell, H., *A Bibliography of Welsh-Americana* 2nd ed. (Aberystwyth, 1977)
Dictionary of Welsh Biography down to 1940 (London, 1959)
Gregory, Winifred (ed.), *American Newspapers 1821-1936: A Union List of Files Available in the United States and Canada* (New York, reprint, 1967)
Hughes, R., *Enwogion Mon 1850-1912* (Dolgellau, 1913)
In Many Voices: Our Fabulous Foreign-Language Press (Norman Park, Ga., n.d.)
Ireland, Sandra L. Jones, comp., E*thnic Periodicals in Contemporary America. An Annotated Guide* (Westport, Conn., 1990)
Jones, Beti, *Newsplan Wales* (Aberystwyth, c1994)
Lewis, I., 'Welsh Newspapers and Journals in the United States', *National Library of Wales Journal*, 2 (Summer 1942)
Nasser, Eugene Paul, *Welsh Imprints of Central New York* (Utica, 1998)
Owen, Bob, 'Welsh American Newspapers and Periodicals', *National Library of Wales Journal*, 6 (Winter 1950)
Thernstrom, Stephan (ed.), *Harvard Encyclopedia of American Ethnic Groups* (Cambridge, Mass., 1980)
U. S. Bureau of the Census, *Historical Statistics of the United States from Colonial Times to 1957* (Washington D.C., 1960).
Williams, J., *Digest of Welsh Historical Statistics*, 2 vols. (Cardiff, 1985)
Wynar, Lubomyr R. and Wynar, Anna T., *Encyclopedic Dictionary of Ethnic Newspapers and Periodicals in the United States* 2nd ed. (Littleton, Colo.: 1976)

Secondary Sources

Articles / Chapters in Books

Baily, Samuel L., 'The Role of Two Newspapers and the Assimilation of the Italians in Buenos Aires and Sao Paulo, 1893-1913', *International Migration Review*, Vol. 12 No. 3, Fall 1978, pp. 321-340

Beijbom, Ulf, 'The Swedish Press' in Miller, Sally M. (ed.), *The Ethnic Press in the United States: A Historical Analysis and Handbook* (Westport, Conn., 1987), pp. 379-392

Berthoff, Rowland, 'Welsh', in Stephan Thernstrom (ed.), *Harvard Encyclopedia of American Ethnic Groups* (Cambridge, Mass., 1980) pp. 1011-1017

Blabey, Margaret Ellis et al, 'Growing up Welsh', *Ninnau*, Vol. 11 Nos. 3-5 (1 Jan.-1 Mar. 1986)

Davies, Phillips G., 'The Welsh in Kansas: Settlement, Contributions and Assimilation', *Welsh History Review*, Vol.14 No. 3 (1989), pp. 380-398

Idem, 'The Welsh Settlements in Minnesota: The Evidence of the Churches in Blue Earth and Le Sueur Counties', *Welsh History Review*, Vol. 13 No. 2 (1986) pp. 139-54

Ellis, David Maldwyn, 'The Welsh in Oneida County in New York State', *Transactions of the Honourable Society of Cymmrodorion*, 1961 Pt. 1, pp. 115-124

Idem, 'The Assimilation of the Welsh in Central New York', *New York History*, Vol. 53 (July 1972), pp. 299-333

Idem, 'The Assimilation of the Welsh in Central New York', *Welsh History Review*, Vol. 6 No. 2 (1973), pp. 424-50

Idem, 'The Welsh in Utica', *Transactions of the Honourable Society of Cymmrodorion*, 1981, pp. 127-135

Idem, 'Cwm Rhondda: The Welsh in Utica' in James S. Pula (ed.), *Ethnic Utica* (Utica, 1994)

Fishman, Joshua A., Hayden, Robert G., and Warshauer, Mary E., 'The Non-English and Ethnic Group Press, 1910-1960' in Joshua A. Fishman et. al., *Language Loyalty in the United States: The Maintenance and Perpetuation of Non-English Mother Tongues by American Ethnic and Religious Groups* (The Hague, 1966), pp. 51-74

Gray, Melinda G., 'Language and Belonging: A Welsh-Language Novel in Late-Nineteenth Century America' in Werner Sollors (ed.), *Multilingual America: Transnationalism, Ethnicity, and the Languages of American Literature* (New York, 1998), pp. 91-102

Hall, Basil, 'The Welsh Revival of 1904-05: A Critique', in C. J. Cuming and Derek Baker (eds.), *Popular Belief and Practice* (Cambridge, 1972), pp. 291-301

Harney, Robert F., 'The Ethnic Press in Ontario', *Polyphony*, 4 (Spring/Summer 1982), pp. 3-14.

Hopkin, Deian Rhys, 'Welsh Immigrants to the United States and their Press, 1840-1930', in Christine Harzig and Dirk Hoerder (eds.), *The Press of Labor Migrants in Europe and North America 1880s to 1930s* (Bremen, 1985), pp. 349-367

Jones, Emrys, 'Some aspects of cultural change in an American Welsh community', *Transactions of the Honourable Society of Cymmrodorion* (1952), pp. 15-41

Jones, Erasmus W., 'The Early Welsh Settlers of Oneida County', *Transactions of the Oneida Historical Society at Utica*, 5 (1889-1892), pp. 60-67

Jones, Robert Owen, 'The Welsh Language in Patagonia' in Geraint H. Jenkins (ed.), *Language and Community in the Nineteenth Century* (Cardiff, 1998), pp. 287-316

Jones, William D., 'The Welsh Language and Welsh Identity in a Pennsylvanian Community' in Geraint H. Jenkins (ed.), *Language and Community in the Nineteenth Century* (Cardiff, 1998), pp. 261-286

Kneller, Pamela, 'Welsh Immigrant Women as wage earners in Utica, New York, 1860-70', *Llafur*, Vol. 5 No. 4 (1991), pp. 71-78

Knowles, Anne Kelly, 'Migration, Nationalism, and the Construction of Welsh Identity' in Guntram H. Herb and David H. Kaplan (eds.), *Nested Identities: Nationalism, Territory, and Scale* (New York, 1999), pp. 289-315.

Idem, 'Religious Identity as Ethnic Identity: the Welsh in Waukesha County' in Robert C. Ostergren and Thomas R. Vale (eds.), *Wisconsin Land and Life* (Madison, Wis., 1997), pp. 282-299

Linnard, Bill, 'Ar Drywydd y Cewri ym Mhatagonia', *Y Casglwr*, 69 (Summer, 2000)

Roberts, D. H. E., 'Welsh Publishing in the United States of America' in Philip Henry Jones and Eiluned Rees (eds.), *A Nation and its Books: A History of the Book in Wales* (Aberystwyth, 1998), pp. 253-264

'Sallie Evans', *Y Gymraes*, Vol. 36 No. 6 (June 1932) pp.121-123

Shenton, James P., 'Ethnicity and Immigration' in Eric Foner (ed.), *The New American History* (Philadelphia, 1990)

Thomas, Howard, 'The Welsh Came to Remsen', *New York History*, Vol. 30 (1949), pp. 33-42

Thomas, Lewis H., 'From the Prairie to the Pampas: The Welsh Migration of 1902', *Saskatchewan History*, Vol. 24 No.1 (Winter 1971), reprint by St. David's Society of New York (no date)

Vasey, Ruth, 'The Media' in Mick Gidley (ed.), *Modern American Culture. An introduction* (London and New York, 1993)

Vecoli, Rudolph J., 'The Italian Immigrant Press and the Construction of Social Reality, 1850-1920' in James P. Danky and Wayne A. Wiegand, *Print Culture in a Diverse America* (Urbana and Chicago, 1998), pp. 17-33

Williams, C. R. W., 'The Welsh Religious Revival of 1904-05', *British Journal of Sociology*, Vol. 8 (1952)

Williams, David, 'Some Figures Relating to Emigration from Wales', *Bulletin of the Board of Celtic Studies*, 7 (1935), pp. 396-415

Books

Badger, Anthony J., *The New Deal: The Depression Years, 1933-1940* (London, 1989)

Berthoff, Rowland T., *British Immigrants in Industrial America* (Cambridge, Mass., 1953)

Danky, James P. and Wiegand, Wayne A., (eds), *Print Culture in a Diverse America* (Urbana and Chicago, 1998)

Davies, Russell, *Secret Sins: Sex, Violence and Society in Carmarthenshire 1870-1920* (Cardiff, 1996)

Davies, William D., *America a Gweledigaethau Bywyd* (Scranton, 1895)

Idem, Llwybrau Bywyd; neu, Haner Can Mlynedd o Oes (Utica, 1889)

Edwards, Ebeneser (William Penn), *Facts about Welsh Factors: Welshmen as Factors in the Foundation and Development of the U.S. Republic* (Utica, 1899)

Edwards, Hywel Teifi, *Eisteddfod Ffair y Byd Chicago, 1893* (Llandysul, 1990)

Ellis, David M., *The Upper Mohawk Country: An Illustrated History of Greater Utica* (Woodland Hills, Calif., 1982)

Ellis, Sam, *Ann y Foty yn Myn'd i'r Mor ac Ystraeon Eraill* (Utica, 1913)

Evans, Eifion, *The Welsh Revival of 1904*, 3rd ed. (Bridgend, 1987)

Fishman, Joshua A. et. al., *Language Loyalty in the United States: The Maintenance and Perpetuation of Non-English Mother Tongues by American Ethnic and Religious Groups* (The Hague, 1966)

Greenslade, David, *Welsh Fever: Welsh Activities in the United States and Canada Today* (Cowbridge, 1986)

Hartmann, E. G., *Americans from Wales* (Boston, 1967)

Hughes, Hugh, *Pryddestau Er Cof am Griffith H. Humphrey, Utica, N.Y.: Gyda Sylwadau ar ei Fywyd* (Utica, 1908)

Jenkins, Dafydd, *Nation on Trial, Penyberth, 1936* (Cardiff, 1996)

Jones, Aled Gruffydd, *Press, Politics and Society: A History of Journalism in Wales* (Cardiff, 1993)

Jones, Alexander, *The Cymry of '76; or Welshmen and their descendants of the American Revolution. An Address* (New York, 1855)

Jones, J. W. and Morris, T. B., *Hanes Y Gwrthryfel Mawr Yn Y Talaethau Unedig* (Utica, 1866).

Jones, John William, *Yr Athrawydd Parod: sef hyfforddydd anffaeledig i ddarllen ac ysgrifenu Cymraeg yn nghyda rheolau barddonaieth Gymreig ac elfenau rhifyddiaeth* (Utica, 1860)

Jones, Thomas, *Lloyd George* (London, 1951), pp. 204-206

Jones, T. M., *Llenyddiaeth Fy Ngwlad sef Hanes y Newyddiadaur a'r Cylchgrawn Cymreig yn Nghymru, America, ac Awstralia* (Holywell, 1893)

Jones, William D., *Wales in America: Scranton and the Welsh, 1860-1920* (Cardiff, 1993)

Knowles, Anne Kelly, *Calvinists Incorporated: Welsh Immigrants in Ohio's Industrial Frontier* (Chicago, 1996)

Lewis, D. Craionog, *Hanes Plwyf Defynog* (Merthyr, 1911)

McCoy, Donald R., *Coming of Age: The United States during the 1920s and 1930s* (Harmondsworth, 1973)

Miller, Sally M. (ed.), *The Ethnic Press in the United States: A Historical Analysis and Handbook* (Westport, Conn., 1987)

Park, Robert E., *The Immigrant Press and Its Control* (New York, 1922)

Roberts, J. C., *Y Trysor Teuluaidd* (Utica, 1877)

Roberts, Samuel, *Hunan-Amddiffyniad S.R.: yn ngwyneb y camddarlunio fu arno drwy adeg cynddaredd, y rhyfel cartrefol yn America* (Conway, 1882, first pub. 1867)

Idem, Pregethau a Darlithiau (Utica, 1865)

Shepperson, Wilbur S., *Samuel Roberts: a Welsh Colonizer in Civil War Tennessee* (Knoxville, 1961)

Thomas, R. D., *Hanes Cymry America* (Utica, 1872). See also Phillips G. Davies, trans., *Hanes Cymry America: A History of the Welsh in America* (Lanham, Md., and London, 1983)

Thomas, William O., *Dwywaith o Amgylch y Byd; sef Hanes Teithiau yn Ewrop, Asia, Affrica, America, ac Australasia, yn ystod Pum Mlynedd o Amser* (Utica, 1882)

Wager, Daniel E., *Oneida County and its People* (Utica, 1896)

Williams, Daniel Jenkins, *The Welsh community of Waukesha County* (Columbus, Ohio, 1926)

Idem, Williams, Daniel Jenkins, *The Welsh of Columbus, Ohio: A Study in Adaptation and Assimilation* (Oshkosh, Wis., 1913)

Williams III, Jay G., *Memory Stones. A History of Welsh-Americans in Central New York and their churches* (Fleischmanns, N.Y., 1993)

Williams, Glanmor, *Samuel Roberts, Llanbrynmair* (Cardiff, 1950)

Williams, Glyn, *The Desert and the Dream: a Study of Welsh Colonization in Chubut, 1865-1915* (Cardiff, 1975)

Theses

Beveridge, Virginia, 'Popular Journalism and Working Class Attitudes 1854-1886' (unpublished Ph.D. thesis, University of London, 1979)

Evans, Paul De Mund, 'The Welsh in Oneida County, New York' (unpublished M.A. thesis, Cornell University, 1914)

Index

Numbers in bold refer to illustrations and their captions on the page concerned.